T0202959

Communications
in Computer and Information Science 1728

Rationale

The CCIS series is devoted to the publication of proceedings of computer science conferences. Its aim is to efficiently disseminate original research results in informatics in printed and electronic form. While the focus is on publication of peer-reviewed full papers presenting mature work, inclusion of reviewed short papers reporting on work in progress is welcome, too. Besides globally relevant meetings with internationally representative program committees guaranteeing a strict peer-reviewing and paper selection process, conferences run by societies or of high regional or national relevance are also considered for publication.

Topics

The topical scope of CCIS spans the entire spectrum of informatics ranging from foundational topics in the theory of computing to information and communications science and technology and a broad variety of interdisciplinary application fields.

Information for Volume Editors and Authors

Publication in CCIS is free of charge. No royalties are paid, however, we offer registered conference participants temporary free access to the online version of the conference proceedings on SpringerLink (http://link.springer.com) by means of an http referrer from the conference website and/or a number of complimentary printed copies, as specified in the official acceptance email of the event.

CCIS proceedings can be published in time for distribution at conferences or as postproceedings, and delivered in the form of printed books and/or electronically as USBs and/or e-content licenses for accessing proceedings at SpringerLink. Furthermore, CCIS proceedings are included in the CCIS electronic book series hosted in the SpringerLink digital library at http://link.springer.com/bookseries/7899. Conferences publishing in CCIS are allowed to use Online Conference Service (OCS) for managing the whole proceedings lifecycle (from submission and reviewing to preparing for publication) free of charge.

Publication process

The language of publication is exclusively English. Authors publishing in CCIS have to sign the Springer CCIS copyright transfer form, however, they are free to use their material published in CCIS for substantially changed, more elaborate subsequent publications elsewhere. For the preparation of the camera-ready papers/files, authors have to strictly adhere to the Springer CCIS Authors' Instructions and are strongly encouraged to use the CCIS LaTeX style files or templates.

Abstracting/Indexing

CCIS is abstracted/indexed in DBLP, Google Scholar, EI-Compendex, Mathematical Reviews, SCImago, Scopus. CCIS volumes are also submitted for the inclusion in ISI Proceedings.

How to start

To start the evaluation of your proposal for inclusion in the CCIS series, please send an e-mail to ccis@springer.com.

Mohamed Tabaa · Hassan Badir ·
Ladjel Bellatreche · Azedine Boulmakoul ·
Ahmed Lbath · Fabrice Monteiro
Editors

New Technologies, Artificial Intelligence and Smart Data

10th International Conference, INTIS 2022
Casablanca, Morocco, May 20–21, 2022
and 11th International Conference, INTIS 2023
Tangier, Morocco, May 26–27, 2023
Revised Selected Papers

 Springer

Editors
Mohamed Tabaa 🄳
EMSI
Casablanca, Morocco

Ladjel Bellatreche 🄳
National Engineering School for Mechanics
and Aerotechnics (ENSMA)
Poitiers, France

Ahmed Lbath 🄳
University Grenoble Alpes
Saint-Martin-d'Hères, France

Hassan Badir 🄳
Abdelmalek Essaâdi University
Tangier, Morocco

Azedine Boulmakoul 🄳
University of Hassan II Casablanca
Casablanca, Morocco

Fabrice Monteiro 🄳
Lorraine University
Nancy, France

ISSN 1865-0929   ISSN 1865-0937 (electronic)
Communications in Computer and Information Science
ISBN 978-3-031-47365-4   ISBN 978-3-031-47366-1 (eBook)
https://doi.org/10.1007/978-3-031-47366-1

This Springer imprint is published by the registered company Springer Nature Switzerland AG
The registered company address is: Gewerbestrasse 11, 6330 Cham, Switzerland

Paper in this product is recyclable.

Preface

This year INTIS – International Conference on New Technologies, Artificial Intelligence and Smart Data (INTIS 2023) – celebrated its 11th anniversary. The first INTIS conference was held in Tangier, Morocco in 2011. Since then, INTIS has taken place annually, with previous editions held in Mohammedia, Morocco (2012), Tangier, Morocco (2013, 2019, 2020), Rabat, Morocco (2014), Fez, Morocco (2016), Casablanca, Morocco (2017, 2022), and Marrakech, Morocco (2018).

The 10th INTIS conference was held in Casablanca, Morocco, during May 20–21, 2022, and the 11th edition in Tangier, during May 26–27, 2023 as a face-to-face event. The two editions' topics cover the main layers of data-enabled systems/applications: data source layer, network layer, data layer, learning layer, and reporting layers, while considering non-functional properties such as data privacy, security, and ethics. INTIS builds on this tradition, facilitating the interdisciplinary exchange of ideas, theory, techniques, experiences, and future research directions, and promoting African and Middle Eastern researchers.

Our call for papers attracted 60 papers (27 papers in INTIS 2022 and 33 papers in INTIS 2023), from which the International Program Committee finally selected 15 full papers and 6 short papers, yielding an acceptance rate of 40%. Each paper was reviewed by an average of three reviewers and in some cases up to four. Accepted papers cover several broad research areas on both theoretical and practical aspects. Some trends found in accepted papers include the following: AI-driven applications, smart data and Internet of Things applications, Big Data Warehouses, and Cyber Security.

INTIS 2022 featured the following three keynote speakers:

- Ladjel Bellatreche – (LIAS/ISAE-ENSMA, Poitiers, France) - "Towards a Generic Infrastructure for Thing Logs Analysis".
- Oussama Cherkaoui (LEENA Senior Solution Engineering Manager Oracle North-Africa, Morocco) - "Fraud Detection Using Machine Learning: Application in Health Insurance".
- Valentina Balas – (University of Arad, Romania) - "New Computational Intelligence Methods and Practical Applications".

INTIS 2023 featured the following three keynote speakers:

- Marjan Mernik (University of Maribor, Slovenia) – "Formal and Practical Aspects of Domain-Specific Languages".
- Sandro Bimonte (TSCF, INRAE, Clermont-Ferrand, France) – "New Supervision and monitoring of agricultural autonomous robots: from design to implementation".
- Mohamed Essaidi, (Moroccan School of Science & Engineering – EMSI, Morocco) – "Sustainable Smart Cities for SDGs Acceleration".

During INTIS 2023, a special tribute was paid to Professor Azedine Boulmakoul, from Hassan II University, Morocco, who passed away in July 2022. He was one of the founders of the INTIS conference. On this solemn occasion, we honored his invaluable contribution to the scientific community and committed ourselves to advancing the fields he held dear. His vision continues to shine through the minds he influenced and the ideas he sowed.

The proceedings of INTIS 2023 include three papers from INTIS 2022 based on the recommendations of Amin Mobasheri, from Springer.

We would like to thank all authors for submitting their papers to INTIS 2023 and we hope they submit again in the future. On the other hand, we express our gratitude to all the Program Committee members who provided high-quality reviews. We want to acknowledge the ease of use and flexibility of the EasyChair system to manage papers. Finally, we would like to thank the local organizers for their support.

Last but not least, we would like to thank Amin Mobasheri from Springer and his staff for their help, support, and advice.

August 2023

Mohamed Tabaa
Hassan Badir
Ladjel Bellatreche
Azedine Boulmakoul
Ahmed Lbath
Fabrice Monteiro

Organization

Honorary Guests

Bouchta El Moumni   Abdelmalek Essaâdi University, Morocco
Ahmed Moussa   ENSATg, Morocco
Karim Alami   EMSI, Morocco
Mohamed Essaaidi   EMSI, Morocco

General Chair

Hassan Badir   ENSATg, Morocco

General Co-chairs

Mohamed Tabaa   EMSI, Morocco
Ladjel Bellatereche   ENSMA, France
Fabrice Monteiro   University of Lorraine, France

Program Committee Chairs

Rachida Fissoune   ENSATg, Morocco
Anirban Mondal   Ashoka University, India
Azedine Boulmakoul   FSTM, Morocco
Zoltán Fazekas   HAS, Hungary
Alessio Ishizaka   University of Portsmouth, UK
Bharat Bhushan   Sharda University, India
Nouria Harbi   Université Lumière Lyon 2, France

Publicity Committee

Amjad Rattrout   AAUJ, Palestine
Rabia Marghoubi   INPT, Morocco
Lilia Sfaxi   INSAT, Tunisia
Wahida Handouzi   Tlemcen University, Algeria

Publication Committee

Achraf Cohen	University of West Florida, USA
Mohamed Tabaa	EMSI, Morocco
Ismail Biskri	Université du Québec à Trois-Rivières, Canada
Ahmed Lbath	Université Grenoble Alpes, France

Organizing Committee Chairs

Rachida Fissoune	ENSATg, Morocco
Sara Ibn Al Ahrach	FMT, Morocco
Hassna Bensag	EMSI, Morocco
Faouzi Kamoun	ESPRIT, Tunisia

Secretary Committee

Lamia Karim	ENSAB, Morocco
Adil Bouziri	FSTM, Morocco

Local Organizing Committee

Rachida Fissoune	ENSATg, Morocco
Sara Ibn El Ahrache	ENSATg, Morocco
Ahmed Moussa	ENSATg, Morocco
Yassine Laaziz	ENSATg, Morocco
Hassan Badir	ENSATg, Morocco
Rabia Marghoubi	INPT, Morocco
Hatim Hafidi	INPT, Morocco
Fatima-Ezzahra Badaoui	FSTM, Mohamedia, Morocco
Aimad Elmourabit	ENSATg, Morocco
Abdelmounaime Lachkar	ENSATg, Morocco
Ahmed Rabhi	ENSATg, Morocco
Kenza Chaoui	ENSATg, Morocco
Mouna Amrou Mhand	ENSATg, Morocco
Lamyae Serhane	EMSI, Morocco
Chaimaa Azromahli	EMSI, Morocco
Ibtihal Mouhib	EMSI, Morocco
Zineb El Khattabi	ENSAH, Al Houceima, Morocco
Houssam Bazza	ENSATg, Morocco

Najlaa El Fathi	EMSI, Morocco
Asmae Chakir	EMSI, Morocco
Meriem Abid	EMSI, Morocco
Younes Tace	EMSI Morocco
Zineb Hidila	EMSI, Morocco

Steering Committee

Hassan Badir	ENSATg, Morocco
Mohamed Tabaa	EMSI, Morocco
Ahmed Lbath	Université Grenoble Alpes, France
Amjad Rattrout	AAUJ, Palestine
Nouria Harbi	Université Lumière Lyon 2, France

Contents

Artificial Intelligence

Machine Learning for the Analysis of Human Microbiome in Inflammatory Bowel Diseases: Literature Review

Nouhaila En Najih[(✉)] and Pr. Ahmed Moussa

Systems and Data Engineering Team ENSA, University Abdelmalek Essaadi, Tangier, Morocco
nouhaila.ennajih@etu.uae.ac.ma, amoussa@uae.ac.ma

Abstract. The pathogenesis of inflammatory bowel disease is related to the imbalance of microbial community composition. A reduction in the diversity of the intestinal microbiota as well as specific taxonomic and functional shifts have been reported in inflammatory bowel diseases and may play a central role in the inflammatory process. The aim was to review recent developments in the structural and functional changes observed in the gastrointestinal microbiome in patients with inflammatory bowel diseases and to survey the use of machine learning to discover the microbiome in inflammatory bowel disease. We start by highlighting the relationship between gut microbiome disorder with inflammatory bowel disease including different studies that confirmed this association, then, we provide an overview of the use of Machine Learning in analyzing the microbiome in inflammatory bowel diseases.

Keywords: Machine Learning · Human microbiome · IBD

1 Introduction

The human body is home to a highly complex and populated microbial ecosystem called the "human microbiome". Microorganisms are more present in the human body than human cells. Their role is vital in almost all aspects of human health and function. High-throughput sequencing (HTS) technology has made it easier to investigate the microbial environment, giving rise to the burgeoning subject of metagenomics. As sequencing becomes cheaper and large amounts of metagenomic sequencing data become publicly available, we can answer two key questions about microbes in the community by studying taxonomic composition and studying these data. The metabolic activity of microorganisms. This in turn prompted computational researchers to develop machine-learning methods to predict patient phenotypes from their metagenomic sequence data. Recent studies have strengthened the view that the pathogenesis of IBD is related to the imbalance of microbial community composition. In this paper, referring to several recent articles, we highlight the relationship between inflammatory bowel diseases (IBD) and the microbiome. After that, we present the recent studies that used machine learning and deep learning for the analysis of the microbiome in Inflammatory bowel diseases.

M. Tabaa et al. (Eds.): INTIS 2022/2023, CCIS 1728, pp. 3–19, 2024.
https://doi.org/10.1007/978-3-031-47366-1_1

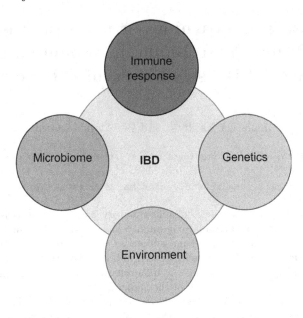

Fig. 1. Risk factors for the development of IBD

2   The Relation Between Inflammatory Bowel Diseases and the Microbiome

Inflammatory bowel diseases (IBDs) are a group of chronic immune-mediated disorders characterized by inflammation of the digestive tract with a relapsing-remitting pattern. IBD may be developed as a result of interactions between environmental, microbial, and immune-mediated factors. Recently, there has been a lot of interest and research on the role played by the microbiome in the development, progression, and treatment of IBD. The disease contains 2 subtypes: ulcerative colitis and Crohn's disease. The clinical symptoms, prognoses, and treatments of these subtypes can vary and they can affect different parts of the digestive tract. Crohn's disease, which has a progressive and debilitating course and is becoming more common worldwide, is characterized by chronic inflammation of any region of the gastrointestinal tract [7]. Several factors have been implicated in the cause of inflammatory bowel diseases, including a dysregulated immune system, an altered microbiothostsenetic susceptibility, and environmental factors, but the cause of the IBD remains unknown.

The gut microbiome is involved in the pathogenesis of inflammatory bowel disease. Reduced gut microbiota diversity, as well as specific classification and functional changes, have been linked to Crohn's disease and may be crucial to the development of the inflammatory process (Fig. 1).

The functional and structural alterations in the gastrointestinal microbiome that have been noticed in people with Crohn's Disease were reviewed by Wright *et al.* [1] in a recent study. They discovered that as a result, Crohn's disease had less microbial diversity. The relative abundance of Firmicutes decreased and Bacteroides increased in Crohn's disease when compared to healthy controls. In particular, E. coli is abundant in Crohn's disease (Table 1).

Table 1. The role of gut microbiome in IBD

Article	Date	Authors	Journal	Objective	Method	Results
Cytometric fingerprints of gut microbiota predict Crohn's disease state	2021	Rubbens, Peter, et al.	The ISME Journal	Demonstrate that cytometric fingerprints can be used as a diagnostic tool in order to classify samples according to Crohn's disease	The recently published data of a disease cohort containing samples diagnosed with Crohn's disease healthy control was analyzed by flow cytometry and 16S rRNA gene amplicon sequencing	Structural differences in function of the disease state were captured by the cytometric fingerprints, which can be summarized in terms of the cytometric diversity. And flow cytometry was proved that it has the potential to perform rapid diagnostics of microbiome-associated diseases
The potential of metabolic and lipid profiling in inflammatory bowel diseases: A pilot study	2020	Tefas, Cristian, et al.	Bosnian journal of basic medical sciences	Identify molecules that could serve as biomarkers for a positive diagnosis of IBD as well as to discriminate UC from colonic CD	Ultra-high-performance liquid chromatography and mass spectrometry were used to quantify Plasma lipid and metabolic profiles. statistical tests univariate and multivariate were employed	Serum lipid and metabolic profiling has a good potential to detect IBD patients non invasively, And can be used to differentiate between colonic CD and UC.

(continued)

Table 1. (*continued*)

Article	Date	Authors	Journal	Objective	Method	Results
Comparative immunophenotyping of Saccharomyces cerevisiae and Candida spp. strains from Crohn's disease patients and their interactions with the gut microbiome	2020	Di Paola, Monica, et al.	Journal of translational autoimmunity	Understand the impact of gut fungal microbiome on crohn's disease patients	The relationship between the composition of the microbiota and the separation of fungi from stool samples was studied through metabarcodes analysis	The gut microbiota profiles showed significant difference according to the presence of Saccharomyces or Candida spp. or the absence of fungal isolates in fecal samples.
The microbiome and inflammatory bowel disease	2020	Glassner, Kerri L., Bincy P. Abraham, and Eamonn MM Quigley	Journal of Allergy and Clinical Immunology	See the relation between IBD and the microbiome	Compare the microbiome in patients with IBD with that in healthy control subjects	The microbiome found in samples with IBD is different from the health control samples
Role of intestinal microbiota and metabolites in inflammatory bowel disease	2019	Dong, Li-Na, et al.	Chinese medical journal	Provide a summary of the latest advances in the microbiota and its metabolites and their impact on the pathogenesis of IBD	The clinical research and animal research of IBD gut microbiota and metabolites were selected. This Organized information explaining the possible pathogenesis of the IBD microbiota.	In patients with IBD, the biological diversity of the fecal/mucosal-related microbiota decreases, and the probiotic microbiota Also decreased, while the pathogenic microbiota increased.
Recent Advances in Characterizing the Gastrointestinal Microbiome in Crohn's Disease: A Systematic Review	2015	Wright, Emily K., et al.	Inflammatory bowel diseases	To review the recent developments in the structural and functional changes observed in the gastrointestinal microbiome in patients with Crohn's Disease.	An electronic search using Medline and PubMed to identify published articles on the GI microbiome and Crohn's disease.	The relative abundance of Bacteroidetes is increased and Firmicutes decreased in Crohn's disease compared with healthy controls

We require new biomarkers to provide patients with the best care and to keep the disease in an inactive state for as long as possible.

Tefas *et al.* [2] suggested a study to find the molecules that could distinguish UC from CD and act as biomarkers of IBD. Utilizing mass spectrometry and ultra-high-performance liquid chromatography, plasma lipid, and metabolic biographies were quantified. Both univariate and multivariate statistical tests were used. As a result, when compared to healthy controls, six lipid species and seven metabolites were significantly altered in IBD cases. Only one metabolite and five lipid species showed a difference between UC and CD. According to this initial study, colonic CD and UC can be distinguished from one another and from IBD cases using serum lipid and metabolic profiling. The study's main flaw is the scant number of cases that were actually included.

Saccharomyces cerevisiae and Candida spp. demonstrated an important role in health and disease in studies pertaining to the fungal communities in animal models of Inflammatory Bowel Diseases (IBD). For this reason, Di Paola *et al.* [3] were motivated by this to learn more about how patients with Crohn's disease were affected by their gut fungus microbiome. They tested Candida spp. and Saccharomyces cerevisiae to determine the effect on the microbiota. It is a strain that researchers isolated from IBD patients' stool samples. They compared the cytokine profiles, stimulated dendritic cells and peripheral blood mononuclear cells (PBMC) with various yeast strains, and assessed the correlation between the immune response and the strain's cell wall sugar content. Additionally, metabarcodes analysis was used to investigate the connection between the microbiota's composition and the removal of fungi from stool samples. Patients with Crohn's disease (CD) had different reactions to "self" and "non-self" strains, which resulted in a pure Th1 or Th17 cytokine pattern. According to the presence of Saccharomyces or Candida spp. or the absence of fungal isolates in fecal samples, the gut microbiota profiles demonstrated significant differences (Raw sequences are available in the European Nucleotide Archive (ENA) with accession number PRJEB22036 and PRJEB22343 (http://www.ebi.ac.uk/ena/data/view/PRJEB22036 and http://www.ebi.ac.uk/ena/data/view/PRJEB22343).

In terms of the microbiota, its metabolites, and their influence on the pathogenesis of IBD, Dong *et al.* [4] provided a summary of the most recent research. The study of IBD gut metabolites and microbiota conducted in animals and in humans was chosen for this. This well-organized information explains how the IBD microbiota may have developed as a pathogenesis. The pathogenic microbiota increases, the probiotic microbiota decreases, and the fecal/mucosal-related microbiota have less biological diversity in patients with IBD. Diagnostic and therapeutic efforts for inflammatory bowel disease may focus on the gut microbiota. The idea that the microbiota and its metabolites play a significant role in IBD by affecting intestinal permeability and the immune response is supported by a lot of studies. In order to show that flow cytometry can quickly diagnose disorders linked to the microbiome, Rubbens *et al.* [5] examined 29 samples of Crohn's disease and 66 healthy samples as controls. This study showed that these differences may be seen in the cytometry data. In the function of CD compared

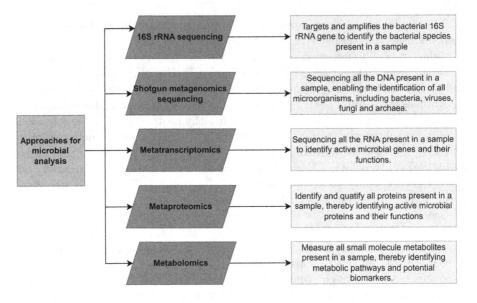

Fig. 2. Existing approaches for microbiome analysis

to HC, both the richness and evenness of the gut microbiota were considerably lower for CD compared to HC samples, and both taxonomic diversity and cytometric diversity were important markers.

3   Existing Approaches for Microbiome Analysis

Microbiome analysis in IBD research involves the use of various techniques to study the taxonomic and functional composition of microbial communities. Among the various technologies available, 16S rRNA sequencing and shotgun metagenomics are two of the most commonly used methods. 16S rRNA sequencing targets conserved regions of the 16S rRNA gene to identify bacterial taxa and their relative abundance in a sample. Shotgun metagenomics, on the other hand, sequences all the DNA in a sample to create a comprehensive profile of microbial communities, including bacteria, archaea, viruses, and fungi. Both methods have been used in studies to diagnose, predict or classify IBD using machine learning methods. Other metagenomic approaches, such as metatranscriptomics, metaproteomics, and metabolomics, can provide more information about the functional potential and activity of the microbiome. However, they are less commonly used in IBD research (Fig. 2).

4   Machine Learning Techniques for Microbiome Analysis

Machine learning techniques are increasingly used in microbiome analysis to develop predictive models and identify key microbial biomarkers associated with various disease states, including IBD. These techniques include supervised and unsupervised learning algorithms such as B. Support Vector Machines (SVM), Random Forests (RF), Neural Networks (NN), and clustering methods, among others. B. k-means clustering and hierarchical clustering. SVM and RF models have been shown to be good at predicting IBD status from microbiome data, while NNs have been used for microbial community classification and trait selection. Clustering methods have also been used for microbial community analysis and identification of microbial symbiosis patterns. Furthermore, deep learning methods such as convolutional neural networks (CNN) and recurrent neural networks (RNN) have shown promising results when analyzing large and complex microbiome datasets.

5   Applications of Machine Learning for the Analysis of the Microbiome in Inflammatory Bowel Diseases

The microbiome has been associated with a number of disorders in recent years, and the revolution in sequencing technology has resulted in a rapid rise in the amount of publically available sequencing data. As a result, efforts to forecast disease states using metagenomic sequencing data have increased. Some of these initiatives have looked into using Machine Learning technique that has been effectively used in a number of biological domains. Reiman et al. [18] defend that the DNN architecture is not ideal for using metagenomic data to predict diseases. Due to the small number of patients sampled, deep architecture frequently requires enormous amounts of data, making it currently impractical. This research presented a framework for predicting diseases from the profile of microbial abundance using CNN architecture. Phylogenetic trees are used by their method, known as PopPhy-CNN, to explain how closely related microbes are. Pasolli *et al.* [19] proposed MetAML (Metagenomic prediction Analysis based on Machine Learning). With this technique, various machine learning strategies for metagenome-based disease prediction tasks are evaluated. IBD was one of six disease datasets that were discussed.

The Met2Img approach was proposed by Nguyen *et al.* [20]. It depends on incorporating taxonomic abundances, like artificial images. Images represent individuals, while pixels represent taxa. They experimented with various color schemes and pixel arrangements, and a CNN was used to forecast the disease from the resulting image.

Another method used was RegMIL [21]. It employs the Multiple Instance Learning methods (MIL). MIL takes into account a "number of instances" without known labels that are contained in "bags," a collection of samples with known labels. In this study, the individuals are represented by the bags, whereas the disease phenotypes are represented by the known labels, and the metagenomic sequence reads are represented by the instances. On IBD datasets, this method produced results that were superior to MetaML in terms of accuracy and AUC.

LaPierre *et al.* [17] used 25 IBD patients and 85 control cases to compare how well these methods worked with IBD.

RegMIL compares their proposed model with the MetAML package and reports that it outperforms the baseline in terms of accuracy and AUC for IBD by 0.5–2%.

Dysbiosis happens in CD, but it's still unclear whether it will contribute to an increase in the risk of recurrent flares given the microbial dynamics in resting CD. Braun *et al.* [8] examined the long-term dynamics of the microbial composition in a prospective observation cohort of CD patients with resting disease (45 cases, 217 samples) who were older than 2 years or up until the onset of clinical onset. The purpose of this study was to find out if changes in the microbiome can predict and precede clinical recurrence. Machine learning was used to prioritize microbiological and clinical factors that separate relapsers and non-relapsers in the quiescent phase. As a result, compared to healthy controls, CD patients had significantly fewer microbes in their clinical, biomarker, and mucosal remissions, while the dysbiosis index was higher in healthy controls. The findings support the hypothesis that individualized microbial variation in resting CD significantly raises the risk of subsequent deterioration and may serve as a model to enhance personalized preventive care.

According to recent studies, each patient's response to ustekinumab (UST) treatment for Crohn's disease (CD) differs, and the causes of this are unknown. Unresponsive to UST are some patients. High placebo rates and insufficient UST induction doses may be to blame for nonresponse to UST. The responsiveness of patients to UST has been evaluated through observational studies. We believe that genes may be related to drug responsiveness. Accordingly, He *et al.* [9] conducted a study to use bioinformatic analysis to examine the expression of genes related to UST response. 26 normal samples and 86 CDs make up the GSE112366 data set, which has been downloaded for analysis. Initially, differentially expressed genes (DEG) were identified. Pathway analysis is done using the Gene Ontology (GO) and Kyoto Encyclopedia of Genes and Genomes (KEGG) databases.

There were 122 DEGs found in all. Display of GO and KEGG analysis The CD of patients has a notable enrichment of immune response pathways. For predicting UST response, four genes (HSD3B1, MUC4, CF1, and CCL11) are included in multiple logistic regression equations.

In order to predict the five-year risk of beginning biological agents in cases with IBD, Choi *et al.* [10] created and validated a machine learning model. The database of the Korean Common Data Model Network was subjected to an ML method. They employed a machine learning (ML) model that included ensemble techniques, support vector machine (SVM) (non-linear model), random forest (RF), XGBoost (XGB), and artificial neural network (ANN). The patients were categorized using SVM and RF. In order to predict outcomes based on one or more feature vectors, SVM specifically compares two classes. Recursive partitioning (RP) algorithms are a collection of classification techniques that combine multiple decision trees. The training made use of ANN and XGB. In a

GMC internal validation study, the ML model produced an area under the curve (AUC) of 0.86. In an independent validation study, the model consistently outperformed a variety of other biological systems, including the K-CDM network (AUC=0.81) (Table 2).

Table 2. The articles that used Machine Learning for the analysis of the microbiome in IBD

Article	Date	Authors	Journal	Objective	Method	Results
Machine learning gene expression predicting model for ustekinumab response in patients with Crohn's disease	2021	He, Manrong, et al.	Immunity, Inflammation and Disease	Develop a predictive model based on the gene transcription profile of CD patients in response to UST.	Least absolute shrinkage and selection operator regression analysis to build a UST response prediction model.	A total of 122 DEGs were identified. GO and KEGG analysis display Immune response pathways are significantly enriched in patients CD. Multiple logistic regression equation containing four genes are used for UST response prediction.
Machine Learning Prediction Model for Inflammatory Bowel Disease Based on Laboratory Markers. Working Model in a Discovery Cohort Study	2021	Kraszewski, Sebastian, et al.	Journal of clinical medicine	Create an IBD machine learning prediction model based on routinely performed blood, urine, and fecal tests	Using some simple machine learning classifiers, they optimized the necessary hyperparameters in order to Obtain reliable few feature predictive models for CD and UC	The most powerful classifier The CD and UC belonging to the random forest family achieved an average accuracy of 97% and 91%, respectively

(*continued*)

Table 2. (*continued*)

Article	Date	Authors	Journal	Objective	Method	Results
LightCUD: a program for diagnosing IBD based on human gut microbiome data	2021	Xu, Congmin, et al.	BioData Mining	Develop an IBD diagnostic method based on the gut microbiome	Developing a tool, named LightCUD, for discriminating UC and CD from non-IBD colitis using the human gut microbiome.	LightCUD demonstrated a high-performance for both WGS and 16S sequencing data. The strains that either identify healthy controls from IBD patients or distinguish the specific type of IBD are expected to be clinically important to serve as biomarkers.
Development of Machine Learning Model to Predict the 5-Year Risk of Starting Biologic Agents in Patients with Inflammatory Bowel Disease (IBD): K-CDM Network Study	2020	Choi, Youn I., et al.	Journal of Clinical Medicine	Develop and validate a machine learning (ML) model to predict the 5-year risk of starting biologic agents in IBD patients.	An ML method was applied to the database of the Korean common data model (K-CDM) network, a data sharing consortium of tertiary centers in Korea.	The ML model yielded an area under the curve (AUC) of 0.86 in an internal validation study carried out at GMC. The model performed consistently across a range of other datasets, including that of the K-CDM network (AUC=0.81) in an external validation study

(*continued*)

Table 2. (*continued*)

Article	Date	Authors	Journal	Objective	Method	Results
Individualized Dynamics in the Gut Microbiota Precede Crohn's Disease Flares	2019	Braun, Tzipi, et al.	Official journal of the American College of Gastroenterology—ACG	Identify if changes in the microbiome can precede and predict clinical relapse.	The long-term dynamics of microbial composition in a prospective observational cohort of patients with quiescent CD (45 cases, 217 samples) were analyzed over 2 years or until clinical flare occurred	Clinical, biomarker, and mucosal remission of CD patients showed a significant reduction in microbes compared with healthy controls and dysbiosis index increased in healthy controls.
Fungal and Bacterial Loads: Noninvasive Inflammatory Bowel Disease Biomarkers for the Clinical Setting	2021	Sarrabayrouse, G., et al.	Msys-tems	Study the use of fungal and bacterial loads as bio markers to detect both CD and UC.	Combining the microbial data with demographic and standard laboratory data to CD and UC and predict disease relapse using the random forest algorithm.	Fungal and bacterial loads were significantly different between healthy relatives of IBD patients and nonrelated healthy controls, between CD and UC patients in endoscopic remission, and between UC patients in relapse and non-UC individuals.

(*continued*)

Table 2. (*continued*)

Article	Date	Authors	Journal	Objective	Method	Results
Ranking microbiome variance in inflammatory bowel disease: a large longitudinal intercontinental study	2021	Clooney, Adam G., et al.	Gut	Clarify the relative contribution of different lifestyle and environmental factors to the compositional variability of the gut microbiota.	Ranking the size effect of disease activity, medications, diet and geographic location of the faecal microbiota composition of CD, UC and control samples .Machine learning separated disease from controls	Reduced microbiota diversity but increased variability was confirmed in CD and UC compared with controls. Significant compositional differences between diseases, particularly CD.
High incidence of glucocorticoid-induced hyperglycaemia in inflammatory bowel disease: metabolic and clinical predictors identified by machine Learning	2020	McDonnell, Martin, et al.	BMJ open gastroenterology	Published prevalence data Risk factors induced by GC Hyperglycemia in IBD The population is limited. They aim to using machine learning Methods to identify key predictors of risk.	Random Forest (RF) regression model were used to extract the prediction modes that exist in the data set.	RF model found that C reactivity increased Protein (CRP) followed by longer IBD duration Risk predictor of significant hyperglycemia.

In another study, Kraszewski *et al.* [11] created a system based on routine blood, urine, And stool test. Based on historical patient data (702 medical records: 319 records of 180 patients 383 records of ulcerative colitis (UC) and 192 Crohn's disease (CD) patients, data was scaled and dimensionality reduced by principal component analysis (PCA) method. Using some simple machine learning classifiers, they optimized the necessary hyperparameters in order to Obtain reliable few feature predictive models for CD and UC respectively. The most powerful classifier The CD and UC belonging to the random forest family achieved an average accuracy of 97% and 91%, respectively*. The research results show that based on basic blood, urine, and fecal markers can support the diagnosis of IBD with high accuracy. However, the test requires validation in a prospective cohort (Fig. 3).

In turn, Xu *et al.* [13] By creating a tool called LightCUD to differentiate between UC and CD from non-IBD colitis based on the human gut microbiome, they emphasize the significance of diagnostic tools developed with machine learning algorithms based on the data of the human gut microbiome. Four extremely high-performance modules make up LightCUD. Each of these modules is made up of a custom reference database and a machine-learning model. Data from high-throughput whole-genome sequencing (WGS) were used to examine the microbial diversity of samples of the gut microbiota. For the purpose of training each model of the corresponding module, this approach was contrasted with five different machine learning algorithms (logistic regression, random forest, gradient boosting classifier, support vector machine, and LightGBM). As a result, LightCUD had the best results. Gubatan *et al.* [12], however, provide a non-invasive mechanism for distinguishing IBD from healthy controls. For either WGS or 16S data, depending on the sequencing depth, the method processes a sample in several hours.

With a long history, glucocorticoids are frequently used as inducers in inflammatory bowel diseases. A known side effect of GC treatment, hyperglycemia affects morbidity and mortality. McDonnell *et al.* [14] described techniques for machine learning to find important risk predictors. They conducted a prospective observational study on IBD patients who were given hydrocortisone intravenously. The data set's existing prediction modes were extracted using the Random Forest (RF) regression model. This study demonstrated the capability of machine learning techniques to pinpoint significant clinical complication risk factors.

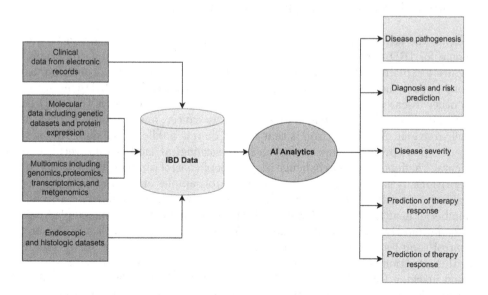

Fig. 3. Location of artificial intelligence (AI) in the medical management of inflammatory bowel disease as proposed by Gubatan et al. [12]

Inflammatory bowel disease (IBD) is significantly influenced by the micro-biome, but it is unclear how much each lifestyle choice and environmental factor contributes to the compositional diversity of the gut microbiota. Clooney *et al.* [15] ranked the size effect of disease activity, drugs, diet, and geographic location of the fecal microbiota of CD, UC, and control samples to explain the relative contribution of various lifestyle and environmental factors to the compositional variability of the gut microbiota. The disease and control were separated using machine learning. As a result, the diversity of the microbiota declines while the variability of CD and UC increases. includes controls. Significant compositional variations between diseases, particularly between samples from CD and controls. A longitudinal analysis of IBD patients, particularly those whose models altered disease activity, reveals a decrease in the temporal stability of the microbiota.

Sarrabayrouse *et al.* [16] studied the use of bacterial and fungal loads as biomarkers to identify relapses of CD and UC as well as both diseases. 294 stool samples from 206 participants were collected, and their fecal fungal and bacterial loads were examined using real-time PCR amplification of the ITS2 region and the 16S rRNA gene. Using the random forest algorithm, the microbial data were combined to predict disease relapse and diagnose ileal or ileocolonic CD and UC. As anticipated, there were significant differences in fungal and bacterial loads between healthy IBD patients' relatives and unrelated healthy controls, between CD and UC patients in endoscopic remission, and between UC patients in relapse and non-UC people.

6   Limitations and Challenges of Using Machine Learning for Microbiome Analysis in IBD

Despite the advantages of using machine learning to analyze the human micro-biome for IBD, researchers in this field face many limitations and challenges. Figure 4 explains these challenges and their consequences. One of our limita-tions is that there are few data on the human microbiome for IBD compared to other diseases. There are two main reasons for this. The first is that IBD is a new disease, most researchers prefer to study cancer, and few include IBD in their research. Another reason is that not all data is public. Small data volumes are a serious problem when using machine learning, as models can overfit and accuracy suffers. Another challenge is the lack of control samples. For supervised algorithms, it is important to have both control samples and patient samples to train the model. Most IBD projects contain only patient samples or a small number of healthy samples. Even studies that provide both control samples and patients mostly do not add metadata. Without specifying which samples are control samples and which samples are patients, the data is not really useful in this situation because we need to provide clear labels for the data in super-vised machine learning models. Another limitation of using data is its quality. Low-quality data limit the accuracy and reliability of disease prediction mod-els. In machine learning predictive models, a large amount of data is required to improve the accuracy and reliability of the model. Dealing with such a huge amount of data is not easy. For example, in a shotgun sequencing sample, only one sample might be 15 to 30 gigabits. For a good model, we need at least 300 samples. This means computing resources are required.

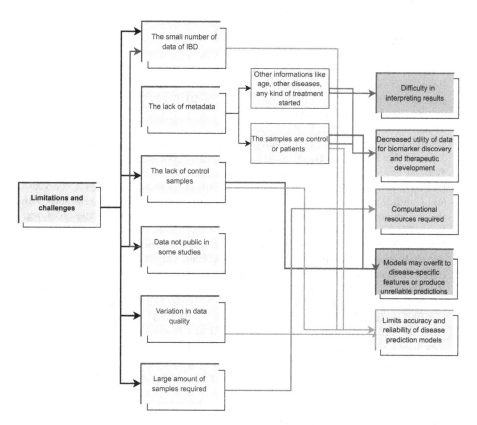

Fig. 4. Limitations and challenges of the use of machine learning for the analysis of human microbiome for IBD

7   Conclusion

Human metagenomic analysis has become an important area of research in the fields of microbiology and human health. Machine learning, with its ability to analyze complex big data, has become an important tool for analyzing human metagenomic data. Machine learning techniques identify patterns and relationships in data that would otherwise be difficult or impossible to detect. This is especially important when studying the human microbiome, as complex interactions between the microbiota and host can have profound effects on health and disease. The use of machine learning can lead to the discovery of new biomarkers, the identification of potential therapeutic targets, and the development of personalized medicine approaches. This review gave instances of AI applications in the field of inflammatory bowel disease microbiome research. This review may be useful to bioinformaticians who wish to use machine learning to study the microbiome in IBD.

References

1. Wright, E.K., Kamm, M.A., Teo, S.M., Inouye, M., Wagner, J., Kirkwood, C.D.: Recent advances in characterizing the gastrointestinal microbiome in Crohn's disease: a systematic review. Inflamm. Bowel Dis. **21**(6), 1219–1228 (2015). https://doi.org/10.1097/MIB.0000000000000382
2. Tefas, C., Ciobanu, L., Tantău, M., Moraru, C., Socaciu, C.: The potential of metabolic and lipid profiling in inflammatory bowel diseases: a pilot study. Bosnian J. Basic Med. Sci. **20**(2), 262–270 (2020). https://doi.org/10.17305/bjbms.2019.423
3. Di Paola, M., et al.: Comparative immunophenotyping of Saccharomyces cerevisiae and Candida spp. strains from Crohn's disease patients and their interactions with the gut microbiome. J. Trans. Autoimmunity **3**, 100036 (2020). https://doi.org/10.1016/j.jtauto.2020.100036
4. Dong, L.N., Wang, M., Guo, J., Wang, J.P.: Role of intestinal microbiota and metabolites in inflammatory bowel disease. Chin. Med. J. **132**(13), 1610–1614 (2019). https://doi.org/10.1097/CM9.0000000000000290
5. Rubbens, P., Props, R., Kerckhof, F.M., Boon, N., Waegeman, W.: Cytometric fingerprints of gut microbiota predict Crohn's disease state. ISME J. **15**(1), 354–358 (2021). https://doi.org/10.1038/s41396-020-00762-4
6. Glassner, K.L., Abraham, B.P., Quigley, E.M.M.: The microbiome and inflammatory bowel disease. J. Allergy Clin. Immunol. **145**(1), 16–27 (2020). https://doi.org/10.1016/j.jaci.2019.11.003
7. Roda, G., et al.: Crohn's disease. Nature reviews. Disease Primers **6**(1), 22 (2020). https://doi.org/10.1038/s41572-020-0156-2
8. Braun, T., et al.: Individualized dynamics in the gut microbiota precede Crohn's disease flares. Am. J. Gastroenterol. **114**(7), 1142–1151 (2019). https://doi.org/10.14309/ajg.0000000000000136
9. He, M., Li, C., Tang, W., Kang, Y., Zuo, Y., Wang, Y.: Machine learning gene expression predicting model for ustekinumab response in patients with Crohn's disease. Immun., Inflamm. Disease **9**(4), 1529–1540 (2021). https://doi.org/10.1002/iid3.506
10. Choi, Y.I., et al.: Development of machine learning model to predict the 5-year risk of starting biologic agents in patients with inflammatory bowel disease (IBD): K-CDM network study. J. Clin. Med. **9**(11), 3427 (2020). https://doi.org/10.3390/jcm9113427
11. Kraszewski, S., Szczurek, W., Szymczak, J., Reguła, M., Neubauer, K.: Machine learning prediction model for inflammatory bowel disease based on laboratory markers. working model in a discovery cohort study. J. Clin. Med. **10**(20), 4745 (2021). https://doi.org/10.3390/jcm10204745
12. Gubatan, J., Levitte, S., Patel, A., Balabanis, T., Wei, M.T., Sinha, S.R.: Artificial intelligence applications in inflammatory bowel disease: emerging technologies and future directions. World J. Gastroenterol. **27**(17), 1920–1935 (2021). https://doi.org/10.3748/wjg.v27.i17.1920

13. Xu, C., Zhou, M., Xie, Z., Li, M., Zhu, X., Zhu, H.: LightCUD: a program for diagnosing IBD based on human gut microbiome data. BioData Mining **14**, 1–13 (2021)
14. McDonnell, M., et al.: High incidence of glucocorticoid-induced hyperglycaemia in inflammatory bowel disease: metabolic and clinical predictors identified by machine learning. BMJ Open Gastroenterol. **7**(1), e000532 (2020). https://doi.org/10.1136/bmjgast-2020-000532
15. Clooney, A.G., et al.: Ranking microbiome variance in inflammatory bowel disease: a large longitudinal intercontinental study. Gut **70**(3), 499–510 (2021). https://doi.org/10.1136/gutjnl-2020-321106
16. Sarrabayrouse, G., et al.: Fungal and bacterial loads: noninvasive inflammatory bowel disease biomarkers for the clinical setting. mSystems **6**(2), e01277–20 (2021). https://doi.org/10.1128/mSystems.01277-20
17. LaPierre, N., Ju, C. J., Zhou, G., Wang, W.: MetaPheno: a critical evaluation of deep learning and machine learning in metagenome-based disease prediction. Methods (San Diego, Calif.) **166**, 74–82 (2019). https://doi.org/10.1016/j.ymeth.2019.03.003
18. Reiman, D., Metwally, A.A., Sun, J., Dai, Y.: PopPhy-CNN: a phylogenetic tree embedded architecture for convolutional neural networks to predict host phenotype from metagenomic data. IEEE J. Biomed. Health Inform. **24**(10), 2993–3001 (2020). https://doi.org/10.1109/JBHI.2020.2993761
19. Pasolli, E., Truong, D.T., Malik, F., Waldron, L., Segata, N.: Machine learning meta-analysis of large metagenomic datasets: tools and biological insights. PLoS Comput. Biol. **12**(7), e1004977 (2016). https://doi.org/10.1371/journal.pcbi.1004977
20. Nguyen, T.H., Prifti, E., Chevaleyre, Y., Sokolovska, N., Zucker, J.D.: Disease classification in metagenomics with 2D embeddings and deep learning (2018). arXiv preprint arXiv:1806.09046
21. Rahman, M.A., Rangwala, H.: RegMIL: phenotype classification from metagenomic data. In: Proceedings of the 2018 ACM International Conference on Bioinformatics, Computational Biology, and Health Informatics, pp. 145–154 (2018)

Systematic Mapping Study on Applications of Deep Learning in Stock Market Prediction

Omaima Guennioui[✉], Dalila Chiadmi, and Mustafa Amghar

Mohammadia School of Engineering, Mohammed V University in Rabat, Rabat, Morocco
omaimaguennioui@research.emi.ac.ma, {chiadmi,amghar}@emi.ac.ma

Abstract. Stock price forecasting is a challenging and complex problem with significant earnings potential for investors and institutes. Thereby, investors, economists and scientists, have studied and developed different approaches to predict stock trend or price. Deep learning methods have shown promising results in different areas such as audiovisual recognition and natural language processing. In the same way, researchers are exploring the effectiveness of the application of deep learning to the problem of stock price prediction. This study aims at reviewing and mapping the works on deep learning applications to stock price prediction. By collecting, analyzing and classifying the existing literature, we explore and give an overview of the latest progress in the studied topic and identify possible future research directions.

Keywords: Deep Learning · machine learning · finance · stock market prediction · mapping study

1 Introduction

The choice of investments is crucial for organizations such as pension funds, where the viability horizon of the funds managed is limited.

Stock market prediction implementations to assist decision-making can help managers better select their investments. Accordingly, they will be able to improve the performance of their portfolios and prolong to a maximum the horizon of viability of their managed funds.

Overall, there are two approaches for predicting the direction of stock prices: fundamental analysis and technical analysis. Fundamental analysis evaluates the stock price based on its intrinsic value. This approach implies an in-depth analysis while exploiting balance sheet, strategic initiatives and microeconomic indicators of the studied company. Whereas, technical analysis studies technical indicators and charts to detect patterns and signals of future price variations. The diversity of technical indicators used for technical analysis makes them an appropriate candidate for machine learning models.

Deep learning as an advanced and promising branch of machine learning has shown a strong ability of learning nonlinear relationship between inputs and dealing with big data. Major advances have been made by deep learning methods in solving complex

M. Tabaa et al. (Eds.): INTIS 2022/2023, CCIS 1728, pp. 20–31, 2024.
https://doi.org/10.1007/978-3-031-47366-1_2

problems that have resisted to the best attempts of the artificial intelligence community for many years [1].

Since the emergence of deep learning models, several studies have investigated their applicability to stock market prediction [2] and have validated the relevance of this approach. Thus, studies are trying to build efficient deep learning prediction models for stock market prediction and compare them to linear and other machine learning models [3, 4].

Our focus in this mapping study is to catch up with the latest advances in the application of deep learning to stock market prediction. For this purpose, we analyze and classify deep learning models, input data, markets and validation metrics used in the literature. We also discuss the results of our analysis and identify possible future research directions.

This paper is organized as follows. Section 2 provides an overview of previous works covering the main topic. Section 3 presents the systematic mapping study protocol used in this research. Section 4 provides and discusses results. Section 5 presents a synthesis and future work possibilities. Finally, Sect. 6 describes our contribution and concludes the paper.

2 Related Works

Stock market prediction is a research topic that has intrigued the scientific community for a long time, several review papers have studied the application of deep learning to this problem. This section enumerates some of them in chronological order.

Back in 2010, Li & Ma [5] publishes a survey on the applications of artificial neural networks in forecasting financial market prices, including stock prices and option pricing. Loughran & Mcdonald (2016) [6] provides a survey about textual analysis in accounting and finance.

More broadly, Hatcher et al. (2018) [7] presents a survey of Deep Learning and its various implementations, platforms, algorithms, and uses. He also provides insight into areas, in which deep learning can improve investigation. Finance and economics are examined and studied in this paper.

Recently, Ozbayogy et al. (2020) reviews the applications of deep learning for finance, including all its domains, with and without using time series [8, 9]. The two papers include a focus on stock market prediction. In the same year Huang et al. [10] presents a literature review of deep learning in finance and banking, including stock market prediction, exchange rate prediction and bank default risk prediction.

In 2021, Hu et al. [11] publishes a survey of forex and stock price prediction using deep learning. He finds that deep learning methods yield great returns and performances when applied to forex and stock price prediction. He finally concludes that, in recent years, the trend of using deep-learning-based methods for financial modeling is rising exponentially.

In summary, we can see from the number of reviews that there is considerable interest in applications of deep learning to stock price prediction. Our study aims at synchronizing with the latest progress and providing a comprehensive paper of the studied topic. To this end, we deeply analyze used deep learning models, input data, evaluation metrics and studied markets.

3 Research Method

The methodology applied in this study was conducted according to the guideline published by Kitchenham et al. [12]. The following sections describe how we followed the guideline to answer the research questions.

Definition of research questions
The research questions (RQs) for this mapping study are defined as:

- RQ 1: Which deep learning models are used for stock market prediction?
- RQ 2: Which data are most used for price prediction? And what time period (input data depth) is the most recurrent?
- RQ 3: Which markets are used to evaluate the proposed model?
- RQ 4: Which prediction horizon is most used?
- RQ 5: Which evaluation metrics are used?

Search on databases
We used an automated searching as a main strategy. For this we used the two databases SpringerLink and ScienceDirect, which index many publications in the field of computer science and related disciplines.

After analyzing different combinations of search terms, we chose to build a search query composed of three different parts. The first one related to the type of financial instrument studied, the second one for the purpose of the study and the third one of the method used (Table 1).

Our evaluation of the results of the different queries, showed that the most relevant results of this study contains the terms 'stock', 'Forecast or Predict' and 'Deep Learning' in the title, abstract or keywords. To this end a filter has been applied. Additionally, no limits were applied on date of publication. Table 1 shows details of the search string used in this paper.

Table 1. Search string used.

Stock Price OR Stock Movement OR Stock Trend OR Stock Market
AND
Forecasting OR Prediction OR forecast OR Predict
AND
Deep Learning

Study selection
The research results were filtered by applying the inclusion, exclusion and validity criteria detailed in Table 2. The purpose of this phase is to select the most relevant papers for study.

After applying all the selection criteria, 41 primary studies were selected for analysis (Fig. 1).

Table 2. Inclusion, exclusion and validity criteria used.

Type	Description
Inclusion	Papers that treat the prediction of stock prices as a main subject
Exclusion	Studies on financial instruments other than stocks
	Duplicates
	Book extracts
	Articles without an abstract
	Studies not presented in English or French
Validity	Study objectives clearly defined
	The proposed architecture is justified and implemented
	The results are discussed and compared with other models

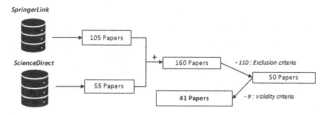

Fig. 1. Breakdown of the selection process.

Data Extraction

The articles were analyzed, and the data were extracted following the template shown in Table 3. The extracted information is either general and gives global information about the article, or specific and answers the research questions.

Paper Statistics

Before presenting mapping study results, we will provide an overview of the included papers.

For the 41 analyzed papers, the publication year is at least 2017. So the activity on the studied topic was not significantly visible until 2017. Figure 2 details the number of papers per year.

Figure 2 highlights a significant increase in the number of papers dealing with the prediction of stock markets by applying deep learning methods. Also, the number of publications has quadrupled from 2017 (date of the first studied publication) to 2020, which shows the growing interest in this recent and challenging topic.

We specify that the number of publications in 2021 is not definitive, since the study was done in May 2021.

Distribution of papers by source type: conference and journal are described in Fig. 3.

The top source conference and journal sorted by number of papers included in this study are detailed in Table 4 and 5.

Table 3. Extracted data template.

Data extracted
Year
Title
Authors
Source
Proposed model
Inputs
Time periods
Output
Evaluation metrics
Comparison models
Stock
Stock market
Timeframe (Horizon)
Environment

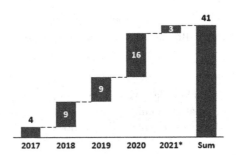

Fig. 2. Paper count per year.

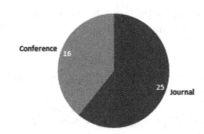

Fig. 3. Papers classification by source type.

Table 4. Ranking of journals by the number of papers included in this study.

Conference	Papers
Procedia Computer Science	5
Lecture Notes in Computer Science	4
Advances in Intelligent Systems and Computing	3
Communications in Computer and Information Science	2
Others	2

Table 5. Ranking of conferences by the number of papers included in this study.

Journal	Papers
Expert Systems with Applications	6
Neural Computing and Applications	4
Journal of Ambient Intelligence and Humanized Computing	2
Others	13

The conference and journal with the most published papers are "Procedia Computer Science" and the "Expert Systems with Applications "accounting for over a quarter of all publications.

4 Systematic Mapping Results

We map 41 papers in order to answer the questions (RQs). In this section, we will present the results of the conducted systematic mapping study.

Based on target output, used approach is either a regression (stock value) or a classification (stock trend). In this study, 16 articles used classification and 25 used regression.

RQ 1: which deep learning models are used for stock market prediction?

There are different models of deep learning of which we define some:

- Long short-term memory (LSTM): is a type of artificial neural network specifically intended to recognize patterns in sequences of data, such as language recognition and time series data forecasting. LSTM networks consist of LSTM units. A common LSTM unit is composed of a cell having an input, an output and forgets gates.
- Convolutional neural network (CNN): is a type of deep neural network, which is widely used for image and object recognition and classification. In general, CNN architectures consist of multiple convolutional layers, pooling layers, fully connected layers and normalization layers.
- Deep neural network (DNN): is a type of artificial neural network composed of an input layer, multiple hidden layers and output layer. The neurons are interconnected by weight.

Figure 4 shows usage percentage of each deep learning model.

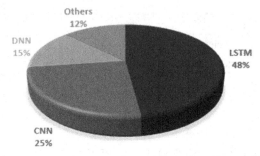

Fig. 4. Percentage of use for each Deep Learning model.

LSTM (long short-term memory) and CNN (convolutional neural network) are the most applied in the literature. In addition, all the proposed models are supervised ones, based on training a data sample from a data source with correct classification already assigned [14].

Furthermore, in order to demonstrate the relevance of their proposed model, studied papers use several comparative models: 9% of papers use linear models, 32% machine learning models and 59% deep learning models (Fig. 5). Performance results of the proposed models show the outperformance of Deep learning models when comparing to other machine learning or linear models.

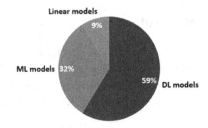

Fig. 5. Distribution of used comparative models.

RQ 2: Which data are most used for price prediction? and what time period is the most recurrent?

Data used

To answer this question, we classify the input data into five different types:

- Market data: market variables related to trading activity, including historical prices (open price, closing price, high, low, volume) and technical indicators.
- Macroeconomic data: information related to the global economic situation of a country or a sector including inflation, reserves and central bank's policy rate.
- Text data: textual information extracted from news, tweets, etc.

- Fundamental data: variables translating the health of the company published generally every six months including net results, assets and liabilities.
- Analytics data: statistical variables such as the number of times the stock name has been searched on Wikipedia, Google or other.

Each document is then mapped to the type of data it uses. Figure 6 details the number of usages of each data type.

Market data is used the most; this data is generally easy to retrieve for long periods of time. Therefore, Market data is an ideal candidate for training deep learning models who require a huge amount of input data. Text data is the second most popular input, more difficult to retrieve than market data, but very useful for capturing sudden abrupt changes in the stock market [13].

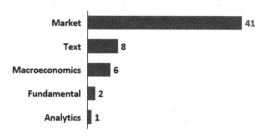

Fig. 6. Paper count per input type.

Input combinations are also used to improve the performance of the proposed models. Figure 7 shows various combinations used in the literature.

Fig. 7. Distribution of used input combinations.

The figure above shows that 37% of the articles use only historical prices, 24% use both historical prices and technical indicators (market data). The combinations of inputs including 3 or more types of data have not been widely explored and represent only 4% of studied papers.

Data depth

Time periods distribution of data in mapped papers is detailed in Fig. 8. The most used data depth is 5 to 9 years. Articles using data collected over less than a year are mostly articles studying intraday prediction.

RQ 3: Which markets are used to evaluate the proposed model?

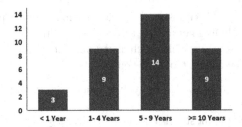

Fig. 8. Paper count per time periods of input data.

Different markets are used in the papers. Figure 9 shows that the US stock market is the most studied with 19 articles, followed by the Chinese market with 13 articles. The whole Asian market has the highest number of publications, which reflects the increased interest of these markets in AI methods. Finally, Tunisian, Guinean and Turkish markets are studied only once.

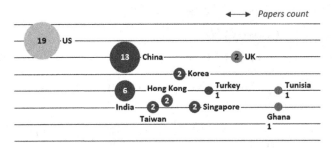

Fig. 9. Stock market used.

All in all, most of the studies focus on one market, only 7 of the studied articles evaluate their models on multiple markets.

RQ 4: Which prediction horizon is most used?

Regarding the prediction horizon (time length of the future to be predicted), daily forecasting is the most studied (Fig. 10). Only four papers in the selection studied multiple timeframes (daily prediction and several days' prediction).

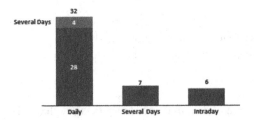

Fig. 10. Paper count by prediction horizon.

Intraday predictions are the rarest, the reason behind could be the complexity of collecting corresponding data.

RQ 5: Which evaluation metrics are used?

In order to measure forecast accuracy of the proposed model, different metrics are used depending on if the approach is a classification or regression (Fig. 11). For Classification: The most used metrics are accuracy and F1 score.

For Regression: The most used metrics are RMSE (Root Mean Square Error), MAE (Mean Absolute Error), and MAPE (Mean Absolute Percentage Error).

However, no study has mentioned that the proposed model has been tested in a real environment.

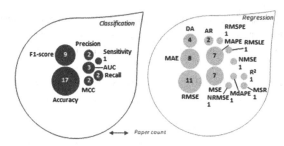

Fig. 11. Paper count by used evaluation metrics.

5   Synthesis and Future Works

In this study, we focus on giving an overview of the achievements in the field of deep learning applications in stock price prediction.

The first question we try to answer, deals with models that were applied to solve this issue. The results show a dominance of LSTM and CNN models. However, deep learning models continue to evolve, and the relevance of integrating many models has not yet been studied or not completely explored, such as for Capsule network, Graph neural network and Generative adversarial network.

Regarding data used for model training, question 2 (RQ2) shows a diversity of input data used for stock price forecasting. The use of combinations of inputs allows improving performance results. Therefore, it appears relevant to explore new data sources in order to further enrich input data, for example using knowledge graph data. In addition, new data processing models could be tested to improve data interpretation for textual information.

As for studied markets, the majority of studied papers focus on one market and only a few of them evaluate their model in different stock markets. Moreover, the relevance of deep learning models for stock price prediction has never been studied or evaluated for some emerging markets.

Studying cross market correlation and integrating it to the predictive model could be relevant. Particularly for intraday forecasting where using time lag between different markets would allow capturing more news/data.

It is worth to mention that, none of the proposed model is tested in a real environment. Performing this test and comparing its results with the theoretical ones could be an area for improvement. Last but not least, proposing an adaptive and intelligent trading or asset management strategy, with an evaluation of risk and profitability is a possibility for future works with noteworthy impact on banking and financial industry.

6   Conclusion

This paper presents the results of a systematic mapping study on applications of deep learning to stock market prediction. Thus, we analyze 41 research publications to answer the five questions of the study.

The findings discussed in this study highlight some literature gaps, such as integrating new deep learning models that appear in recent years, varying data sources and merging them in an intelligent way, proposing a trading strategy and testing it in a real environment, and others.

To the best of our knowledge, this will be the first systematic mapping study covering deep learning and stock market forecasting.

References

1. Lecun, Y., Bengio, Y., Hinton, G.: Deep learning. Nature **521**(7553), 436–444 (2015). https://doi.org/10.1038/nature14539
2. Jayanth Balaji, A., Harish Ram, D.S., Nair, B.B.: Applicability of deep learning models for stock price forecasting an empirical study on BANKEX data. Procedia Comput. Sci. **143**, 947–953 (2018)
3. Nikou, M., Mansourfar, G., Bagherzadeh, J.: Stock price prediction using DEEP learning algorithm and its comparison with machine learning algorithms. Intell. Syst. Account. Financ. Manag. **26**(4), 164–174 (2019)
4. Xu, Y., Cohen, S.B.: Stock movement prediction from tweets and historical prices. In: ACL 2018 - 56th Annual Meeting of the Association for Computational Linguistics, Proceedings of the Conference (Long Papers), vol. 1, pp. 1970–1979 (2018)
5. Li, Y., Ma, W.: Applications of artificial neural networks in financial economics: a survey. In: Proceedings - 2010 International Symposium on Computational Intelligence and Design, ISCID 2010, vol. 1, pp. 211–214 (2010)
6. Loughran, T., Mcdonald, B.: Textual analysis in accounting and finance: a Survey. J. Account. Res. **54**(4), 1187–1230 (2016)
7. Hatcher, W.G., Yu, W.: A Survey of deep learning: platforms, applications and emerging research trends. IEEE Access **6**, 24411–24432 (2018)
8. Ozbayoglu, A.M., Gudelek, M.U., Sezer, O.B.: Deep learning for financial applications : a survey. Appl. Soft Comput. **93**, 106384 (2020)
9. Sezer, O.B., Gudelek, M.U., Ozbayoglu, A.M.: Financial time series forecasting with deep learning : a systematic literature review: 2005–2019. Appl. Soft Comput. **90**, 106181 (2020)
10. Huang, J., Chai, J., Cho, S.: Deep learning in finance and banking: a literature review and classification. Front. Bus. Res. China **14**(1), 1–24 (2020)
11. Hu, Z., Zhao, Y., Khushi, M.: A survey of forex and stock price prediction using deep learning. Appl. Syst. Innov. **4**(1), 1–30 (2021)

12. Kitchenham, B., Charters, S.: Guidelines for Performing Systematic Literature Reviews in Software Engineering, Technical Report EBSE 2007–001, Keele University and Durham University Joint Report. - References - Scientific Research Publishing (2007)
13. Deng, S., Chen, J., Zhang, N., Pan, J. Z., Zhang, W., Chen, H.: Knowledge-driven stock trend prediction and explanation via temporal convolutional network. In: The Web Conference 2019 - Companion of the World Wide Web Conference, WWW 2019, 678–685 (2019)
14. Sathya, R., Abraham, A.: Comparison of supervised and unsupervised learning algorithms for pattern classification. In: International Journal of Advanced Research in Artificial Intelligence, vol. 2(2) (2013)

Exploring the Knowledge Distillation

Yasssine Khaider[1]([✉])[iD], Dounia Rahhali[1][iD], Hamza Alami[2],
and Noureddine En Nahnahi[1][iD]

[1] LISAC Laboratory, Faculty of Sciences Dhar EL Mehraz, Sidi Mohamed Ben
Abdellah University, Fez, Morocco
{yassine.khaider,dounia.rahhali,noureddine.en-nahnahi}@usmba.ac.ma
[2] Department of Engineering, Innov-Tech Laboratory, High Technology School,
Rabat, Morocco

Abstract. Knowledge distillation is a well-known method of model compressing but it is largely under-used. Knowledge distillation has the ability to reduce the size of a model by transferring the knowledge from a large (pre-trained or not) model into a smaller one with minimum loss to the accuracy, for a better fit in edge devices and the devices with low computational power. Furthermore, it can be used also as a performance enhancer for the student model as we'll see in the experiments since it doesn't need any additional data to be effective. This paper argues that the knowledge distillation method or one of its variations should always be used on deep learning models. In our experiments we trained and tested our models on some well-known datasets (MNIST, CIFAR10 and CIFAR100) to prove that the knowledge distillation and two of its variations give positive results when applied on over-fitted or under-fitted teacher models.

Keywords: Deep learning · knowledge distillation · teacher student · convolutional neural network · teacher assistant knowledge distillation

1 Introduction

In recent years, deep learning models have become popular and very successful in various fields such as computer vision, natural language processing, robotics, etc. This is due to these models great scalability to both large-scale data samples and billions of model parameters. Thus, their deployment in devices that have limited resources and their use in applications with strict latency requirements are hindered. For example, edge and embedded devices (mobile, Arduino, raspberry Pi, and drones). Therefore, some techniques have arisen to compress and accelerate deep learning models (e.g. pruning [1] and quantization [2], etc.). The paper [3] presented a method for "compressing" large, complex ensembles into smaller, faster models, usually without significant loss in performance. They used an ensemble model to label large unlabeled dataset and then trained a single model that performs as well as the ensemble. They developed a new algorithm called MUNGE to generate pseudo data based on shallow neural networks.

M. Tabaa et al. (Eds.): INTIS 2022/2023, CCIS 1728, pp. 32–44, 2024.
https://doi.org/10.1007/978-3-031-47366-1_3

Authors [4] proposed the idea of teacher-student learning method. They show that after training a shallow neural networks with a complex teacher, the model can achieve almost the same performances of deep neural networks. Instead of using the softmax output, the logits are then treated as labels to train the shallow student network. Therefore, the student network benefits from the teacher model generalization, without losing information via the softmax layer.

As a modern technique for model compression, knowledge distillation (KD) [5] aims to increase the student model's performance through training it to imitate a pre-trained, larger model. This process is frequently named "teacher-student", where the teacher is the largest model and the student is the small model. With its simplicity and effectiveness, it has received increasing attention from the community.

In this paper, we built various deep neural networks models based on KD, teacher assistant knowledge distillation (TAKD) [6], and self-distillation (SD). We used badly trained teacher models (with minimal effort of increasing their performance) to prove that those techniques can be used with overfitted or underfitted models and give better results (increase of student model performance compared to training it without those methods). Although the paper [7] had a similar idea but it remains limited to the vanilla KD due to the purpose of that paper. We performed these various experiments using publicly available datasets namely MNIST, Cifar10 [8], and Cifar100 [8]. The obtained results show the effectiveness of these techniques.

This paper is organized as follows: Sect. 2 states some works related to our study, Sect. 3 briefly describes the methods used, Sect. 4 presents in a detailed manner the results and findings of our experiments. Finally, Sect. 5 contains a global conclusion of the work and also outlines the future work.

2   Related Work

In this section we highlight the research done on some of the well-known compression and acceleration methods for deep learning models.

Usually, large models tend to be over-parameterized and not all of those parameters are being used or have a low impact on the models result. Therefore, Pruning aims to locate and remove those parameters [9]. This paper [10] introduces a technique to prune convolutional filters and set the ones with the least contributions to 0 after each training epoch.

The main objective of the quantization method is the reduction of the total amount of bits used when representing each weight, the papers [11,12] presented a low bit-width models utilizing weight and activation quantization with results that yields a high level of accuracy, while this paper [13] used k-means as a method of clustering on the weight values, to result in storage of the model weights in compressed format when the training is completed, since it helps reducing the storage and the computational required.

Numerous variations of the knowledge distillation appeared such as attention distillation that implements map functions to transfer the knowledge about feature embedding [14,15]. The lifelong distillation which depends on accumulating the knowledge previously learned and transfers it into future KD without forgetting or loosing too much information [16,17]. The multi-teacher distillation consists of helping the student model to learn from the knowledge transferred by multiple large models via averaging the prediction of all the teacher models or any other method [18,19]. The data-free distillation adds the generation of the data needed for training to the basic KD from the feature representation of the pre-trained teacher model [20,21]. The adversarial distillation utilizes generative adversarial networks to create synthetic data [22], increase the size of existing training dataset [23] or generate examples for transferring the knowledge [24]. The NAS-based distillation is based on neural architecture search (NAS) which automatically design deep neural models and learn adaptively the optimal structure for the those models, since the architecture of the student model in the knowledge distillation influence its performance, this method yields great results [25,26]. The Quantized distillation revolves around combining the quantization with the knowledge distillation either on the teacher model alone or on both the teacher and the student models [27,28]. The Cross-modal distillation aims transfer the knowledge from the teacher model to the student model that has a different modality (temporal data to spatial data [29], RGB images to depth images [30]. Finally, the Graph-based distillation can either use the graph to carry teacher knowledge or to control the knowledge transfer of the teacher [31,32] (Fig. 1).

Fig. 1. Distillation Algorithms

All the different variation of the knowledge distillation method are follow-ing a specific form of knowledge distillation. The three forms of the knowledge distillation are the Response-Based Knowledge which relies on transferring the knowledge from the output of the model (last layer) to help the student model mimic the output of the teacher model [33], the Feature-Based Knowledge that transfers the knowledge from the intermediate layers of the model (last layer) to help the student model mimic how the teacher model extract the features [34], and the Relation-Based Knowledge combines the previous two forms and adds the knowledge obtained from the relationship between data samples or feature maps [35].

3 Methods and Background

In this section, we give a detailed definition of the vanilla KD and all of its characteristics. Also we explain how the two interesting variants (TAKD, SD) work while highlighting the similarity to the original method.

3.1 Knowledge Distillation

KD allows to transfer the knowledge learnt by an oversized model to a smaller one, that may not be able to easily learn it directly from the information itself, producing a brand-new model that's faster to train and test, and so deployable on less powerful hardware (such as a mobile device), while at the same time experiencing a noticeable increase in the accuracy of the smaller model com-pared to it being trained without KD.

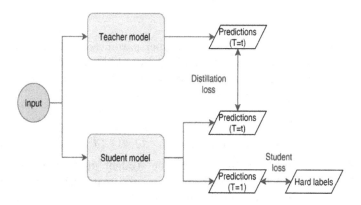

Fig. 2. The architecture of the KD

Model distillation can be achieved as illustrated in Fig. 2. Through a teacher model and a student model. Obviously, what we need is the teacher's predictions and then soften them with the temperature parameter, then give those soften prediction to the student model as the true label for him to train on (named as "distillation loss"). Finally, we train the student model on the hard labels to increase its accuracy (named "student loss"), and that can be tuned by the alpha hyper-parameter. Another thing to keep in mind is that the architecture of the model can change depending on the distillation scheme chosen. The main characteristics of KD are the temperature that extract how the model generalize, and the alpha hyper-parameter which enables the possibility of how much to learn from the teacher model's predictions. We will fine-tune those hyper-parameters manually just enough to prove our concept, also other methods for hyper-parameter optimization and fine-tuning can be used such as grid search or random search, and while they give better performance, they are insanely computationally expensive.

Temperature. Normally, the knowledge is transferred from the teacher model to the student model by minimizing a loss function in which the target is the distribution of class probabilities predicted by the teacher model. In other words, the output of a softmax function on the teacher model's logits. Although, in a lot of cases, this probability distribution has the correct class with a probability close to 1, and all other class probabilities very close to 0. Therefore, it doesn't differ much from the ground truth labels already provided in the dataset. To tackle this issue, [5] introduced the concept of "softmax temperature", T is the temperature hyper-parameter added where the increase of it gives more information about how the teacher generalizes its prediction. The probability p_i of class i is calculated from the logits z as:

$$p_i = \frac{e^{\frac{z_i}{T}}}{\sum_j e^{\frac{z_i}{T}}} \tag{1}$$

Alpha Hyper-parameter. The alpha hyper-parameter is used when we try to increase the influence of the predictions by adding directly the hard loss (comparing with true labels) to the distillation loss (comparing with the teacher predictions) in the global loss which looks like:

$$
\begin{aligned}
L(x; W) = {}& \alpha * H(y, \sigma(z_s; T = 1)) \\
& + \beta * H(y, \sigma(z_t; T = \tau), \sigma(z_s; T = \tau))
\end{aligned} \tag{2}
$$

where x represents the input and W are the student model parameters given to the global loss, while H is the loss function used (categorical cross-entropy), the logit of the teacher and student are z_t and z_s respectively, T is the temperature hyper-parameter and finally α and β coefficients are how to control the predictions influence.

3.2   Teacher Assistant Knowledge Distillation

TAKD consists of introducing another model between the teacher and the student to help the student model to further learn how to generalize from the teacher. When the student model is too small to learn from all the information given by the teacher model, the assistant model comes to simplify that knowledge for the student model. The Fig. 3 illustrates the difference in the hidden layers as well as the flow of transferring the knowledge.

The other interesting fact is that we are not limited by just one teacher assistant model, the paper [6] showed that the more teacher assistant models the more the student model learns and its accuracy improves, since it helps by reducing the amount of generalization information loss.

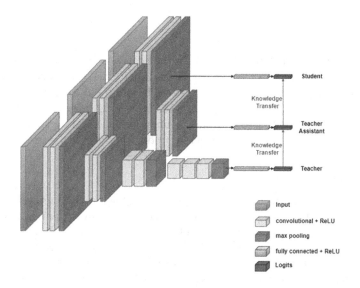

Fig. 3. Teacher Assistant fills the gap between student & teacher [6]

3.3   Self-distillation

The SD scheme is used when we want to further improve our model by learning from its own prediction. In other words, when the architecture of the student and the teacher models are identical, then it's called self-distillation.

To do that, we give the prediction produced by the trained model to a new model that has the same architecture which helps it enhance its performance. It is interesting due to the ambiguity and the lack of rigorous understanding to how the model learns from its own predictions without any external data or influence.

There is a lot of techniques to achieve SD [36,37], for example, in the paper [38] introduced that after every epoch they take the predictions and give them to the new model to learn from, which means that the student model transforms to become the teacher model after every epoch. But in our experiment, we used the final prediction after the teacher model has finished training as shown in the Fig. 2.

4   Experimental Results

In our experiments, we used "Colaboratory" as an online platform of executing our work, combined with some famous libraries of model classification problems training and performance assessment which are: tensorflow, keras, numpy, matplotlib.

4.1   Datasets

Our training was on the CIFAR10 dataset that consists of 50000 training images and 10000 test images of 32×32 color images in 10 classes, CIFAR100 dataset that has 100 classes containing 600 images each, and finally, the MNIST dataset that contains 60,000 training images and 10,000 testing images. We chose these datasets for they are well-known in the classification field and for they are heavily used in benchmarking, all to give a better understanding of our results.

4.2   Experiment Settings

We realized experiments on different datasets following the method proposed by [5] and due to time constraint we found the optimal hyper-parameters (temperature/loss coefficients) only for the VGG16 trained on CIFAR10 and applied them to all of our work, until we don't obtain the increase of performance in the student then we change it, such as in TAKD, because those hyper-parameters are the core of the KD. To further explain we will detail below:

In the Vanilla KD: We tried multiple hyper parameters but the ones with the highest results are: Temperature = 5, Loss_weight for the output with temperature = 0.7, Loss_weight for the output with only the softmax = 0.3.

- For CIFAR10: we used the pre-trained VGG16 model as a teacher and a student model with an architecture shown in Fig. 4.

- For CIFAR100:
  Teacher: used a different model illustrated in Fig. 5, Student: followed the same architecture as the one in Fig. 4.

- For MNIST dataset: we used the architecture Fig. 4 as a teacher model and a student model with an architecture as in Fig. 6.

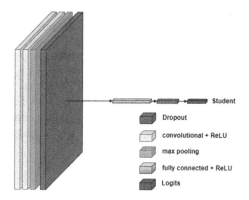

Fig. 4. Student model used for KD and SD with cifar10 and cifar100

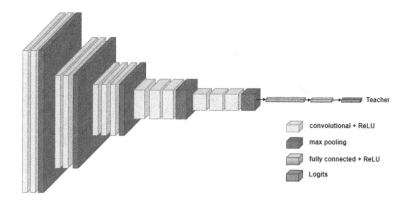

Fig. 5. Teacher model used for KD with cifar100

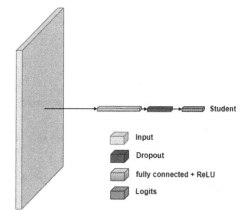

Fig. 6. Student model used for KD with Mnist

In the TAKD Method: We used Temperature = 5, Loss_weight for the output with temperature = 0.3, Loss_weight for the output with only the softmax = 0.7.

– We used for CIFAR10 a teacher model with 4 blocks, a teacher assistant model with 3 blocks and a student model with 2 block Fig. 7.
– We used for CIFAR100 a teacher model with 4 blocks and a teacher assistant model with 3 blocks same architecture as in Fig. 7 and a different student model with 2 block illustrated in Fig. 8.

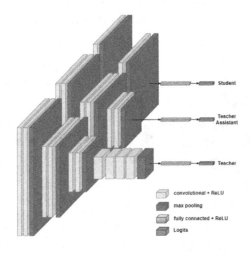

Fig. 7. All the models used for TAKD with cifar10

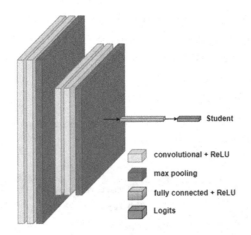

Fig. 8. Student model used for TAKD

In the SD Method: We used the architecture in Fig. 4 for both CIFAR10 and CIFAR100, with Temperature = 5.

Loss_weight for the output with temperature = 0.7.

Loss_weight for the output with only the softmax = 0.3.

4.3   Evaluation Metric

Since our data is balanced we relied on the categorical cross-entropy loss and the keras metrics categorical accuracy that verifies the percentage of the true predicted values. The equations for the accuracy is as follows:

$$Accuracy(\%) = \frac{\text{Number of the true predicted images}}{\text{Number of all the images in the datatset}} * 100 \qquad (3)$$

4.4   Performance Evaluation

The results in Table 1 show the increase of accuracy proven on different datasets with different models while using the same hyper-parameters for all the tests as described before.

Table 1. The accuracy obtained with the knowledge distillation on different datasets.

Datasets	Performances		
	Teacher's accuracy	Student accuracy	Distilled student accuracy
MNIST	99.129%	97.939%	98.32%
CIFAR10	80.729%	55.909%	66.100%
CIFAR100	43.23%	32.55%	36.689%

Moreover, while we test the same basic KD method on multiple datasets, we kept the same hyper-parameters (temperature and loss coefficients), all this is for the simple reason of keeping the experiments fair, in Table 1 we can see that the increase of the performance with is due purely to the KD, and this method works with various datasets whatever your models state.

Table 2. Performance of the self-distillation method on CIFAR10 and CIFAR100.

Datasets	Performances	
	Teacher's and student's accuracy (same model)	Distilled student accuracy
CIFAR10	69.569%	71.23%
CIFAR100	38.269%	40.029%

In the SD distillation, we also used the same hyper-parameters and obtained an increase in the accuracy on both datasets CIFAR10 and CIFAR100. From Table 2 SD pushes us to assume that we should always use this method to enhance the performance of our model.

Table 3. The accuracy obtained with the TAKD on CIFAR10 and CIFAR100.

Datasets	Performances		
	Teacher's accuracy	*Student accuracy*	*TAKD's student accuracy*
CIFAR10	72.769%	61.229%	62.08%
CIFAR100	38.989%	32.73%	32.789%

Finally, we have the results of the TAKD's method in which we see the increase of the performance even if it's a small improvement because we used the same parameters for all the tests, but for the loss coefficients we change it into 0.3 on the distillation loss and 0.7 on the student loss (basically a switch) (Table 3).

5   Conclusion

In this work, we experimented with different neural network distillation techniques KD, TAKD, and SD using the well-known datasets CIFAR10, CIFAR100, and MNIST. As the KD compresses the model, TAKD also does the same thing but gives a solution to the huge gap between the teacher and the student. On the other hand, we have the SD that aims to improve the performance of the model without any new data or external influence. In the initial testing on TAKD with different models and before obtaining the results above, we had an assistant model bigger than a student model but gave a lesser accuracy than the student model. After distilling the student model, its accuracy has improved even with the defected predictions of the teacher assistant model. These experiments showed the value of using KD and its variations for compressing models or improving the performance even with badly trained models.

Future studies could investigate the association between several methods of KD since there are numerous, and being published continuously. Another important area for future research is to further study the results of combining the KD with pruning and quantization. Also finding a logical explanation of how the model can learn from its own predictions without any new information is an interesting field for researchers to tackle and start unraveling.

References

1. Zhu, M., Gupta, S.: To prune or not to prune: exploring the efficacy of pruning for model compression (2017)

2. Sung, W., Shin, S., Hwang, K.: Resiliency of deep neural networks under quantization (2015)
3. Bucila, C., Caruana, R., Niculescu-Mizil, A.: Model compression, vol. 10(1145), pp. 535–541 (2006)
4. Ba, L.J., Caruana, R.: Do deep nets really need to be deep? Adv. Neural. Inf. Process. Syst. **3**, 2654–2662 (2014)
5. Hinton, G., Vinyals, O., Dean, J.: Distilling the knowledge in a neural network (2015)
6. Mirzadeh, S.I., Farajtabar, M., Li, A., Levine, N., Matsukawa, A., Ghasemzadeh, H.: Improved knowledge distillation via teacher assistant. In: AAAIth AAAI, editor, AAAI 2020–34th AAAI Conference on Artificial Intelligence, pp. 5191–5198 (2020)
7. Yuan, L., Tay, F., Li, G., Wang, T., Feng, J.: Revisiting knowledge distillation via label smoothing regularization, vol. 10(1109), pp. 3902–3910 (2020)
8. Krizhevsky, A., Nair, V., Hinton, G.: Learning multiple layers of features from tiny images (2009)
9. Ding, X., Ding, G., Zhou, X., Guo, Y., Liu, J., Han, J.: Global sparse momentum SGD for pruning very deep neural networks (2019)
10. He, Y., Kang, G., Dong, X., Fu, Y., Yang, Y.: Soft filter pruning for accelerating deep convolutional neural networks, vol. 10(24963), pp. 2234–2240 (2018)
11. Zhou, A., Yao, A., Guo, Y., Xu, L., Chen, Y.: Incremental network quantization: towards lossless CNNs with low-precision weights (2017)
12. Zhao, Y., Gao, X., Bates, D., Mullins, R.D., Xu, C.: Focused quantization for sparse CNNs. In: NeurIPS (2019)
13. Wu, J., Leng, C., Wang, Y., Lin, Q., Cheng, J.: Quantized convolutional neural networks for mobile devices (2015)
14. Zagoruyko, N., Komodakis, S.: Paying more attention to attention: improving the performance of convolutional neural networks via attention transfer (2016)
15. Srinivas, S., Fleuret, F.: Knowledge transfer with Jacobian matching (2018)
16. Li, Z., Hoiem, D.: Learning without forgetting. In: ECCV (2016)
17. Jang, Y., Lee, H., Hwang, S.J., Shin, J.: Learning what and where to transfer. In: Proceedings of the 36th International Conference on Machine Learning, in Proceedings of Machine Learning Research (2019)
18. Zhao, H., Sun, X., Dong, J., Chen, C., Dong, Z.: Highlight every step: knowledge distillation via collaborative teaching. IEEE Trans. Cybern. **52**, 2070–2081 (2022)
19. Yuan, F., et al.: Reinforced multi-teacher selection for knowledge distillation (2020)
20. Nayak, G.K., Mopuri, K.R., Chakraborty, A.: Effectiveness of arbitrary transfer sets for data-free knowledge distillation, vol. 10(1109), pp. 1429–1437 (2021)
21. Shen, C., Wang, X., Yin, Y., Song, J., Luo, S., Song, M.: Progressive network grafting for few-shot knowledge distillation (2020)
22. Ye, J., Ji, Y., Wang, X., Gao, X., Song, M.: Data-free knowledge amalgamation via group-stack dual-GAN, vol. 10(1109), pp. 12513–12522 (2020)
23. Liu, R., Fusi, N., Mackey, L.: Model compression with generative adversarial networks (2018)
24. Micaelli, P., Storkey, A.: Zero-shot knowledge transfer via adversarial belief matching (2019)
25. Li, C., et al.: Block-wisely supervised neural architecture search with knowledge distillation (2019)
26. Peng, H., Du, H., Yu, H., Li, Q., Liao, J., Fu, J.: Cream of the crop: distilling prioritized paths for one-shot neural architecture search (2020)

27. Kim, J., Bhalgat, Y., Lee, J., Patel, C., Kwak, N.: QKD: quantization-aware knowledge distillation (2019)
28. Shin, S., Boo, Y., Sung, W.: Knowledge distillation for optimization of quantized deep neural networks, vol. 10(1109), pp. 1–6 (2020)
29. Roheda, S., Riggan, B., Krim, H., Dai, L.: Cross-modality distillation: a case for conditional generative adversarial networks, vol. 10(1109), pp. 2926–2930 (2018)
30. Tian, Y., Krishnan, D., Isola, P.: Contrastive representation distillation (2019)
31. Chen, H., Wang, Y., Xu, C., Tao, D.: Learning student networks via feature embedding. IEEE Trans. Neural Networks Learn. Syst. **10**(1109), 1–11 (2020)
32. Yao, H., et al.: Graph few-shot learning via knowledge transfer (2019)
33. Meng, Z., Li, J., Zhao, Y., Gong, Y.: Conditional teacher-student learning, vol. 10, p. 1109 (2019)
34. Chen, D., et al.: AAAI (2021)
35. Passalis, N., Tzelepi, M., Tefas, A.: Heterogeneous knowledge distillation using information flow modeling (2020)
36. Zhang, Z., Sabuncu, M.R.: Self-distillation as instance-specific label smoothing (2020)
37. Mobahi, H., Farajtabar, M., Bartlett, P.: Self-distillation amplifies regularization in Hilbert space (2020)
38. Kim, K., Ji, B., Yoon, D., Hwang, S.: Self-knowledge distillation: a simple way for better generalization. arXiv:abs/2006.12000 (2020)

Intelligent Traffic Congestion and Collision Avoidance Using Multi-agent System Based on Reinforcement Learning

Israa Alqatow[1] , Majdi Jaradat[1] , Rashid Jayousi[2]([✉]) ,
and Amjad Rattrout[1]

[1] Arab American University, Ramallah, Palestine
{israa.alqatow,amjad.rattrout}@aaup.edu, m.saleh24@student.aaup.edu
[2] Al-Quds University, Jerusalem, Palestine
rjayousi@staff.alquds.edu

Abstract. The number of vehicles in Palestine has significantly increased over the past decade leading to significant traffic congestion in cities. The narrow structure of roads within cities, coupled with a lack of development and updates, has exacerbated this problem. Congestion causes air pollution and driver frustration and costs a significant amount in fuel consumption. Additionally, collisions between vehicles waiting at traffic lights can occur due to high speeds or small distances between waiting cars. Finding solutions for this dynamic and unpredictable problem is a significant challenge. One proposed solution is to control traffic lights and redirect vehicles from congested roads to less crowded ones. A multi-agent system is utilized in this study. Based on the JaCaMo platform was developed to address the issue of traffic congestion and collision avoidance. Simulation using SUMO and JADE platforms demonstrated that traffic congestion could be reduced by 52.7% through traffic light timing control.

Keywords: multi-agent system · JaCaMo · SUMO

1 Introduction

The number of vehicles in the world is increasing rapidly, and this will lead to the emergence of many problems, such as traffic congestion and Collision between vehicles. This issue has a huge impact on the environment and economy, one of these problems is Pollution [7]. They are spread in the atmosphere as a result of gas emissions from vehicles. These issues' magnitude fluctuates depending on the density of vehicles and the type of roads, varying from one region or country to another. On the other hand, the transportation system does not develop as it does in technology. In addition, the capacity of the old road infrastructure is not able to accommodate the huge numbers of vehicles [5]. In Palestine, we can

M. Tabaa et al. (Eds.): INTIS 2022/2023, CCIS 1728, pp. 45–59, 2024.
https://doi.org/10.1007/978-3-031-47366-1_4

say that the prevailing situation in the cities of Palestine has become crowded roads all the time, and daily collisions occurred between vehicles. In addition, the capacity of the old road infrastructure is not able to accommodate the huge numbers of vehicles. This is due to the weakness in controlling the flow of vehicles through traffic lights; also, there is no control on deviation from highly crowded roads to less crowded roads. Managing and controlling Traffic lights is an important role in mitigating and solving traffic congestion, and also reducing the number of collisions between vehicles. The aim of the proposed system is to efficiently manage and regulate traffic lights by creating a period for each traffic signal based on the level of road congestion. This process is known as a traffic light plan. It is essential to establish and monitor an optimal timing plan for traffic signals to alleviate high. Our proposed system is applied to a crowded city in Palestine which is Ramallah city with the most significant traffic congestion. The Sumo platform was employed to obtain an overview of the roads in Palestine.

2   Literature Review

In several studies conducted on traffic congestion and collision between vehicles in different articles, the multi-agent system has played a major role in solving these problems. In this section, we make a summary of a multi-agent system and related works of intelligent traffic congestion and collision avoidance systems.

2.1   Multi-agent System

MAS is an entity placed in an environment with various parameters used to make decisions based on its goals. To make a necessary action performs based on the decision taken [3]. MAS has the ability to address complex computing problems, By breaking down a complex task into smaller tasks, it becomes possible to assign each task to a unique agent instead of solved by one single powerful entity [2,6]. MAS can be used to address problems in different domains, including controlling smart grids, traffic controls, distributed control, telecommunications, and robotics [1,3]. MAS can be used to address problems in different domains, including controlling smart grids, traffic controls, distributed control, telecommunications, and robotics [6]. In real-world scenarios, it requires using heterogeneous agents with various constraints, structures, and complexity [2,4,6]. Every agent is considered a decision-maker based on its goal and can share knowledge with other agents [2].

2.2   Intelligent Traffic Congestion

The modern world because of rapid urbanization created many challenges. One of these challenges is the rapid spreading of vehicles that leads to traffic congestion and to non-green cities, because of pollution emitted from vehicles. Furthermore, it creates an obstacle for emergency vehicles like ambulances and security vehicles. According to statistics studies in 2017, 20% of patient deaths were because of traffic bottlenecks because ambulance vehicles could not arrive at the patient in time or transmit him to the healthcare center [7]. By the study [12], people waste approximately 6.9 billion hours because of traffic congestion in urban areas, on the other hand, they also consumed about 3.1 billion gallons of fuel, costing a total of 160 billion dollars. The traffic light timing behavior is the primary cause of traffic congestion, author of [8] focuses on the timing of the traffic signal to solve the congestion problem that happened on the road intersections. They used a multi-agent system called DALI (Distributed Agent-based Traffic Lights). This system reduces the delay by 40.12%. The author in [9] pro- pose a new architecture based on reinforcement learning which is a methodology used in the Artificial Intelligence field and a multi-agents system to simulate the real-time changes in the road state to predict congestion level in order to avoid it. The authors of [10] proposed a system called Efficient Intelligent Traffic Light Control and Deviation (EITLCD) and plan to solve the problem based on a multi-agent system. This route model help to find alternative routes to avoid traffic congestion before it occurs.

2.3   Collision Avoidance

Collision avoidance at intersections is one of the most vital issues we have to focus on. Based on a report issued by the U.S Federal Highway Administration in 2020, 50% of collisions occurred close to intersections [11]. In order to mitigate these disastrous facts, the researchers proposed a solution based on Hybrid Norms Synthesizing (HNS), which enables vehicles to consider their local traffic flow, in order to decrease their waiting time and avoid collisions. The authors of [13], proposed a model, It is computationally efficient and specifically designed for real-time simulation of large crowds. The communication between agents is implemented allowing them to share information about their location, speed, and intended actions.

2.4   Reinforcement Learning

The methodology for applying reinforcement in traffic light timing starts by defining the problem as a Markov Decision Process (MDP), in which the traffic light timings are treated as actions, the traffic conditions are treated as states, and the wait times for vehicles are treated as rewards. The objective is to define the optimality in policy, which represents a function mapping states to actions that increase the cumulative reward within a specific time. To solve MDP, a reinforcement-learning algorithm, such as Q-Learning or SARSA, is used. These algorithms work by estimating the optimal action-value function, it is necessary to calculate the anticipated cumulative reward associated with taking a specific action in a given state [17]. The algorithm updates the action-value function by taking into account both the observed rewards and state transitions. The reinforcement-learning algorithm is trained using real-time traffic data, such as vehicle speeds, road occupancy, and traffic volume, to make decisions about when to change the traffic lights. The algorithm continually learns from its experiences and adjusts the traffic light timings accordingly [17]. It provides a dynamic and adaptive solution to traffic light timing, allowing the system to respond quickly to changing traffic conditions and improve overall traffic efficiency.

3   Proposed System

The proposed system is an intelligent multi-agent system based on the reinforcement learning approach to make it adaptive to the continuous changes in the traffic environment. First, we design a conceptual model for the system architecture then we use the JaCaMo platform to define the system environment and its organization and Agents participating in the system.

3.1   System Architecture

The proposed system is made within the integration between two subsystems; First subsystem is called Traffic congestion controller TCC used to control traffic congestion and the second subsystem is called Traffic collision avoidance TCA used to alert drivers before the occurrence of a collision between the waiting vehicles exists on the road intersection, which consists of a traffic light system (see Fig. 1).

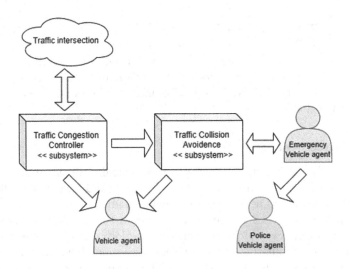

Fig. 1. Architecture of proposed system

The traffic congestion controller TCC defined by six agents (Traffic lights timing agent, Decision making agent, Data Processing agent, Data collector agent, Road traffic status agent, and Road Deviation Agent), Second subsystem is the

Traffic collision avoidance TCA defined by two agents (Supervisor agent and Emergency Detector agent). In addition, the system consists of three external agents (Emergency Vehicle agent, Police Vehicle agent, and Vehicle agent) which interact with the two subsystems (see Fig. 2).

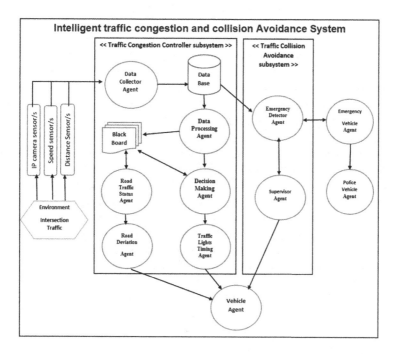

Fig. 2. Architecture of proposed system

3.2 Methodology

In this research, we use simulation-based optimization by applying SUMO opensource software with Python programming language to build a reinforcement learning multi-agent system, to model the traffic network and optimize traffic signal timings. Sumo simulation results were used to help us to propose an appropriate model to be applied in solving traffic congestion and collision avoidance. We use the JaCaMo framework to build the conceptual overview of our MAS system (see Fig. 3). JaCaMo framework also provides a set of features for building MAS including:

- Coordination mechanisms: such as roles and protocols, which can be used to coordinate the actions of the agents and achieve common goals (see Fig. 4).
- Modularity: JaCaMo provides a set of modularity mechanisms, such as modules and components, which can be used to decompose the system into smaller, more manageable parts (see Fig. 5).

– Environments: JaCaMo provides a set of environments, such as the Cartago environment, which can be used to simulate and test MAS applications (see Fig. 6).

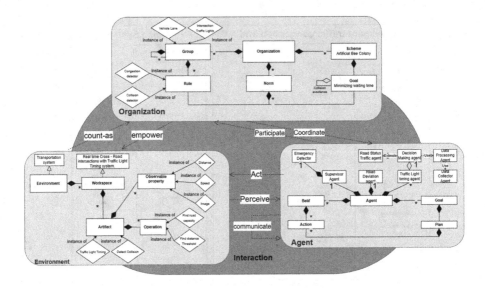

Fig. 3. JaCaMo model for our system

3.3 Design Objectives

The objective of using a multi-agent system involves creating a decentralized and adaptive system that can coordinate the behavior of vehicles and manage traffic flow in order to improve traffic efficiency and reduce congestion, while also ensuring the safety of all road users by avoiding collisions and reducing the number of accidents. The intelligent agents have their own decision-making rules that can communicate and coordinate with one another [17]. Reinforcement learning algorithms assist the system to continually improve and adapt over time, based on real-world data and feedback. The system takes into consideration various factors that contribute to traffic congestion and collisions, such as traffic volume, road conditions, and vehicle behavior. The objective design of a traffic congestion and collision avoidance system using a multi-agent system is a complex and challenging task, but the potential benefits are significant and include improved traffic flow, reduced delays, and increased road safety. Our proposed system aims to satisfy two main goals:

– Traffic congestion avoidance, by minimizing the waiting time for each vehicle in the road intersection, which has traffic lights on it. This is done by controlling the timing duration of each traffic light in the traffic light system.

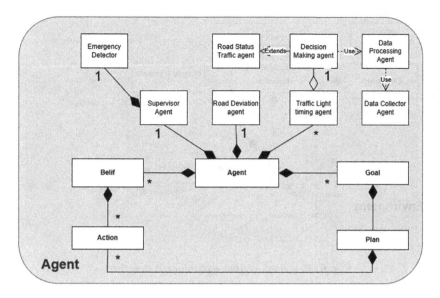

Fig. 4. Agents coordination to achieve their goals

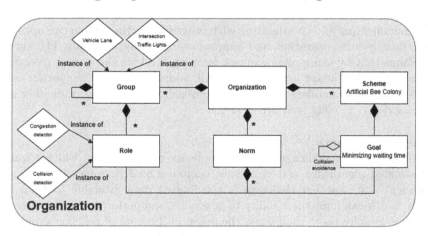

Fig. 5. An overview of the organization of the proposed system

– Collision avoidance, by managing the distances between waiting vehicles at the traffic light and monitoring the speed of the entering vehicles to the intersection area.

Addressing Traffic Congestion
We employ a multi-agent system to overcome congestion by involving multiple intelligent agents to coordinate the behavior of vehicles and manage traffic flow. The proposed approach has the ability to improve traffic flow and reduce delays. The reason behind that, the system responds quickly and is adaptive to changing

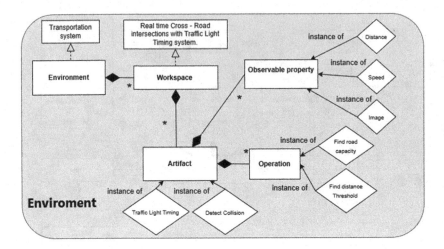

Fig. 6. Proposed system environment overview

traffic conditions. Each agent in the system has its own decisions based on its sensors and information from other agents, such as traffic lights and road sensors. By communicating and coordinating with other agents, the system can optimize traffic flow, reduce congestion, and improve overall traffic efficiency. The author [17] claims that by using reinforcement learning it allows the system to continually improve and adapt over time. Overall, addressing traffic congestion using a multi-agent system offers a promising approach for improving traffic flow and reducing delays in congested urban areas.

Collision Avoidance
One of the biggest challenges is the complexity of the system, which requires sophisticated algorithms and significant computational resources to train and implement [13]. Another challenge is the limited data available to train the agents, which can limit their ability to generalize and perform well in real-world scenarios. Despite these challenges, the potential benefits of collision avoidance using a multi-agent system are significant, and further research and development in this field are expected to result in novel and more efficient methods for enhancing road safety. Our proposed system contains a collision avoidance subsystem with the main role of alersting vehicles depending on the collision indicator before the collision occurs based on Eq. (4). The collision avoidance algorithm is clarified in the following pseudo-code.

Pseudo-code for Collision Avoidance Algorithm
Calculate D between Vf, Vm, Vr where:
Vf= front vehicle, Vm = middle vehicle and Vr = rear vehicle D = distance between vehicles, Allowed D = Th;
for (i=0; $i < n$; i++)

Vf = Vfi - Vfnext;
Vm = Vmi - Vmnext;
Vr = Vri - Vrnext;
$D = \sqrt{Vf^2 + Vm^2 + Vr^2}$;
if ($D >= allowed$)   Do Nothing
else   Critical D, make Alert.

Route Optimization

The goal is to reduce travel time, fuel consumption, and congestion while also ensuring that all vehicles arrive at their destinations as quickly as possible [15]. The system is designed using multiple agents, each representing a single vehicle that can communicate and coordinate with one another. The use of machine learning algorithms allows the system to continually improve and adapt over time, based on real-world data and feedback. Every agent within the system can access information pertaining to the present traffic conditions, road network, and the destinations of other agents. Based on this information, each agent makes decisions about which routes to take in real-time, taking into account factors such as traffic volume, road conditions, and vehicle behavior [14]. By communicating and coordinating with other agents, the system can optimize the routes taken by all vehicles and find the most efficient routes in real time. The route optimization system can also use real-time traffic data, such as vehicle speeds and road occupancy, to update the routes as needed and respond to changing traffic conditions. This approach offers a dynamic and adaptive solution to route optimization, allowing the system to respond quickly to changing traffic conditions and improve overall traffic efficiency [14]. Vehicles can optimize their routes and achieve real-time route optimization. Our proposed system uses the Bee colony scheme to solve traffic congestion by finding the best route from a set of alternative routes and directing vehicles to pass through it. Please see the pseudo-code for more details.

Pseudo-code for Road Deviation Algorithm

Function TLightSwarmOptimization(numTLight, numIterations, lightTLight, CrowdTLight)
bestRoute = initializeBestRoute()
for i = 1 to numIterations
TLight = createTLight(numTLight)
evaluateRoute(TLight) Light = selectLightTLight(TLight, LightTLight)
bestRoute = updateBestRoute(bestRoute, Light)
Crowd = generateNewRoute(TLight, CrowdTLight)
evaluateRoute(CrowdTlight)
bestSolution = updateBestRoute(bestRoute, CrowdTLight)
return bestRoute
end function

3.4   Mathematical Model

Our proposed system reduces congestion and improves safety by collecting data from real-time traffic, such as traffic density and speed that is used for dynamic route optimization and respond quickly to changing traffic conditions. The model can be extended to include variables such as road conditions and the presence of incidents, to further improve its accuracy in representing real-world traffic scenarios. The end goal of such a model is to inform traffic management decisions that lead to a reduction in congestion and a decrease in the risk of collisions. A mathematical model used to describe traffic flow and collision avoidance by the extraction of the equations based on the following subsystems:

- Traffic congestion controller subsystem: The relation between traffic light timing, and congestion status. As Congestion increases, the traffic light timing decreases. Congestion Coefficient (Low, Medium, High) :
  $Number of waiting Vehicles > threshold.$
  TLT = GLT *1 ; in case $Th <= 1$; In Low congestion
  TLT = GLT *2; in case Th between 1.01 and 1.10; In Medium congestion
  TLT = GLT *3; in case $Th > 1.10$; In High congestion
  where: TLT: Traffic Light Time GLT: Green Light Time TH: Threshold
  We can calculate the threshold by the following formula:

$$TH = \frac{WV}{RC} \tag{1}$$

where:
RC: Road Capacity calculated from Eq. (2), WV: Waiting Vehicles
We find Road capacity using the following formula:

$$RC = \frac{RA}{AVS} \tag{2}$$

where:
RA: Road Area, AVS: Average Vehicle Space

$$GreenDuration = BGD + (TV - TH) * AF \tag{3}$$

BasedGreenDuration (BGD): This is the base green light duration, which is set ac- cording to the normal traffic volume. TrafficVolume (TV): This is the measured traffic volume at the intersection. Threshold (TH): This is the traffic volume threshold for the intersection calculated from Eq. (1). AdjustmentFactor (AF) is a constant that determines the rate at which the green light duration changes with respect to changes in traffic volume. We also apply reinforcement in traffic light timing involves using reinforcement-learning techniques to optimize the timing of traffic lights in real time based on current traffic conditions. The system learns the best traffic light timings through trial and error, using a reward signal to reinforce good behavior and a penalty signal to discourage poor behavior. The goal is to find the optimal timing that minimizes wait times for vehicles while also reducing congestion and improving overall traffic flow. The methodology for applying reinforcement in traffic light timing is a promising approach for improving traffic flow and reducing congestion in urban areas. See Eq. (4)

$$GreenDuration = BGD + Kp * (OV - PV) + Ki * IE \qquad (4)$$

BaseGreenDuration (BGD): Starting point for the traffic light. Kp: This is the proportional gain constant utilized to modify the green light duration, accounting for the difference between the anticipated traffic volume and the observed traffic volume. ObservedVolume (OV): This is the count of vehicles identified by the traffic signal during the present time interval. PredictedVolume (PV): This is the estimated count of automobiles expected to be present at the traffic signal during the current time interval, based on historical data. Ki: This is an integral gain constant that adjusts the green duration based on the cumulative deviation over a period of time. IntegralError (IE): This is the cumulative disparity between the predicted traffic volume and the actual traffic volume over a specified duration.

- Traffic Collision Avoidance subsystem
  Collision indicator
  if $D >= DTh$ then collision indicator is low
  if $D > 0.50 * DTh$ then collision indicator is medium
  if $D < 0.50 * DTh$ then collision indicator is high
  Where:
  D : is the current distance between waiting vehicles calculated using Eq. (5)
  DTh: Minimum distance between waiting vehicles.
  By using the distance equation

$$D = \sqrt{(vai - vanext)^2 + (vbi - vbnext)^2} \qquad i = 1, 2, ..n \qquad (5)$$

if $D >= allowed$ then "Safety D" else "Critical D make alert"
The required Time per second for a probability of collision between two vehicles is calculated by the equation below:

$$T = \frac{D}{(Va - Vb)} \qquad (6)$$

where:
  T = time (second)
  D = distance between vehicles calculated by Eq. (5)
  Va = rear vehicle speed (m/s)
  Vb = front vehicle speed (m/s)

4   Findings

The simulation of an intelligent traffic congestion and collision avoidance system based on a multi-agent system and reinforcement learning was conducted using a computer model of a real-world city environment. The agents in the system were programmed to make decisions based on the reinforcement learning algorithm and real-time traffic conditions. The results of the simulation were very promising and showed significant improvements in traffic flow and a reduction in collisions compared to a traditional traffic management system. The multi-agent system was able to make real-time decisions that optimized traffic flow, reduced congestion, and prevented collisions. In terms of traffic flow, the simulation showed a significant improvement in average vehicle speed, a reduction in traffic jam formation, and a reduction in the number of vehicles that were stuck in traffic. The average vehicle speed was found to increase compared to the traditional traffic management system, the number of vehicles stuck in traffic was reduced, and the traffic flow increased by over 52.7%. In terms of collision avoidance, the results showed a significant reduction in the number of collisions, by alerting another agent (vehicles) before the collision occurred compared to the traditional traffic management system. The multi-agent system was able to make real-time decisions to prevent collisions, such as slowing down vehicles approaching intersections or changing the lane assignments of vehicles. We take three cases and test our system in those cases based on random traffic generated and the scale of the traffic changes to test two cases, normal random traffic and reinforcement random traffic, (see Table 1) and (see Fig. 7).

Table 1. Random traffic generation using normal and reinforcement traffic

Experiment	Normal random traffic (NRT)	Reinforcement random traffic (RRT)	(RRT - NRT) x 100%
1	0.23137812	0.95681377	72.54%
2	0.31533247	0.84658438	53.13%
3	0.33599661	0.80011551	46.41%
4	0.40150038	0.87827629	47.68%
5	0.45257893	0.82026007	36.77%
6	0.1527654	0.75032056	59.76%
7	0.34505569	0.95341696	60.84%
8	0.1317361	0.96438035	83.26%
9	0.21232619	0.51907433	30.67%
10	0.25483413	0.62075569	36.59%
11	0.23852635	0.74810578	50.96%
12	0.38068375	0.92303409	54.24%

Mean	0.2850833	0.81509481	0.527368638
SDV	0.10002319	0.13897938	0.151136452
Min	0.1317361	0.51907433	0.306748141
Max	0.45257893	0.96438035	0.832644253

To implement Multi-Agent Reinforcement Learning (MARL) in this scenario, each traffic light acts as a single agent. This approach can help in optimizing

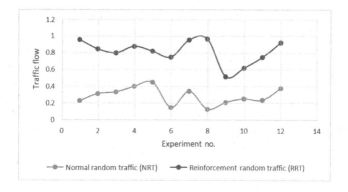

Fig. 7. Traffic Flow distribution

the overall traffic flow by allowing the traffic lights to interact with each other and learn from each other's actions. By using MARL, the traffic lights can adapt to changing traffic patterns and learn to coordinate with each other, leading to smoother traffic flow and reduced congestion, (see Fig. 8).

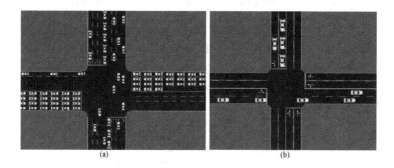

Fig. 8. Two intersections with multiple traffic lights interact with each other, (a) Normal random traffic flow and (b) Reinforcement Learning traffic flow

Our proposed mathematical model showed a perfect match with the simulation that was conducted using SUMO and JADE, as the results obtained were accurate and promising in solving the collision and congestion problem.

5   Conclusion

In this paper, we present a new model that we have developed for intelligent traffic congestion and collision avoidance, which is based on the integration between two subsystems. The first subsystem is Traffic Congestion Controller (TCC) which works by controlling the traffic light's duration to minimize the waiting time for each vehicle to enter the road intersection. The second subsystem is

Traffic Collision Avoidance (TCA), which is designed to decrease the percentage of collisions between waiting vehicles at the traffic light by alerting drivers within a time before the collision to avoid it. Using a multi-agent system based on reinforcement learning for intelligent traffic congestion and collision avoidance has the potential to revolutionize the way in which traffic is managed and optimized. By using a multi-agent system based on leveraging Reinforcement learning, this approach can make real-time decisions to manage traffic flow and prevent collisions, leading to safer, more efficient, and less congested roads. The results of this study and simulation have shown that this approach can significantly improve traffic flow and reduce accidents, making it a promising solution for addressing the complex challenges of modern traffic management.

6   Future Work

With further research and development, the integration of reinforcement learning into traffic management systems could bring us one step closer to realizing a safer, more efficient, and sustainable transportation future. In the future, we will take into account unexpected events such as the failure of traffic lights or diversion to roads without traffic lights. In the first case, defining alternative plans to make the system work all the time without causing errors that lead to the return of traffic congestion again. In the second case, it will be to rely on changing the data through sensors and radar identified at all road intersections, even if they do not contain traffic lights, to know the road condition before diverting traffic on it.

References

1. Mascardi, V., et al.: Engineering multi-agent systems: state of affairs and the road ahead. ACM SIGSOFT Softw. Eng. Notes **44**(1), 18–28 (2019)
2. Dorri, A., Kanhere, S.S., Jurdak, R.: Multi-agent systems: a survey. IEEE Access **6**, 28573–28593 (2018)
3. González-Briones, A., De La Prieta, F., Mohamad, M.S., Omatu, S., Corchado, J.M.: Multi-agent systems applications in energy optimization problems: a state-of-the-art review. Energies **11**(8), 1928 (2018)
4. Afanasyev, I., et al.: Towards blockchain-based multi-agent robotic systems: analysis, classification and applications. arXiv preprint arXiv:1907.07433 (2019)
5. Ali, A., Ayub, N., Shiraz, M., Ullah, N., Gani, A., Qureshi, M.A.: Traffic efficiency models for urban traffic management using mobile crowd sensing: a survey. Sustainability **13**(23), 13068 (2021)
6. Rattrout, A., Jayousi, R., Benouaret, K., Tissaoui, A., Benslimane, D.: Designing intelligent marine framework based on complex adaptive system principles. In: Hameurlain, A., Tjoa, A.M. (eds.) Transactions on Large-Scale Data- and Knowledge-Centered Systems L. LNCS, vol. 12930, pp. 63–76. Springer, Heidelberg (2021). https://doi.org/10.1007/978-3-662-64553-6_4
7. Mahmud, U., Hussain, S., Sarwar, A., Toure, I.K.: A distributed emergency vehicle transit system using artificial Intelligence of Things (DEVeTS-AIoT). Wirel. Commun. Mob. Comput. **2022**, 1–12 (2022). https://doi.org/10.1155/2022/9654858

8. Torabi, B., Zalila-Wenkstern, R., Saylor, R., Ryan, P.: Deployment of a plug-in multi-agent system for traffic signal timing. In: Proceedings of the 19th International Conference on Autonomous Agents and MultiAgent Systems, pp. 1386–1394 (2020)
9. Rezzai, M., Dachry, W., Moutaouakkil, F., Medromi, H.: Design and realization of a new architecture based on multi-agent systems and reinforcement learning for traffic signal control. In: 2018 6th International Conference on Multimedia Computing and Systems (ICMCS), pp. 1–6. IEEE (2018)
10. Sathiyaraj, R., Bharathi, A.: An efficient intelligent traffic light control and deviation system for traffic congestion avoidance using multi-agent system. Transport **35**(3), 327–335 (2020)
11. Riad, M., Golpayegani, F.: A normative multi-objective based intersection collision avoidance system. In: Jezic, G., Chen-Burger, Y.-H.J., Kusek, M., Šperka, R., Howlett, R.J., Jain, L.C. (eds.) Agents and Multi-Agent Systems: Technologies and Applications 2022: Proceedings of 16th KES International Conference, KES-AMSTA 2022, June 2022, pp. 289–300. Springer, Singapore (2022). https://doi.org/10.1007/978-981-19-3359-2_25
12. Rios-Torres, J., Malikopoulos, A.A.: A survey on the coordination of connected and automated vehicles at intersections and merging at highway on-ramps. IEEE Trans. Intell. Transp. Syst. **18**(5), 1066–1077 (2016)
13. Buisson, J., Galland, S., Gaud, N., Gonçalves, M., Koukam, A.: Real-time collision avoidance for pedestrian and bicyclist simulation: a smooth and predictive approach. Procedia Comput. Sci. **19**, 815–820 (2013)
14. De Souza, A. M., Yokoyama, R. S., Maia, G., Loureiro, A., Villas, L.: Real-time path planning to prevent traffic jam through an intelligent transportation system. In: 2016 IEEE Symposium on Computers and Communication (ISCC), pp. 726–731. IEEE (2016)
15. Jin, Q., Wu, G., Boriboonsomsin, K., Barth, M.: Multi-agent intersection management for connected vehicles using an optimal scheduling approach. In: 2012 International Conference on Connected Vehicles and Expo (ICCVE), pp. 185–190. IEEE (2012)
16. Xia, Y., Na, X., Sun, Z., Chen, J.: Formation control and collision avoidance for multi-agent systems based on position estimation. ISA Trans. **61**, 287–296 (2016)
17. Malialis, K., Devlin, S., Kudenko, D.: Resource abstraction for reinforcement learning in multiagent congestion problems. arXiv preprint arXiv:1903.05431 (2019)

BERT for Arabic NLP Applications: Pretraining and Finetuning MSA and Arabic Dialects

Chaimae Azroumahli[1($\boxtimes$)], Yacine Elyounoussi[2], and Hassan Badir[3]

[1] Laboratory of Intelligent Systems and Applications (LSIA), Moroccan School of Engineering Sciences (EMSI), Tangier, Morocco
c.azroumahli@emsi.ma

[2] SIGL Laboratory, ENSA, Abdel Malek Essaadi University, Tetuan, Morocco

[3] SDET, ENSA, Abdel Malek Essaadi University, Tangier, Morocco

Abstract. In recent practices, the BERT model that utilizes contextual word Embedding with transfer learning has arisen as a popular state-of-the-art deep learning model. It improved the performance of several Natural Language Processing (NLP) Applications [1]. In this paper, following the effectiveness that these models demonstrated, we use the advantages of training Arabic Transformer-based representational language models to create three Arabic NLP applications for two Arabic varieties; MSA and Arabic Dialects. We build an Arabic representational language model using BERT as the Transformer-based training model [2]. Then we compare the resulting model to the pre-trained multi-lingual models. This step is accomplished by building multiple Arabic NLP applications and then evaluating they are evaluating their performances. Our system had an accuracy of 0.91 on the NER task, 0.89 on the document classification application, and 0.87 on the sentiment Analysis application. This work proved that using a language-specific model outperforms the trained multilingual models on several NLP applications.

Keywords: Arabic NLP · NER · Sentiment Analysis · Document Classification · word Embeddings · BERT

1 Introduction

The last decade witnessed an increased interest to learn word representations known as word Embeddings using a large amount of unlabeled data. These word Embeddings learn the syntactic and semantic features of words in a context. For complex languages like Arabic, which suffer from language's lack of resources, the automatically extracted features are used in unsupervised or supervised NLP machine learning approaches. They can also be used to adjust to the morphological complexity of complex languages thus simplifying the processing of natural languages.

The first models that were used to create word Embeddings are Word2Vec (Words to Vectors) [3], and Glove (Global Vectors) [4]. Each model creates word-level vector representations that depend on the hypothesis of distributional properties ("You shall know a word by the company it keeps" (Firth, 1957)). Following the great popularity and

© The Author(s), under exclusive license to Springer Nature Switzerland AG 2024
M. Tabaa et al. (Eds.): INTIS 2022/2023, CCIS 1728, pp. 60–72, 2024.
https://doi.org/10.1007/978-3-031-47366-1_5

effectiveness that these models are gaining in the NLP community, two models BERT (Bidirectional Encoder Representations from Transformers) [2] and ELMO (Embeddings from Language Models) [5] were introduced. The architecture of creating and fine-tuning these models is slightly different from the classical word-level vector representations. These word representations provide general-purpose word Embeddings models for natural languages. Although, the word Embeddings created by BERT or ELMO can carry considerable information including the grammatical structure, which, consequently can hold a deep general encapsulation of linguistic information. This feature is important for complex languages like Arabic.

Literature showed that the BERT model can improve the performance of NLP applications for several natural languages [6, 7]. More specifically, BERT is adjustable and can handle any type of natural language dataset while delivering impressive results.

In this work, we use the BERT model to create a Word Embeddings model for three Arabic NLP applications, namely, the Named Entity Recognition task (NER), Sentiment Analysis (SA), and Document Classification (DC). The word Embeddings is pre-trained and then fin-tuned for the specific NLP application. We used two different Arabic varieties datasets as input to pre-train BERT models. The two datasets used in our experiments contain both the Modern Standard Arabic variety (MSA) and the Arabic Dialects variety (AD). Then we compare their performance with the multi-lingual pre-trained BERT model employing different Arabic NLP applications.

This paper is structured as follows; We start with an overview of the word Embeddings approach. Then, a BERT model description that we used in this paper. This section highlights the two main steps for creating an NLP application using BERT. Afterwards, an experiment setups description was carried out; We describe the training datasets used for pre-training the two Arabic BERT models and the procedure of fine-tuning a word Embeddings model for Arabic NLP applications. Finally, we discuss the obtained results of the experiments, then, we explain the outperformance of the pre-trained model in creating downstream NLP applications.

2   Word Embeddings and BERT

To process natural texts, we need to create word representations by searching for key terms using other NLP tasks on the training dataset [8]. Commonly, these representations have no semantic or syntactic features, thus, they are not as beneficial for machine learning mathematical and statistical models.

With models like Word2Vec [3] and GloVe [4], we can skip the use of other NLP tasks by directly building real-valued vectors. These vectorized representations are created using words' distributional properties and context in a non-annotated corpus.

Different works in literature have proved that these generated word representations – word Embeddings models – can hold the semantic and the syntactic properties of words, thus, greatly improving the accuracy of the targeted NLP application like the work described in [9] and [10]. Although, for natural languages known by their complexity like Arabic and Persian, these models fall a little short while handling the different linguistic complexity. One of the most known challenges of word Embeddings models is processing polysemy words. E.g., Word2Vec stores the feed-forward information only, thus resulting in creating similar representations for several words that carry poly-semy features of different contexts. Moreover, the resulting word Embeddings are more context-independent; each word has a real-valued vector, and this vector reassembles the word's features.

The deep learning approaches used in models like BERT and ELMO upgraded the performance of word Embeddings in NLP applications. These two newer models can offer different representations for each word while capturing the different positions and contexts in one sentence. Further, unlike Word2Vec and Glove – traditional contextual-ized word representations –, the newer models consider the words' order in a sentence. Thus, they can generate different representations according to the word's distributional property in a context [11].

For the work described in this paper, we adopted the BERT model instead of ELMO for several reasons. Notably, an important number of research papers in literature pre-ferred the BERT model; the work described in [12] proved that BERT outperformed ELMO for different NLP applications in the clinical domain. The creators of the BERT model [2] claimed that BERT surpassed human performance by 2.0. In addition, BERT has the possibility of incorporating the fine-tuning step using an integrated task-specific architecture of an NLP application.

3   The BERT Model: Background

3.1   Bert Architecture

BERT adopted the transfer learning approach and the tuning language model for training NLP applications. BERT transformers architecture was introduced in [13] where the pre-trained models are built using a stack of Transformers; a multi-layer bidirectional transformer encoder-decoder. The transformers of the BERT architecture replace the LSTM (Long Short Term Memory) layers to improve on long-term dependencies [14]. Figure 1 illustrates how the structure of transformers in the BERT architecture.

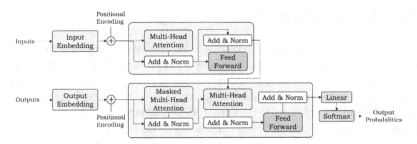

Fig. 1. The architecture of the Transformers

The attention mechanism layer is employed to decide the text's context contributing to the word Embedding. This mechanism calculates V as the output of the weighted sum value Vector as shown (1), Q is the matrix of the queries and K is the matrix of the keys.

$$Attention(Q, K, V) = softmax\left(\frac{QK^T}{\sqrt{d_k}}\right)V \tag{1}$$

The word Embeddings is the input of the encoder-decoder used in the structure of BERT transformers. The input of the encoders is fed to a self-attention layer. This layer processes different words and encodes a specific word, then outputs a layer that goes through a feed-forward neural network. Words with different positions in context follow different paths throughout the encoders. The input of a decoder is fed to a self-attention layer as well, an encoder-decoder attention layer, and finally a feed-forward neural network [15].

This architecture proves that transformers handle long-term dependencies better than LSTM. The dependencies that exist between the different self-attention layers, do not appear in the feed-forward layer. Thus, the various parallel execution of the self-attention pathways can go through the feed-forward layer. [14].

3.2 BERT Pre-training and Fine-Tuning

To create BERT based NLP application, we need to follow two main steps. (1) Pretraining BERT representation using a large corpus containing unlabeled data. (2) Using the labelled data of the NLP application to fine-tune the parameters of the pre-trained [2].

BERT Pre-training. The step of the next sentence prediction task and the masked language model task are part of the pre-training. The input Embeddings is a combination of position Embeddings. They deduce the position of words in a sentence. Segment Embeddings are created to distinguish between two sentence pairs. The sentence pairs are inputted in the fine-tuning step. The objective of this technique is to produce a better pre-trained BERT model that can be trained for several NLP applications without making any changes to the pre-trained model itself [14]. The pretraining phase relies on the masked language model (MLM), and Next Sentence Prediction (NSP).

The MLM is used to train deep bidirectional representations while preventing words from recognizing themselves in a multi-layer context. This task masks a random 15% of the input tokens and then predicts them using the unmasked input words and an additional classification layer on top of the transformers' blocks [2]. The NSP is used in BERT since the MLM does not process relationships between sentences in a context, and NSP pre-trains the binary next-sentence prediction tasks.

BERT Fine-tuning. BERT adopt transfer learning and uses the fine-tuning approach, where the pre-trained model is expanded with a classification layer, and the parameters are fine-tuned on the targeted NLP application keeping the head of the model [2].

4 BERT for Arabic NLP Applications: Pre-training and Fine-Tuning

We use BERT to create two Arabic BERT pre-trained models using two different Arabic datasets; MSA and AD. Then, we fine-tune the created two models and the pre-trained BERT multi-lingual model on three NLP applications, namely, Named Entity Recognition, Document classification and Sentiment Analysis. Then, we compare their performances. Figure 2 illustrates our approach to creating an NLP application using BERT.

We change the annotated corpora that were used for the fine-tuning steps according to the targeted NLP application. In this section, we describe the following approach thoroughly including; The creation of the non-labelled and the labelled datasets. The pre-training of the language-specific BERT model. And the fine-tuning of the pre-trained BERT model for the three Arabic NLP applications.

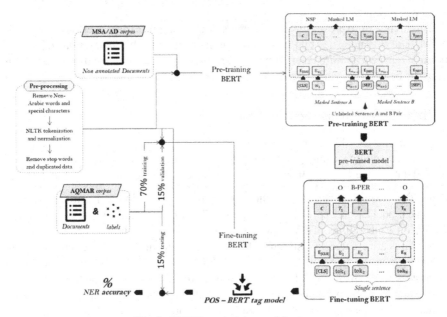

Fig. 2. BERT pre-training architecture

4.1 Training Datasets

The Arabic-speaking community exhibits the diglossia phenomenon where several Arabic varieties are used by the same speakers for different purposes [16]. For the work described in this paper, we process the two most used varieties: MSA and Arabic Dialects. MSA is the formal variety used in Arabic-speaking countries. It is mostly employed in formal communications and educational environments. Arabic Dialect is the informal variety used in day-to-day conversations. This variety varies from one region to another across Arabic countries and is known for not having any orthographic standards.

Pre-training Datasets: MSA. In a previous work [16], we created and preprocessed an Arabic dataset by collecting data from different text sources. The used dataset was collected from two main web sources; Wikipedia and social media. Wikipedia provided more the 810k Arabic articles written in MSA. We used a function-based algorithm provided by Wikipedia Library[1] to harvest this dataset. Table 1 shows the statists of pre-training and the fine-tuning datasets used to create the Arabic BERT models.

---

[1] https://pypi.org/project/wikipedia/

Table 1. The statistics of the pre-training datasets.

Source	Wikipedia	Social Media	
		Facebook	Twitter
Arabic Variety	*MSA*	MSA & North African dialects	MSA & Middle Eastern dialects
Vocabulary size	325, 544	256, 226	

Fine-Tuning Dataset for the NER Task. NER is the task of locating and separating Named Entities (NE) from a larger context, and then categorizing them into semantic categories that were defined according to the NER task [17]. We used an annotated dataset provided by the AQMAR project [18]. There are a total of 28 hand-annotated articles in this dataset. This dataset contains 28 hand-annotated articles. Table 2 illustrates the statistics of the NER annotated dataset. The articles were tagged to nine NE using the BIO system tags i.e., O (outside), B-PER (Beginning of person's entity), B-MIS (Beginning of miscellaneous' entity), B-ORG (Beginning of an organization's entity), B-LOC (Beginning of location's entity), I-PER (Inside of person's entity), I-MIS (Inside of miscellaneous' entity), I-ORG (Inside of an organization's entity), I-LOC (Inside of location's entity).

Table 2. Statistics of the NER annotated corpus.

Total	71, 247							
Distribution of the entity tokens								
Beginning				Inside				Outside
PER	MISC	ORG	LOC	PER	MISC	ORG	LOC	
1, 328	2, 258	388	1, 369	875	3, 505	453	572	60, 952

Fine-Tuning Dataset for the Sentiment Analysis Application. Sentiment Analysis is the task of detecting people's sentiments, opinions and attitudes, towards specific entities that hold key information about certain products, services, issues, or topics [17]. For this experiment, we perform the Sentiment Analysis on a sentence level, where the application identifies the orientation of the opinion held by an input sentence. In prior work, we collected and preprocessed several annotated sentiment analysis Arabic datasets. We use the same dataset as an annotated fine-tuning dataset (see Table 3). It is a fusion of ArsenTD, annotated Arabic blogs from [19] and a Twitter dataset for Arabic sentiment analysis provided by the authors of [20].

Fine-Tuning dataset for the Document Classification application. Document Classification is the task of assigning one or more labels to a document. It is used in environments that deal with a lot of content such as libraries, and publishing companies. For our experiment, the application aims at assigning specific labels to many articles,

Table 3. Statistics of the Sentiment Analysis annotated corpus.

Total of inputs	Positive	Negative	Neutral
6, 166	2, 238	2, 931	997

these labels present six different categories namely: Culture, Economy, International, Local, Religion and Sports. Table 4 summarizes the statistics of the training dataset for Document Classification. We used Kalimat Multipurpose Arabic Corpus which contains 20, 291 articles, collected from an Omani newspaper, divided into the 6 categories mentioned above [21].

Table 4. Statistics of the Document Analysis annotated corpus.

Total of articles	Culture	Economy	International	Local	Religion	Sports
20, 291	2, 782	3, 468	2, 035	3, 596	3, 860	4, 550

Pre-processing the Datasets. To pre-process the pre-training and the finetuning datasets, we apply several pre-processing respecting the Arabic characteristics. To Pre-process the social media datasets, we removed the non-Arabic, the diacritics signs – they present a set of symbols used to alter the pronunciation of phonemes. We removed all stop words, then we normalize all the Arabic characters throughout the different dialects. Lastly, we tokenize the different sentences using the NLTK library [16].

4.2 Pre-training BERT Models

The main objective of this study is to observe the impact of using the unsupervised pre-training approach using the BERT model. This study is conducted on three different NLP applications, we started by pre-training two Arabic BERT models, and we also used the pre-trained multilingual BERT model. There are five major experiments to follow: (1) Creating the pre-trained unsupervised BERT model using two unlabeled datasets, (2) Fine-tuning three pre-trained BERT models on the NER task, the Sentiment Analysis application, and the Document Classification application. (3) Comparing the accuracy of each application. Our implementations were created using BERT's original codebase[2], and TensorFlow which contains several libraries, thus making it possible to create outperforming NLP applications.

BERT Base Model. We used the BERT-base multilingual model in the finetuning phase. As it was described in [2], the pre-trained model was created using a large amount of data. This data contains 104 languages including Arabic. In general, this multilingual version can be used as a pre-trained model for multiple languages to create several task-specific

---

[2] BERT pre-trained models for TensorFlow https://github.com/google-research/bert

NLP applications. In literature, we found that many works such as [1] and [22], reported that the performance of the multilingual model isn't as outperforming as the single-language model. In this work, we decided to pre-train our own Arabic BERT model, in addition to the step of fine-tuning the multilingual model and the single-language model. Afterwards, we can apply a fair comparison of the two Arabic pre-trained models.

BERT for Pretraining the MSA and AD Models. We follow BERT's original pre-training script (the Python version) to create the pre-trained Arabic single-language BERT models. This method takes a large file containing the separated sentences representing our pre-training dataset. In addition to the model's configuration and parameters. Due to the Wikipedia dataset size, we have to distribute the input file text that should be kept in memory during training. To create the MSA model, we implemented the MLM and the NSP task. On the other hand, to create the social media model, we implemented only the MLM task. This choice is justified by the fact that social media content (i.e., Tweets, Facebook comments) lacks the same understanding of sentence flow as text in articles. This model won't work well for problem-solving tasks, but it will not have an impact on categorization task performance such as NER, Sentiment Analysis and Document Classification. Both MSA and Arabic Dialects models are trained using the configuration described below:

The training instances. The maximum length of sequences was set to 512. The masked LM probability was set to 0.15. The masked LM maximum number of predictions per sequence was set to 77.

The base configuration. We chose the Bidirectional transformer pre-training. For the non-linear layer, we chose "GuLu" as the activation function. For the dropout ratio, we chose the value of 0.1 as the attention probability. For the fully connected layer in the encoder embeddings, we chose the value of 0.1 as the probability dropout. For the encoder layers, we chose the value of 768 as the dimensionality. For the weight matrix initialization, we chose the value of 0.02 as the deviation score. For the transformer encoder feed-forward layer, we chose the value of 3072 as a dimensionality. For the sequence length maximum value that this model uses, we chose the value of 2048. For the transformer encoder, both, the attention layer heads and the number of hidden layers were set to 12. For the BERT model forward method, we permitted the passing of different tokens. Finally, the vocabulary size of the BERT model is 156226 for MSA and 325544 for the Arabic Dialect.

The pipeline Input Data configuration. The maximum number sequence length was set to 512 for MSA and 128 for the Arabic Dialect model. The training batch size was set to 32. The maximum number of MLM predictions per sequence was set to 77 for MSA and 20 for the Arabic Dialect model. Finally, the number of warmup steps was set to 100 and the learning rate was set to $2e^5$.

4.3 Fine-Tuning for Arabic NLP Applications

The three pre-trained BERT models (i.e., BERT-base model, MSA model and Arabic Dialect models) are used to fine-tune each dataset's model independently for each NLP application. We trained each and fine-tuned each model for the three applications separately. We strictly follow the BERT original fine-tuning script (the Python version). This version is relatively easier to adopt for NLP. It fine-tunes the deep bidirectional representations on a wide range of tasks including NER, Sentiment Analysis, and Document Classification where the input is a set of sentences instead of separated word tokens. Fine-tuning is done with minimal task-specific parameters and obtains state-of-the-art results according to BERT developers [2].

The same procedure is followed for the three applications. The annotated training datasets need to be pre-processed and prepared before starting training. The pre-processing steps are the same steps explained in Sect. 4.1. Preparing the dataset includes the addition of these steps: The tokenization of the input sequence. Adding the tokens [CLS] at the beginning of the tokens, and [SEP] between the token's sentences. Generate Ids segments to identify the first sentence from the second sentence, and generate the sequence length. The training dataset is divided afterwards into a 15% validation part, a 15% testing part and a 70% training part.

After preparing the training datasets, we start loading the pre-trained BERT model which inputs the vocabulary alongside with model. The BERT model is wrapped in the fine-tuning BERT script, which also layers a token-level classifier on top of the pre-trained BERT model. The final hidden state of the sequence serves as the input for this classifier, which is a linear layer. The loaded pre-trained BERT model provides the number of possible labels. The optimizer and tuning parameters are altered and an objective is developed to reduce the learning rate linearly throughout the epochs. The training uses this configuration; Three epochs (2 epochs for the multilingual model). A Learning rate of $5e^{-5}$. The maximum number of training steps was set to 10000. The training batch size was set to 32. Finally, the maximum sequence length was set at 512.

4.4 The Computational Cost

Pre-training BERT models are notoriously expensive e.g., 4 days in a machine with a 16 Cloud TPUs. However, when a model is generated for a specific language, it can be fine-tuned to generate an assortment of NLP applications. Fine-tuning is inexpensive e.g., 1 h on a single TPU or a few hours on a GPU.

We used the recommended settings to reduce the costs of the computations, such as increasing 10000 steps with a sequence length of 512. BERT pre-training and fine-tuning were performed on a GeForce GPU with significant CPU power memory for pre-processing activities (64 Gb RAM, and 1 Tb SSD).

Our pre-trained models required an extensive amount of computational time, within 360 h, and fine-tuning all of the pre-trained models took 16 h in total. This runtime does not include collecting datasets, pre-processing, or preparing training dataset tokens.

5   Results and Discussion

The results reported in Table 5 summarize the accuracies of the Sentiment Analysis, the NER task and the Document classification applications obtained by fine-tuning the three pre-trained models. A quick look at the results of our studies reveals a few intriguing findings.

Table 5. Results of the MSA model, the AD model and the BERT-base

	Bert-base model	MSA model	Arabic Dialect model
NER	0.893	0.915	0.902
Sentiment Analysis	0.761	0.824	0.825
Document Classification	0.826	0.854	0.772

For the NER task, the accuracy levels achieved by earlier Arabic NER systems in the literature have been outperformed by the BERT technique. A hybrid technique [23] generated an accuracy of 73%, followed by the maximum entropy combined with POS-tag information [8] with an accuracy of 83%, and the recall-oriented learning approach [18] at 84%. This can be explained by the fact that the supervised approaches have limitations that the knowledge of the unsupervised ways can help to overcome. The model that was pre-trained using the Wikipedia dataset had the best accuracy with the least amount of loss, at 91%, followed by the Arabic Dialect model at 90%, and the multilingual BERT model at 89%.

For the Document Classification application, the best result was again obtained by the MSA model which achieved an accuracy of 85% followed by the BERT-base model with an accuracy of 82%, and then the Arabic Dialect model with an accuracy of 77%. The reported results are significant since they do outperform several Arabic Document Classification applications in the literature. E.g. the application of [24] reported an accuracy of 74% where the authors used different algorithms such as vector space model (VSM), K-Nearest Neighbor algorithms (KNN), and Naïve Bayes (NB).

The Best result of Sentiment Analysis is the result reported by the two applications obtained by the Arabic Dialect model and the MSA model with an accuracy of 82% with an insignificant difference of 0.1%, followed by the BERT base model that results in an accuracy of 76%. Repeatedly, BERT has proven to be very beneficial for utilizing smaller annotated data with a pre-trained BERT model. The results outperformed several Arabic Sentiment Analysis applications such as the application described in [25] where they used their Arabic Sentiment Ontology to obtain a precision of 78%.

Even though the MSA is the best model out of the three, there is only a 2% margin of error separating the three models' accuracy. It is important to note that only the MSA variety is present in the fine-tuning datasets for NER and Document Classification. Whereas the Arabic Dialect BERT comprises a portion of the MSA content in addition to the many Arabic Dialect variants, the content of the social media dataset utilized for pre-training does not. Additionally, compared to the social media dataset, the Wikipedia dataset used to pre-train the MSA BERT model is much bigger. Since both models produced meaningful results with a 1.2% difference, these facts didn't have a substantial impact on the NER task's accuracy. In theory, this result will stay true even if we increase the pre-training dataset size. As for the BERT base, similar to reports for other languages like the study detailed in [1] and [6], it did perform somewhat worse than the single language model for Arabic. Even Though, for a complex language like Arabic, the BERT-base model's stated accuracy is impressive.

For developing Arabic NLP applications, the BERT technique and the need for a task-specific model architecture were helpful. In addition to the pre-trained model's impressive results (such as the single language pre-trained model and the multi-lingual model), Sect. 4.4 reported that the computational cost of developing a particular NLP-task system (such as Text Summarization, Language translation, Chatbots, etc.) can be significantly reduced. Using BERT fine-tuning or combining the fine-tuning classification layers with other connected neural network components, many task-specific applications can be developed at a significantly reduced computational cost after the expensive representation (i.e., the single language BERT model) is pre-computed.

6 Conclusion

In this paper, we outline the method we used to pre-train and develop three NLP applications for the various Arabic verities: NER, Sentiment Analysis, and Document Classification. In addition to a multilingual model made public by BERT, we pre-train two Arabic models: one for the MSA, the official Arabic language, and one for the Arabic Dialect, which comprises the majority of Arabic dialects. We then compare their performances on the three NLP applications. The models were fine-tuned using various annotated training datasets accessible for various Arabic NLP applications, which were trained using the standard BERT source code. Computationally, the construction of the task-specific model is particularly advantageous. Further, the accuracy of the MSA model on the document classification application, the NER task, and the sentiment analysis application were 85%, 91% and 82%, accordingly. The results were also exceptionally positive. To properly investigate the performance of BERT on Arabic and to improve the annotated training datasets so they will contain all the varieties of Arabic dialects in addition to MSA, we plan to incorporate additional NLP tasks with different processing views in future works.

References

1. Polignano, M., Basile, P., de Gemmis, M., et al.: AlBERTo: Italian BERT language understanding model for NLP challenging tasks based on tweets. In: CEUR Workshop Proceedings, vol. 2481 (2019)
2. Devlin, J., Chang, M.-W., Lee, K., Toutanova, K.: BERT: pre-training of deep bidirectional transformers for language understanding. arXiv Prepr arXiv181004805. arXiv:1811.03600v2 (2018)
3. Mikolov, T., Chen, K., Corrado, G., Dean, J.: Efficient estimation of word representations in vector space. In: ICLR 2020 Conference Blind Submission, pp. 4069–4076 (2013). https://doi.org/10.48550/arXiv.1301.3781
4. Pennington, J., Socher, R., Manning, C.: Glove: global vectors for word representation. In: Proceedings of the 2014 Conference on Empirical Methods in Natural Language Processing (EMNLP), pp. 1532–1543 (2014)
5. Peters, M.E., Neumann, M., Iyyer, M., et al.: Deep contextualized word representations. In: Proceedings of the 2018 Conference of the North American Chapter of the Association for Computational Linguistics: Human Language Technologies, pp. 2227–2237 (2018)

6. Li, X., Zhang, H., Zhou, X.H.: Chinese clinical named entity recognition with variant neural structures based on BERT methods. J. Biomed. Inform. **107**, 103422 (2020). https://doi.org/10.1016/j.jbi.2020.103422

7. Moradshahi, M., Palangi, H., Lam, M,S., et al.: HUBERT untangles BERT to improve transfer across NLP tasks. 1–13 (2019)

8. Benajiba, Y., Rosso, P.: ANERsys 2.0 : Conquering the NER task for the Arabic language by combining the maximum entropy with POS-tag information. In: 3rd Indian International Conference Artificial Intelligence, pp. 1814–1823 (2007)

9. Tang, D., Wei, F., Qin, B., et al.: Sentiment embeddings with applications to sentiment analysis. IEEE Trans. Knowl. Data Eng. **28**, 496–509 (2016). https://doi.org/10.1109/TKDE.2015.2489653

10. Li, J., Li, J., Fu, X., et al.: Learning distributed word representation with multi-contextual mixed embedding. Knowl.-Based Syst. **106**, 220–230 (2016). https://doi.org/10.1016/j.knosys.2016.05.045

11. Rajasekharan, A.: Examining BERT's raw embeddings - towards data science (2019). https://www.quora.com/q/handsonnlpmodelreview/Examining-BERT-s-raw-embeddings-1?ch=10&share=4afe89e5. Accessed 26 Jun 2020

12. Alsentzer, E., Murphy, J.R., Boag, W., et al.: Publicly available clinical BERT embeddings. In: Proceedings of the 2nd Clinical Natural Language Processing Workshop, pp. 72–78 (2019)

13. Ashish, V., Noam, S., Niki, P., et al.: Attention is all you need. In: Advances in Neural Information Processing Systems, pp. 6000–6010 (2017)

14. Alammar, J.: The Illustrated Transformer – Jay Alammar – Visualizing machine learning one concept at a time. Jay alammar Github **27** (2018)

15. Chaimae, A., Yacine, E.Y., Rybinski, M., Montes, J,F.A.: BERT for Arabic named entity recognition. In: 2020 International Symposium on Advanced Electrical and Communication Technologies (ISAECT), pp. 1–6 IEEE (2020)

16. Chaimae, A., El Younoussi, Y., Moussaoui, O., Zahidi, Y.: An Arabic dialects dictionary using word embeddings. Int. J. Rough Sets Data Anal. **6**, 18–31 (2019). https://doi.org/10.4018/IJRSDA.2019070102

17. Chaimae, A., Rybinski, M., Yacine, E.Y., Montes, J.F.A. Comparative study of Arabic word embeddings : evaluation and application. Int. J. Comput. Inf. Syst. Ind. Manag. Appl. ISSN-2150-7988 **12**, 349–362 (2020)

18. Mohit, B., Schneider, N., Bhowmick, R., et al.: Recall-oriented learning of named entities in Arabic Wikipedia. In: EACL 2012 - 13th Conference of the European Chapter of the Association for Computational Linguistics Proceedings, pp. 162–173 (2012)

19. Baly, R., Khaddaj, A., Hajj, H., El-Hajj, W., Shaban, K.B.: ArSentD-LEV : a multi-topic corpus for target-based sentiment analysis in arabic levantine tweets. In: OSACT3, pp. 37–43 (2018)

20. Abdulla, N.A., Ahmed, N.A., Shehab, M.A., Al-ayyoub, M.: Arabic Sentiment Analysis: lexicon-based and corpus-based. In: Jordan Conference Applied Electrical Engineering Computing Technologies, vol. 6, pp.1–6 (2013). https://doi.org/10.1109/AEECT.2013.6716448

21. El-haj, M., Koulali, R.: KALIMAT a multipurpose Arabic corpus. In: Second Work Arab Corpus Linguist, pp. 22–25 (2013)

22. Polignano, M., De Gemmis, M., Basile, P., Semeraro, G. A comparison of word-embeddings in emotion detection from text using BiLSTM, CNN and self-attention. In: ACM UMAP 2019 Adjun - Adjun Publ 27th Conference User Model Adapt Pers, pp. 63–68 (2019). https://doi.org/10.1145/3314183.3324983

23. Shaalan, K., Oudah, M.: A hybrid approach to Arabic named entity recognition. J. Inf. Sci. **40**, 67–87 (2013). https://doi.org/10.1177/0165551513502417

24. Al-Zoghby, A., Eldin, A.S., Ismail, N.A., Hamza, T.: Mining Arabic text using soft-matching association rules. In: ICCES'07 - 2007 International Conference on Computer Engineering and Systems (2007)

25. Tartir, S., Abdul-Nabi, I.: Semantic sentiment analysis in arabic social media. J. King Saud Univ. – Comput. Inf. Sci. **29**, 229–233 (2017). https://doi.org/10.1016/j.jksuci.2016.11.011

VacDist MAS for Covid-19 Vaccination Distribution: Palestine as a Case Study

Amjad Ratrout[1]([✉])[iD], Ashar Natsheh[2,3][iD], Aya Mousa[2,3][iD], and Daniel Voskergin[1,3][iD]

[1] Arab American University, Ramallah, Palestine
amjad.rattrout@aaup.edu
[2] Palestinian Neuroscience Initiative, East Jerusalem, Palestine
[3] Al-Quds University, East Jerusalem, Palestine

Abstract. The infectious COVID-19 outbreak has put an enormous load on the healthcare systems and the economy. It significantly impacted death rates and overall society immunity. Fortunately, vaccines have an apparent effect on enhancing an individual's immunity to specific diseases. In the early periods of the COVID-19 pandemic, health authorities had limited quantities of the vaccine and urgently needed to optimize vaccine purchase and allocation. This study introduced the VacDist framework, a multi-agent system for COVID-19 vaccination distribution for the Palestinian population during the COVID-19 pandemic. VacDist provides a complete vaccination system starting from the effective purchase of the vaccine until vaccinated citizens. The results of VacDist significantly outperform the traditional strategy in fairly distributing the vaccine to reach the most significant number of citizens. The multi-agent model developed in this study can be used to support decision-makers and aid in designing dynamic, optimal health interventions to counter COVID-19 and other disease outbreaks.

Keywords: Mutli-agent · covid-19 · vaccination · Vaccine distribution · pandemic · deep Q-learning learning · ACL messages

1 Introduction

Since December 2019, the world has witnessed an ongoing global outbreak, known as the COVID-19 pandemic, which originated from a severe acute respiratory syndrome coronavirus 2 (SARS-Cov-2). Since then, this pandemic has registered more than 168 million cases and has claimed more than 3.5 million lives worldwide, making this pandemic one of the deadliest in history [9].

At the beginning of this pandemic, many countries took precautionary policies to contain the current pandemic. Lockdown measures, quarantine, face masks, physical distancing, restrictions on public and private places, and public

---

Supported by organization x.

M. Tabaa et al. (Eds.): INTIS 2022/2023, CCIS 1728, pp. 73–87, 2024.
https://doi.org/10.1007/978-3-031-47366-1_6

awareness, are the most commonly used interventions to suppress virus transmission. In synchronization with those measures, researchers around the world are working persistently to produce an effective vaccine against COVID-19, since the implementation of mass vaccination programs has been a powerful containment measure to control the virus spread during the infectious disease outbreaks that happened throughout history.

As a result of vaccination, an individual's immune system is enhanced to safely recognize and defend against specific diseases. In this aspect, the COVID-19 vaccines produce an immune response to the SARS-Cov-2 virus [10]. Hence, developing mass vaccination programs enables health authorities to protect a huge number of people from an infectious disease outbreak by reducing the risk of individuals developing the illness, and as a consequence, preventing them from infecting others. Until now, there are more than 14 COVID-19 vaccines that have achieved regulatory authorization or approval across the globe [11].

Unfortunately, during pandemics, vaccines are often in shortage supply. There are various reasons for this scarcity. First, the time for vaccine research and development is lengthy extended to confirm the effectiveness of the vaccine on human health and to handle the emergence of new COVID-19 virus strains, and this impedes the mass production of vaccines. Second, due to the impact of the COVID-19 pandemic on global economic growth, some countries lack sufficient purchasing power, especially in third-world countries such as Palestine, to obtain vaccines. Due to the very limited quantities of developed vaccines, health authorities have an urgent need to devise a strategy to optimize how the vaccines are to be distributed across different cities within a country, and how to be allocated to individuals, to equitably distribute this shortage in vaccines and to minimize the further spread of the virus infection.

Distributed Artificial Intelligence (DAI) is regarded as one of the most promising fields in computer science and artificial intelligence. It is mainly utilized to solve complex computing problems. DAI algorithms are classified into three categories: parallel AI, Distributed Problem Solving (DPS), and MAS (MAS). MAS can be defined as a system that composes multiple interacting agents within an environment. The collaboration and cooperation between agents aim to solve complex problem tasks. Agents learn new contexts and actions through interactions with neighboring agents and the environment. Therefore, agents decide and perform actions in the environment based on their knowledge to complete their assigned tasks. Furthermore, the agents in the MAS system have several essential characteristics: Autonomy, Locality, and decentralization. In addition, MAS can display self-organization and self-steering, as well as other control paradigms and complex behaviors. MAS agents can share knowledge within the constraints of the system's communication protocol, such as Knowledge Query Manipulation Language (KQML) and FIPA's Agent Communication Language (ACL) [6].

FIPA stands for "The Foundation for Intelligent, physical agents," an international non-profit association to develop a set of standards relating to software agent technology. One of the key achievements of FIPA during the past years was the creation of a set of standard specifications supporting inter-agent communication and a well-specified agent communication language called FIPA-ACL. It is based on speech act theory, where each message represents an action or communicative act (known as performative). Each FIPA-ACL message contains a set of message parameters, i.e., performative, sender, receiver, replay-to, content, etc. In this aspect, FIPA-ACL consists of 22 communicative acts, where every act is described using both a formal semantic and a narrative form that provides an explanation of how sending a message affects the mental attitudes of both the sender and the receiver agents, consistent with BDI - or Belief, Desire, and Intention reason model. Some commonly used performatives are request, inform, proposal, refuse, agree, and not understood [12].

In this study, we developed the VacDist framework, a MAS that provides an adaptive smart framework for Covid-19 vaccination distribution and allocation, starting from efficiently purchasing the vaccine until the citizens get vaccinated.

Our proposed framework includes four main parts that cooperatively work to achieve the proposed aim. The main contributions of the VacDist framework can be summarized in the strategies it provides as follows:

First: supporting decision-makers in purchasing vaccines based on meaningful factors.

Second: providing fairness in the vaccine distribution based on two strategies of distribution, on the level of cities based on their pandemic status and on the citizen level based on their personal information.

Third: providing a persuader to encourage people to get the vaccine to increase the number of vaccinated people.

The three contributions of the system were achieved via merging three main subsystems, purchasing system, smart distribution system, and social advisor system. Each subsystem contains hybrid agents collaborating and cooperating with each other and with the other subsystems to successfully complete the system's tasks. Many different models used MAS to simulate pandemic spreading. However, only a few models studied vaccination distribution using a multi-agent framework, which can effectively contribute to increasing the performance of such model simulations.

Article sections are outlined as follows: first, we provide a review of the studies that used MAS in simulating several pandemics spreading as well as vaccination strategies proposed in the literature. Then, we provide the methodology section that introduces the proposed system and the following methodology in designing and implementing the VacDist framework. After that, we include the results of the VacDist framework along with the results of the naive framework and the comparison between them. Then, we provide the discussion section to discuss the results and VacDist limitations. Finally, we provide the conclusion sections and future directions of the study.

2   Related Work

This section provides a review of several studies that focused on MAS for both pandemic spreading and vaccination allocation strategies.

In [1], the authors proposed a COVID-ABS model based on a new SEIR (Susceptible-Exposed-Infected-Recovered) agent-based model that aims to simulate the pandemic behaviors via a society of agents that emulate people, businesses, and government. Various epidemiological and economic effects of seven government intervention scenarios were examined. The results showed that the COVID-ABS approach succeeded in simulating social intervention scenarios in line with the results reported in the literature. In addition, they found that the Governments that preferred to preserve the economy by neglecting the isolation policies suffered great human losses and bitter economic losses.

Many studies used MAS to demonstrate vaccine allocation strategies for different pandemics. These systems can, in turn, be borrowed for several types of pandemics. For example, in [2], the authors developed a novel vaccine distribution policy model using reinforcement learning algorithms. The model aims to find the best distribution policy for vaccines at the state level. They utilized a pipelined Actor-Critic (ACKTR) model with the Bandit model in a feedforward way. The outputs of the actor-critic model (action and reward) are used as input to the Contextual Bandit model to provide a rational context to compromise action and reward. In addition, the Contextual Bandit model is used to optimize the model policy by analyzing the demographic metrics, such as the population of each state and the characteristics of COVID-19 spreading in each state. The model was evaluated by applying projection scenarios since there is no vaccine available. The authors defined the Naïve policy as the percentage of vaccines given to a state equals the percentage of infected People in that state and compared it with the proposed policy. The results showed that the ACKTR-based policy reduced infected cases in cities compared with the Naive policy.

Further, Chowell, G., et al. introduced the age-structured agent-based transmission model that provides a vaccination distribution strategy against pandemic influenza in Mexico. The model comprises a set of differential equations that describe the time-dependent movement of individuals in a population, considering various infection and vaccination statuses. They followed two main distribution strategies to compare their performance. The first strategy prioritized vaccination for the youngest children and individuals over the age of 65. The second strategy dynamically prioritized age groups based on disease patterns observed in previous pandemics. Each age group was classified into nine states to represent specific disease patterns. The objective of the strategy was to prevent hospitalizations and reduce the number of deaths by strategically allocating vaccinations. The outcomes of implementing the adaptive strategy surpassed those of the initial age-only vaccination allocation approach across a broad spectrum of disease and vaccine coverage parameters. This study was recommended to be used to support healthcare policymakers in other pandemics in countries with similar demographic features and vaccine resource issues [3].

Also, in [8], the authors aim to optimize the vaccine distribution plan by formulating a multi-objective linear programming model and applying it to their previous work, an agent-based version of the ASQ-SEIR-NLIR compartmental model. ASQ-SEIR-NLIR compartmental model is an enhancement of the classical SEIR model with non-linear incidence rates, considering three additional factors, age-stratified, quarantine-modified, and disease-resistance and behavioral factors that suppress virus transmission. The authors converted this model into Agent-based modeling (ABM) to simulate individuals (closed society) living in a common finite environment, and to ease the capturing process of the virus spread during agent interactions. Simulations were performed to analyze the effect of different vaccination scenarios on the number of infectious people and the protection coverage over the target population. The obtained results showed that prioritizing the mobile workers yield the lowest number of infections while prioritizing the elderly ensures the highest protection of the population (the lowest mortality cases). On the other hand, other studies provided vaccination allocation strategies based on surveys and citizens' reviews regarding vaccines. In [4], Marco-Franco, J. E., et al. conducted a study investigating the potential for implementing regulations aimed at mitigating the spread of misinformation surrounding COVID-19 vaccines. The research examined various aspects, including the establishment of compulsory vaccination against COVID-19, the impact of misinformation, particularly when disseminated by healthcare professionals, and the acceptance of vaccination measures by the general public. Analysis of data obtained from multiple surveys revealed a prevalent sense of hesitancy, rather than outright opposition, towards vaccines. Among the concerns expressed, the most common complaint was related to the fear of experiencing side effects associated with the COVID-19 vaccination. Based on the performed analysis, the study outputs three main recommendations, including that (1) compulsory vaccination for certain jobs, (2) government regulation of fake News, especially Misinformation provided by medical professionals in collaboration with media, and (3) education and truthful information for persuading the population of the benefits of a vaccine on a voluntary basis to reduce fake news about vaccines.

3   Methodology

3.1   The Proposed MAS

The proposed MAS provides three strategies to effectively purchase and distribute the Covid-19 vaccine:

First: Decision-Making Strategy that supports decision-makers in purchasing vaccines from suppliers based on several factors.

Second: Vaccine distribution based on two levels: (1) Machine Learning Distribution Strategy based Cities, which implies using real data of the covid-19 pandemic spreading in each Palestinian city and then borrowing the elements of the reinforcement learning VacSIM model in [3] to prioritize these cities to allocate vaccine amounts based on this priority. (2) Distribution Strategy based Citizens, which implies distributing the vaccine to citizens based on their data, including their age, job, and health status. Some of them will get compulsory vaccination based on their job, and others will follow a prioritizing strategy based on their age, job, and health status.

Third: Persuading People Strategy to repeatedly notify citizens to get the vaccine based on scientific advice.

The basic structure of our proposed MAS includes several environments that interact with each other; the main environment is the health ministry environment; it is responsible for (1) the completion of the vaccine purchasing method by interacting with the supplier environment, (2) it should work too with a machine learning unit to process cities pandemic data in order to distribute the vaccines for the cities, (3) organizing the strategy of vaccine distribution for registered citizens in coordination with the population environment, and (4) interacting with the advisor environment to check the number of vaccinated people and persuading them to get the vaccine until having 60% of the population vaccinated Fig. 1.

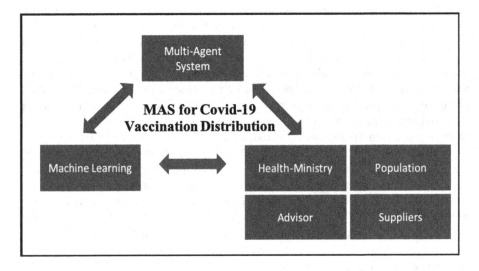

Fig. 1. Basic Structure of the Proposed Vaccination Distribution MAS.

3.2 System Environments and Their Agents

Each environment of the four environments represents a container and is divided into several agents that cooperate with each other to accomplish their environmental goals using Jade specifications and ACL message communication. Figure 2 summarizes the full Structure of the Proposed Vaccination Distribution MAS.

3.3 Data Source

We obtained four types of data to be integrated and processed through the proposed system, as follows:

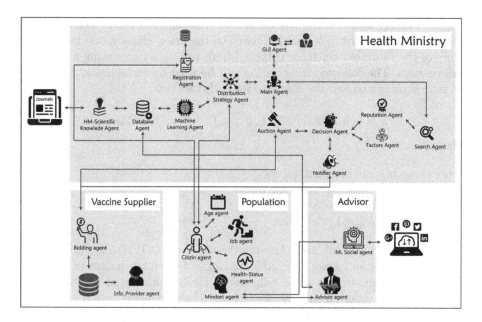

Fig. 2. Full Structure of the Proposed Vaccination Distribution MAS.

Pandemic Status Real-Data: The source of the real data for pandemic spreading for each of the 12 Palestinian cities.

Citizen Information Data: The data of the population and citizen registration assumed using different proposed scenarios, we mimic some inputs based on the platform of vaccine covid-19 registration form on the Health ministry web page.

Vaccine Reputation Data: The vaccine reputation data is collected via a reputation survey that is distributed to citizens from different Palestinian cities.

Population Data: We obtained the real numbers of cities' populations and overall population from the Palestinian Central Bureau of Statistics website.

3.4   VacDist Framework

The following sections provide a detailed description of each phase of the VacDist framework strategies.

Decision-Making Strategy Main Goal: The main goal of this strategy is to help decision-makers in the health sector and government to make informed decisions about adding a COVID-19 vaccine to their immunization program. The subsystem consists of six main agents that communicate and cooperate to achieve the specified goal. When the auction agent is requested to buy COVID-19 vaccines within a budget constraint, it enters into a negotiation process with supplier bidding agents using the FIPA-ACL message structure. The decision-maker agent makes the final decision based on the price, efficacy, and reputation values of the vaccines, which are collected from various sources using a QUERY performative. The collected information will be used by an equation defined in the next equation to find the Ps value for each vaccine.

$$Ps = (w_R.R_{norm}) + (w_E.E_{norm})) + (w_P.(1 - P_{norm})) \qquad (1)$$

Where:

w_R, w_E, w_P are constant values
R_{norm} : Normalized reputation value
E_{norm} : Normalized efficacy value
P_{norm} : Normalized price value

The proposed strategy involves choosing the top three COVID-19 vaccines with the best Ps values and using 50%, 30%, and 20% of the total budget to purchase them. The decision-maker agent will inform the auction agent of the chosen biddings and the required amount of vaccines to be purchased from their suppliers. After the purchasing process is finalized, the main agent will distribute the vaccines in the second stage. A clearing signal will be sent to all participating agents, and the auction agent will pass control to the main agent and terminate itself.

Machine Learning Distribution Strategy Based Cities. Instead of using the naive approach for vaccine distribution that depends only on cities' populations, we utilized a reinforcement learning algorithm and the Contextual Bandits to develop an optimal vaccine distribution over 12 Palestinian cities. In VacDist, we deployed the VacSIM system proposed by Awasthi et al. to achieve optimal vaccine distribution [2]. VacSIM is a novel pipeline system that merged a feed-forward Sequential Decision-based RL model (Deep Q Learning) into a Contextual Bandit for optimizing the distribution of the COVID-19 vaccine. Whereas the Deep Q learning model finds better actions and rewards, contextual bands allow online modifications that may need to be implemented on a day-to-day basis in the real-world scenario. Furthermore, to reach the best utility of the vaccine to vulnerable populations and overcome the covid 19 infections spreading, they selected multiple features as input to the feed-forward neural network and the contextual bandit model, such as death rate, recovery rate, and population.

In the VacDist model, we used a real dataset representing the pandemic situation in 12 Palestinian cities to extract the pandemic features for the VacDist system. We employed the VacSIM model to carry out the best distribution of the vaccine over 12 Palestinian cities according to their pandemic situation. We extracted the main features that represent the inputs of the feed-forward neural network and the contextual bandit. These features include the daily number of Covid-19 patients, the death rate, the recovery rate, the population, the available number of beds, the daily number of the available ICUs, and the daily number of the available ventilator.

We supposed that the vaccine would distribute over the city on the last day of the month; therefore, we used 28 d for model training and the last two days for model testing. The final output represents the percentage of vaccines for the 12 cities.

Deployment Machine Learning Distribution Strategy in MAS

The machine learning (ML) model for vaccine allocation and distribution over cities is one of the system parts. Multiple agents cooperated and collaborated to achieve the goals. Firstly, the main agent sends an ACL Inform massage to the Machine learning agent to inform it that we have the vaccine. Then ML agent sent a Query ACL message to the HM database agent in the health ministry container to get the actual data for model training and testing. After the HM database agent receives a message from the ML agent, it sends a directory of the ACL messages. After that, the ML agent runs the model using the data. Finally, the ML agent sent each city's vaccine portion via ACL messages to the vaccine distribution strategy agent.

Distribution Strategy Based Citizen. In this phase of the VacDist System, we distribute the vaccine to citizens based on their personal information in order to achieve fairness in distributing the limited amount of the vaccine. This phase receives the output of the decision-making strategy-based cities phase that gets the amount of the available vaccine and distributes it among cities, as illustrated in the previous section. The output of Decision Making Strategy Based Cities is the percentage of the vaccine amount for each city.

After receiving this amount in the current phase, the Distribution strategy agent announces to the registration agent the availability of the vaccine. In order to get the information of registered citizens, the registration agent announces the same announcement to the citizen agent in the population environment in order to inform the citizens about vaccine availability.

In our applied scenario, the Citizen agent creates several citizens as a whole population, each one with his name, city, and mindset. Each one of the citizens is an independent agent with a unique name, that can connect with the registration agent if he wants to get the vaccine. The mindset of each citizen impacts the willingness of the agent to get vaccinated or not. The name, city, and mindset of the agents are stored on the database agent of the health ministry agent as a whole population. When the citizen wants to be vaccinated, he should provide his job, health status, and age to be registered with the registration agent, along with his name, city, and mindset.

Each citizen should have all or some of the following attributes, along with his unique name, according to his registration status to the registration agent. These attributes are **City**, **Age**, **Job**, **Health status** and **Mindset** as we assumed that the mindset towards getting a vaccination for each citizen agent would belong to one of these categories: persuaded, hesitated, never minded, and anti-vaxxers.

Once the citizen is created, citizens of hesitated, never minded, and anti-vaxxer mindset will be classified as "not registered" to get the vaccination. On the other hand, the citizen with persuaded mindset is the citizens that want to get the vaccine, so they info registered with the registration agent and pass it to the distribution strategy agent in order to get their date of getting the vaccine.

Two main strategies followed here as follows:

Strategy1-The Compulsory Vaccination. In this strategy, if citizens work in a medical sector that directly contacts covid-19 patients, they must immediately get the vaccine once the vaccines are available.

Strategy2-Getting Priority

In this strategy, priority numbers from 1 to 3 will be assigned to each citizen based on his age, job, and health status. For each attribute of these three attributes, we put a rank out of 10 based on the registered values (Age Rank (AR), Job Rank (JR), Health-Status Rank (HSR)), then we put them in a priority formula where each one of the attributes has a weight of the priority to get the overall priority.

The weight of health status of 50% of the priority decision, while the weight of the age forms 40% of the priority decision along with 10% weight for the job according to this assumed formula:

$$priority = 0.5HSR + 0.4AR + 0.1JR \qquad (2)$$

Before entering the distribution strategy for each citizen, the amount of available vaccine is checked for the citizen city since the amount of vaccines are limited, as we assumed at the beginning of our study. If no vaccine is available, the citizen will be notified that he cannot get the vaccine, otherwise, the citizen will receive the strategy of getting vaccination along with the data of getting the vaccine.

Persuading People Strategy. This strategy represents the advisor environment. The advisor subsystem plays an influential role in encouraging people to get the Covid-19 vaccine and combat the spreading of rumors and fake news on social media. The Advisor frequently sends messages to the unregistered people in the vaccination system to pursue them to get their vaccine. The messages are in the form of bits of advice; we collected them from the World Health Organization website. In the VacDist system, the Advisor represents one of the primary containers in the MAS. It starts working once the main agent announces that the vaccination registration is open. Firstly, the Advisor agent sends an ACL query massage to the HM database to get bits of advice from it. Then, the HM database sends the pieces of advice by informing ACL messages. After that, the advisor agent requests the information of the population from the HM database; information includes their names, phone numbers, and vaccination registration status [Registered, not registered]; then the HM database sends the information of the population to the Advisor. The Advisor checks the people's registration status if they are not registered, then the Advisor sends messages to them until they are registered or reach 60% of the population vaccinated.

4 Results

4.1 Decision-Making Strategy Results

We have created a survey to measure the reputation of each of the following vaccines, i.e., Pfizer-BioNTech, Sinopharm, AstraZeneca, Novavax, Moderna, and Sputnik, within the Palestinian community. Based on the survey responses, a reputation value between 0 and 5 was calculated for each COVID-19 vaccine. In this aspect, the Pfizer vaccine got the highest reputation score with a value of 4.1, followed by Sputnik, Moderna Sinopharm, AstraZeneca, and Novavax, respectively, with the following values in order, 2.4, 2.3, 2.0, 1.7, 1.5. Figure 3, represents the calculated Ps values for each vaccine. Pfizer got the highest value with 0.81, while Sinopharm reported the lowest Ps with 0.44. Based on the calculated values of Ps for each vaccine, and following the proposed strategy discussed in the methodology section for purchasing vaccines, three vaccines with the highest Ps values were chosen for purchasing: Pfizer-BioNTech, Sputnik, and Moderna. In this aspect, 40% of the total number of vaccines to be purchased will come from Pfizer, 48% will come from Sputnik, and 12% will come from Moderna.

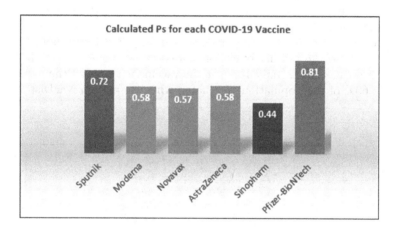

Fig. 3. Calculated Ps for each COVID-19 Vaccine.

4.2 Machine Learning Distribution Strategy Based Cities Results

Here, we reported the vaccine percentage of each city using the machine learning algorithm and naive strategy. At the naive approach, we calculated the vaccine portion of cities by dividing the population of each city over the people of Palestine, Fig. 4

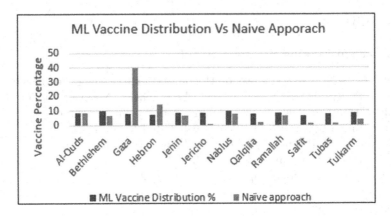

Fig. 4. Vaccine Distribution Based Cities stratigies

4.3   Distribution Strategy Based Citizen Results

In this section, we illustrate the results obtained from the VacDist framework Decision Making Strategy Based Citizen, and we compared these results with the naïve distribution strategy results. We assumed that the naïve strategy of distributing the vaccine (1) distributes the vaccine to the cities based on population percentage instead of the machine learning model percentage (Fig. 6), and (2) calculates the priority of citizens based on citizen age only. The overall number of citizens is 112, only 15% get the vaccine when using the naïve strategy, while 69% of the population vaccinated when we use our VacDist strategy (Fig. 5).

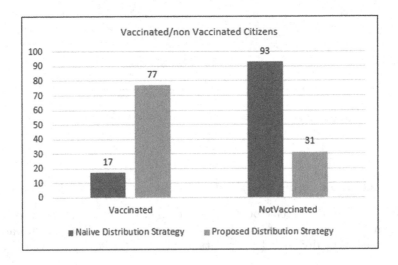

Fig. 5. Number of vaccinated/not vaccinated citizens for each strategy

Health-Status Attribute Impact. In the VacDist strategy, we added the health status attribute to rank the priority of getting the vaccine. We showed the results of the Health-status impact by calculating the percentage of vaccinated people using the naïve strategy to the percentage of vaccinated people using the VacDist strategy (Fig. 6).

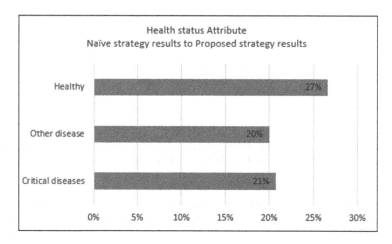

Fig. 6. Percentage of the vaccinated citizens in naïve strategy to overall citizens getting vaccinated in the VacDist strategy based on health-status distribution

Job Attribute Impact. In our strategy, we used the job attribute to rank the priority of getting the vaccine, where this attribute has not been taken into consideration in the assumed naïve strategy. We showed the results of job impact by calculating the percentage of vaccinated people using the naïve strategy to the percentage of vaccinated people using our strategy (Fig. 7).

Advisor Agent and Mindset Impact. Adding an advisor agent to VacDist significantly increases the number of citizens that register to get the vaccine. In the naïve strategy, only persuaded mindset persons can get the vaccine i.e. 15% of the overall population, while in the VacDist strategy, all of the persuaded citizens, hesitated and never-minded citizens get the vaccine because of the repeatedly received notifications by the advisor agent.

5 Discussion

During the development of the VacDist framework, we faced a lot of challenges in terms of obtaining the required data from main sources to perform our research. At first, we were unable to obtain real data about for epidemic spreading from the

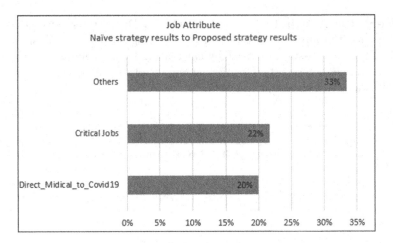

Fig. 7. Percentage of vaccinated people using naïve strategy to the percentage of vaccinated people using VacDist strategy based on job type distribution

Palestinian health ministry. Second, we were unable to obtain real data related to the vaccinated people (i.e., age, job, health status), nor the data related to the purchasing process (e.g., budget) from the health ministry. For these reasons, we have put many assumptions using random data. In addition, we have used random generators utilizing minimum and maximum values to fill the missing values in the utilized data (e.g., features related to the hospitals, i.e., number of beds, number of Ventilator, and the daily number of people in the ICU). Third, due to the lack of knowledge about the utilized strategy within health ministries for purchasing vaccines, we were not able to compare our proposed strategy with the naïve approach used. Concerning the survey responses, the number of respondents was not enough or satisfactory. However, this is explainable since many people in our community do not have the culture to interact with the research community. Few people would interact and volunteer to answer scientific questionnaires that are distributed on social media platforms. Finally, the Main agent in our system has a centralized role. It is the main controller that coordinates the interaction of different environments (health ministry, suppliers, advisor, and population). This could lead to bottlenecks and failure in the system over time. And thus, decentralizing the main agent tasks would improve the system's performance, and this will be considered in future work.

6   Conclusion

This study provided a VacDist tool; it is a MAS that provides four primary strategies to control the vaccination process from vaccine purchasing to pursue the population to get their vaccine and vaccinate them.

The VacDist tool contains four primary subsystems: The vaccine purchasing subsystem; it aims to help the decision-makers to select and purchase the vaccine according to multiple factors such as price and the vaccine's reputation. The second subsystem is the vaccine distribution over cities; we deployed a pipeline reinforcement learning algorithm to find the optimal policy to distribute the vaccine over cities according to their pandemic status. The third subsystem is vaccine distribution among citizens; our system provides a strategy to vaccinate the most vulnerable people as a priority. Finally, the advisor subsystem plays an essential role in educating and pursuing the citizens who are not persuaded to get their vaccine by sending them messages containing scientific information about the vaccines.

Our simulation results found that the VacDist tool speeds up the vaccination process compared with the current naive strategy applied in Palestine. Furthermore, our system succeeded in vaccinating the most vulnerable population once the vaccine is available. Up to our knowledge, the VacDist tool is the first tool that deployed all the services needed to control the whole vaccination process.

References

1. Silva, P.C.L., Batista, P.V.C., Lima, H.S., Alves, M.A., Guimarães, F.G., Silva, R.C.P.: COVID-ABS: an agent-based model of COVID-19 epidemic to simulate health and economic effects of social distancing interventions. Chaos Solitons Fractals **139**, 110088 (2020). https://doi.org/10.1016/j.chaos.2020.110088
2. Awasthi, R., et al.: VacSIM: learning effective strategies for COVID-19 vaccine distribution using reinforcement learning. Intell. Based Med. **6**, 100060 (2022). https://doi.org/10.1016/j.ibmed.2022.100060
3. Chowell, G., Viboud, C., Wang, X., Bertozzi, S.M., Miller, M.A.: Adaptive vaccination strategies to mitigate pandemic influenza: Mexico as a case study. PLoS ONE **4**, e8164 (2009). https://doi.org/10.1371/journal.pone.0008164
4. Marco-Franco, J.E., Pita-Barros, P., Vivas-Orts, D., González-de-Julián, S., Vivas-Consuelo, D.: COVID-19, fake news, and vaccines: should regulation be implemented? IJERPH. 18, 744 (2021). https://doi.org/10.3390/ijerph18020744
5. Minoza, J.M.A., Bongolan, V.P., Rayo, J.F.: COVID-19 Agent-Based Model with Multi-objective Optimization for Vaccine Distribution (2021)
6. Cardoso, R.C., Ferrando, A.: A review of agent-based programming for multi-agent systems. Computers. **10**, 16 (2021)
7. Hassan, A., Sawan, A., Rattrout, A., Sabha, M.: Human tracking in cultural places using multi-agent systems and face recognition. In: Jezic, G., Chen-Burger, J., Kusek, M., Sperka, R., Howlett, R.J., Jain, L.C. (eds.) Agents and Multi-Agent Systems: Technologies and Applications 2020. SIST, vol. 186, pp. 177–186. Springer, Singapore (2020). https://doi.org/10.1007/978-981-15-5764-4_16
8. Dorri, A., Kanhere, S.S., Jurdak, R.: Multi-agent systems: a survey. IEEE Access **6**, 28573–28593 (2018). https://doi.org/10.1109/ACCESS.2018.2831228
9. COVID-Coronavirus Statistics-Worldometer. https://www.worldometers.info/coronavirus/
10. Coronavirus Disease (COVID-19): Vaccines and Vaccine Safety. https://www.who.int/news-room/coronavirus-disease-(covid-19)-vaccines
11. Covid-19 Vaccine Tracker: Latest Updates - The New York Times. https://www.nytimes.com/2020/science/coronavirus-vaccine-tracker.html
12. Bellifemine, F.L., Caire, G., Greenwood, D.: Developing Multi-agent Systems with JADE. John Wiley & Sons (2007)

Smart E-Waste Management System Utilizing IoT and DL Approaches

Daniel Voskergian[(⊠)] and Isam Ishaq

Computer Engineering Department, Al-Quds University, Jerusalem, Palestine
Daniel2vosk@gmail.com, isam@alquds.edu

Abstract. Electronic waste is presently acknowledged as the rapidly expanding waste stream on a global scale. Consequently, e-waste represents a primary global concern in modern society since electronic equipment contains hazardous substances, and if not managed properly, it will harm human health and the environment. Thus, the necessity for more innovative, safer, and greener systems to handle e-waste has never been more urgent. To address this issue, a smart e-waste management system based on the Internet of Things (IoT) and TensorFlow-based Deep Learning (DL) is designed and developed in this paper. This innovative system offers the potential to manage e-waste more efficiently, supporting green city initiatives and promoting sustainability. By realizing an intelligent green city vision, we can tackle various contamination problems, benefiting both humans and the environment.

Keywords: E-waste Management · Internet of Things (IoT) · TensorFlow Lite · Deep Learning · Object Detection · Smart Green City

1 Introduction

Electronic waste - also called e-waste - is discarded electronic devices that are no longer needed, do not function, or are obsolete. The rapid technological advancement today and increasing consumer demand make lots of electronic devices reach the end of their estimated lifespan after short periods of use.

Nowadays, e-waste is currently recognized as the waste stream experiencing the most rapid growth worldwide, entitled by the United Nations as a "tsunami of e-waste" [1]. As mentioned in [2], global e-waste production reached around 53.6 million metric tons in 2019, with a noticeable increase of 44.4 million metric tons in only five years. The study anticipates that the entire mass of e-waste will increase to 74 million metric tons by 2030. As documented, only 17.4% of collected e-waste is properly recycled.

According to some estimates in Europe, an average household has 72 electronic devices, out of which 11 are either broken or no longer in use [3]. Alongside, Cisco provided in its annual report in 2018 an estimate of 28.5 billion smart devices to be connected to the Internet by 2022 and anticipated that 5% of IoT-enabled devices would be trashed per year by consumers; as a consequence, this could lead to 1.5 billion new e-waste items annually [4].

M. Tabaa et al. (Eds.): INTIS 2022/2023, CCIS 1728, pp. 88–103, 2024.
https://doi.org/10.1007/978-3-031-47366-1_7

Thus, e-waste management is a primary growing concern today, especially in developing countries like Palestine. Improper disposal and mishandling of e-waste can lead to hazardous effects on both human health and the environment. Certain e-waste remnants contain toxic and flammable chemicals, such as cadmium, beryllium, lead, and brominated flame retardants, which may easily catch fire in an open environment, thus, threatening lives, increasing diseases, economic loss, and pollution [5]. Hence, the realization of intelligent systems for e-waste management to significantly reduce their harmful effects is of immense importance and has become a hot topic.

Technological advancement and the appearance of novel technologies, i.e., the Internet of Things (IoT) and Deep Learning (DL), facilitate numerous new improvements to the existing infrastructures and systems in various domains. IoT refers to a system of interconnected things (e.g., devices) enriched by the ability to exchange data through the Internet [6]. In contrast, DL offers cutting-edge solutions for comprehensively understanding human behavior [7] and facilitates numerous new improvements to the existing infrastructures and systems in various domains. Considering the e-waste management challenges, implementing IoT and DL solutions is becoming compulsory for smart city vision since it allows objects to interconnect and interact with humans in a pervasive and intelligent way [8].

This study proposes the design and development of a smart e-waste management system utilizing the IoT and TensorFlow-based DL. The proposed system holds the potential to manage e-wastes better to support Green city initiatives and meet sustainability goals. By realizing a smart green city vision, we will be able to realize numerous human health and environmental contamination problems.

Our proposed system performs e-waste object detection and identification using a pre-trained object detection model within the TensorFlow Lite framework. The model is trained on an electronic object dataset using the concept of transfer learning for e-waste object detection in images. In addition, the system continuously monitors the condition of the e-waste bin, such as the temperature and humidity inside the bin, to detect and prevent fires. Moreover, the system provides up-to-date, real-time information to various stakeholders (i.e., municipalities, service waste managers, and system administrators) regarding e-waste count, e-waste weight/volume, and the filling level of the bin. We have utilized the ThingSpeak cloud platform to store and retrieve all the monitoring data using two main protocols, HTTP and MQTT protocol over the Internet and displayed for system administrators via an interactive Web-based interface (UI).

We structure the remainder of this paper as follows: Section 2 explores the related works on e-waste management. In Sect. 3, we present the used Object Detection model, and in Sect. 4, we present our proposed system in detail. Finally, Sect. 5 concludes the work and outlines potential areas for future research.

2 Related Work

The majority of waste management articles found in literature suggest the implementation of smart dustbins or waste bins that prioritize IoT-based segregation and recycling mechanisms for items such as plastics, papers, bottles, and glasses. Researchers for waste management have devised several methods; however, e-waste management is still an unresolved issue, with the current focus primarily on monitoring the condition of e-waste bins, such as the e-waste level. A very modest number of articles have proposed ideas for e-waste management. This section will highly concentrate on what has been published in the literature on smart e-waste management systems.

Kang et al. in [9] developed a smart collection system for the Malaysian e-waste management and recycling sector. They designed a smart e-waste collection box for households equipped with ultrasonic sensors to measure the e-waste level. They recorded it in a cloud-based database system called Google Firebase. A backend server was developed that schedules e-waste collectors to pick up e-waste once the box's volume reaches a specific threshold. In addition, they developed a mobile application for the public end-users to use when they want to dispose of their household e-waste.

Singh et al. [10] presented an e-waste management solution using an IoT-based collection vendor machine (CVM). To use the system, the customer must register and receive a QR code that contains all relevant information about the customer. The customer then attaches the QR code to their e-waste object and deposits it into the CVM. The prototype uses ultrasonic sensors to measure the CVM's capacity and alert the authorities when it reaches a certain threshold. The e-waste items are collected by a collector and transported to a warehouse for recycling and billing. The project uses the Arduino Uno platform to connect the sensors and gather sensor data.

Ali et al. [11] developed an IoT-based smart e-waste monitoring system that utilizes a DS18B20 temperature sensor and a KY-026 flame sensor to monitor the condition of the e-waste bin. The system also uses an HC-SR04 Ultrasonic sensor to measure the waste level. A Raspberry Pi 3 was employed as a microcontroller to process the input signals and generate the desired output. Additionally, ThingSpeak was utilized as an IoT web platform to enable system administrators to analyze and visualize the collected data.

Sampedro et al. [12] have proposed a smart e-waste bin that utilizes YOLOv4, an object detection model, and Raspberry Pi 3 to identify the types of e-waste, including cellphones, chargers, batteries, and others. The bin segregates the waste and provides e-wallet credit to the user. All transactions are logged in a server, which enables operators to monitor usage and determine when e-waste collection is necessary via an admin dashboard. The bin's crediting and monitoring functionalities are facilitated through GSM and WIFI modules.

Rani et al. [13] suggested an IoT-based mobile e-waste management system for smart campuses. The system involves using a Raspberry Pi 3 microcontroller to identify e-waste objects in an image by employing a Single Shot Multibox Detector Lite-MobileNet-v2 model that was trained on the Microsoft Common Objects in Context dataset. Additionally, the system keeps track of the e-waste count and bin percentage level. The monitoring data is stored on a cloud platform, and an interactive Android-based mobile user interface was created to display the monitored data.

Nonetheless, the e-waste management systems reported in the literature do not integrate object detection with thorough and detailed monitoring aspects of the e-waste bin; the majority only focus on one of those in their systems. In fact, object detection is not well explored in the e-waste management domain. Thus, in this paper, we propose a smart e-waste management system that integrates various sensors for monitoring the current condition of bins and a TensorFlow Lite framework to train a deep learning model to perform real-time e-waste object detection, providing a more comprehensive view of the e-waste management process. By combining object detection and detailed monitoring, the system will not only improve the efficiency of e-waste collection and management but also provide valuable data for policymakers and researchers to understand better and address the issue of e-waste. Overall, the proposed system has immense potential to contribute to the sustainable management of e-waste significantly.

3 Object Detection Model

The present study outlines five key stages for developing object detection, namely: determining the computing paradigm (cloud, fog, or local) for object detection; selecting the deep learning framework (TensorFlow Lite or TensorFlow); choosing the model and architecture for object detection; selecting the method for obtaining the dataset; and determining the method for exporting the trained model to a hardware application.

3.1 Cloud, Fog, or Local Computing

Recently, various IoT projects utilized cloud computing and fog computing due to the limitation of computing power and the battery life faced by current technologies. Both approaches can shift the vast amount of data and computation previously processed locally in the device to the fog or remote cloud nodes. Compared to cloud computing, fog computing achieves superior latency and faster response time in IoT systems [14].

However, performing fog computing by transmitting images for e-waste object detection to the fog node is not suitable for our project for the following reasons: For our proposed approach, we will utilize GSM communication for data transmissions, which has the desirable range characteristics (i.e., several kilometers between the GSM module and the tower) suitable to be implemented in the e-waste trash bin since these bins will be scattered along with the city. However, since the Pi camera in our project will capture a 5 MP image of e-waste objects with a file size of 15 MB, fog computing will not be suitable in our case since GSM has limited data rates per channel. Consequently, this will result in higher latency and reduce the response time compared with the processing on the device. Table 1 illustrates the typical transfer time to upload an image of 15 MB in size via different GSM standards.

In addition, with the development of TensorFlow Lite (TFLite), we can convert and optimize TensorFlow models for deployment on mobile devices such as raspberry pi and Android. In this aspect, we will utilize EfficientDet-Lite, an advanced object detection model architecture specifically optimized for mobile devices, providing the required accuracy, faster inference speed, and smaller model size when compared to the original model. The lowest version (EfficientDet-Lite0) pre-trained on COCO 2017 dataset has a size of 4.4 MB and latency of 37 ms, while the highest version (EfficientDet-Lite4) has 19.9 MB and 260 ms latency. Thus, processing object detection on the local device is more resource-efficient and assists in making data-driven decisions faster.

We will use the cloud platform mainly to store the collected data (i.e., filling level, e-waste object count, e-waste object type, bin weight, humidity, temperature, etc.) and perform further analysis (e.g., predictive models).

Table 1. Transfer time of 15 MB image via different GSM network types when considering a 15% amount of overhead attached to the payload packet.

Network Type	Typical Upload Speeds (Mbps) [15]	Transfer Time [16] (hh:mm:ss)
3G	0.4	00:04:41
3G HSPA+	3	00:01:00
4G LTE	5	00:00:28
4G LTE-Advanced	10	00:00:14

3.2 Choosing a Deep-Learning Framework

In our project, we have chosen TensorFlow Lite instead of TensorFlow for one main reason. A TensorFlow object detection model typically requires a powerful Graphical Processing Unit (GPU) to perform efficiently. However, such a requirement is unsuitable for a smart e-waste management system that utilizes a low-power embedded mobile device like a Raspberry Pi. Fortunately, TensorFlow Lite enables the use of object detection models on these constrained resources.

TensorFlow Lite is a deep learning framework that is open-source and can be used across different platforms. It transforms pre-trained models in TensorFlow into an optimized portable format called FlatBuffers, identifiable by the.tflite file extension, that can be tailored for speed or storage [17]. In essence, TensorFlow Lite is a collection of tools that facilitates on-device machine learning, particularly on devices with limited computational and memory resources. Consequently, developers can execute their models on mobile, embedded, and IoT devices, including Linux-based embedded devices like Raspberry Pi or microcontrollers. Since models at resource-constrained devices need to be lightweight and have low latency, the amount of computation required for prediction must be reduced. TensorFlow Lite addresses this challenge by employing two optimization methods: quantization and weight pruning. Quantization involves reducing the precision of the numbers used to represent various TensorFlow model parameters, thereby reducing the model's weight (e.g., 32-bit floating points weights can be converted to 8-bit floating or integer points). On the other hand, weight pruning involves removing parameters within a model that have minimal impact on the model's performance [18].

TensorFlow Lite model addresses five key constraints: 1) low latency by eliminating the round-trip from the device to the server, 2) privacy protection by ensuring that personal data is not shared across the network, 3) no need for permanent internet connectivity, 4) reduced model and smaller binary size, 5) efficient power consumption as the inference is made locally irrespective of network connectivity [19].

3.3 Choosing an Architecture for Object Detection

This project has used a pre-trained TensorFlow Lite model called EffiecentDet-Lite4, a mobile/IoT-friendly object detection model derived from the EfficientDet architecture and pre-trained on the COCO 2017 dataset. EfficientDet [20] is a family of object detectors that is lightweight and optimized for running on devices with resource constraints.

It utilizes a weighted bi-directional feature pyramid network (BiFPN) and employs a compound scaling technique that uniformly scales the resolution, depth, and width for all backbone, feature networks, and box/class prediction networks simultaneously. We have chosen EfficientDet-Lite 4 since it has the highest mean average precision (mAP) among other models in its family, with 41.96%. Although it has the lowest inference time (260 ms), this is an acceptable speed for our project.

3.4 Dataset Collection

To train the pre-trained object detection model, we have collected around 1000 images of five electronic objects, namely a Monitor, Keyboard, Mouse, Headphone, and Smartphone, from the Open Images Dataset [11]. Open Images Dataset is a collaborative release that comprises around nine million images annotated with image-level labels, object bounding boxes, object segmentation masks, and visual relationships. To ensure equal e-waste class coverage, we collected two hundred images per e-waste type with different backgrounds, orientations, and lighting conditions. In this study, we randomly selected 80% of the original images as the training set, 10% as the validation set, and 10% as the test set. Additionally, we used stratified sampling to preserve the percentage of samples for each class in the training and testing data.

3.5 Training Phase

To perform the training phase, we have used the TensorFlow Lite Model Maker library [12] to train a custom object detection model capable of detecting e-waste objects within images on a Raspberry Pi 4. The Model Maker library uses transfer learning to simplify training a TensorFlow Lite model using a custom dataset. Transfer learning is a technique that takes an already trained model for a related task as input and uses it as the starting point to create a new custom model [14]. Retraining a TensorFlow Lite model with a custom dataset reduces the required training data and will shorten the training time. In addition, transfer learning enables object detection even if the dataset is small. We trained the model until the model consistently achieved an error of less than 1.0000. Once we had generated the frozen graph, we exported it to the Raspberry Pi 4 for use in object detection. The mAP of the obtained model from the test images evaluation is 76.9%. Figure 1 shows the pipeline for developing the TensorFlow Lite object detection model needed for the proposed system.

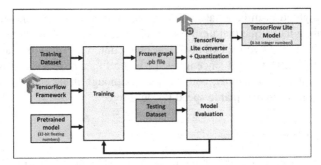

Fig. 1. Pipeline for developing the e-waste TensorFlow Lite Object Detection Model.

4 The Proposed System

4.1 System Architecture

Figure 2 illustrates the overall architecture of our proposed system. It uses 1) a Raspberry Pi 4 microcontroller for performing e-waste object detection and identification, 2) an Electron Particle kit with 3-G cellular connectivity that is responsible for: a) continuously monitoring the condition of the e-waste bin, such as the temperature, and humidity inside the bin, to detect and prevent fires from happening, b) providing up-to-date real-time information to different stakeholders (i.e., municipalities, service waste manager, system administrator) regarding e-waste count, e-waste weight/volume, and the filling level of the bin.

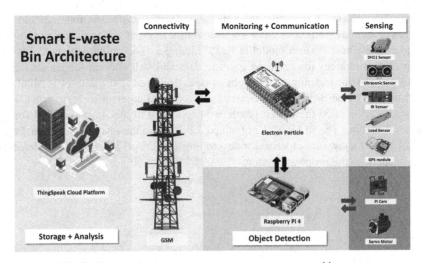

Fig. 2. Proposed smart e-waste management system architecture.

This project uses the TensorFlow Lite application programming interface (API) to run the EfficientDet-Lite model trained on an electronic object dataset for image e-waste object detection. In addition, we utilized the ThingSpeak cloud platform to store and retrieve all the monitoring data using two main protocols: Hypertext Transfer Protocol (HTTP) and Message Queuing Telemetry Transport (MQTT) protocol over the Internet. An interactive Web-based interface displays stored data to system administrators.

4.2 System Components

Table 2 lists all the components and modules used in our project, with their corresponding functionalities. These components work together to form an integrated system to achieve smart, green, healthy, and sustainable environments and cities.

4.3 System Workflow

This subsection describes the working mechanisms of the proposed smart e-waste bin as follows:

1) The system starts by checking if every component (i.e., sensors) is working correctly and examines the filling level of the trash bin. Suppose the system needs maintenance or the trash bin is full. In that case, it will communicate with its neighbors (trash bins in the neighborhood) via a GSM module embedded within Particle Electron Kit and try to retrieve different information, such as their locations, working status, filling level, etc. This information will be used to find the trash bin that satisfies the shortest path to the user and holds the required capacity. Then the system will display all the information regarding the nearest trash bin to the user through an LCD.

2) If the system works properly and the filling level does not exceed a predefined threshold, it will accept waste in its compartment. Suppose the user presses the 'run' button. In that case, the system begins by capturing an image of the waste object using a five-megapixel (5 MP) Pi camera connected to the Raspberry Pi and located above the trash bin. Then the TensorFlow Lite API will take the waste object image as input and run the EfficientDet-Lite object detection model for object detection and identification. If e-waste is detected, a servo motor controlled by the Raspberry Pi will actuate the opening container lid. Figure 3 shows the results of e-waste object detection for some electronic devices, based on the quantized EffiecientDet-Lite4 object detection model, trained and run by TensorFlow Lite API. In Fig. 3.b, the keyboard is detected with a score of 87%. The mouse is detected with a score of 90%, and the smartphone is detected with a score of 81%, respectively. The score indicates confidence that the object was genuinely detected.

An infrared sensor will count the number of e-waste objects thrown in the trash bin (refer to Fig. 4). The basic concept of an IR Sensor is to transmit an infrared signal by an IR light-emitting diode; if an obstacle appears in front of the LED, this infrared signal bounces from the surface of an object and is received at the infrared receiver (photodiodes or phototransistors). In this project, we gave 10 s duration to this process to ensure the counting of every e-waste object thrown. Then, the same servo motor will actuate the closing of the container lid.

Table 2. System components with their corresponding functionalities in the smart e-waste bin.

	Components	Functions
Sensors / Modules	Ultrasonic sensor	Measures the percentage filling level of e-waste within a bin
	Flame sensor module	Detects fire inside the e-waste bin
	Temperature / Humidity sensor	Measures the temperature and humidity within a bin Predicts an upcoming fire or non-favorable events
	Gas sensor	Identifies the presence of harmful gas
	Load sensor	Measures the actual weight of collected e-waste
	Infrared sensors	Counts e-waste objects being thrown in a bin
	GPS module	Provides location identification of waste bin (latitude, longitude) and real-time of the bin from the satellite Ensures the physical security of the bin
	Camera module	Captures real-time images of e-waste object → an input data for pre-trained e-waste object detection model
Microcontrollers	Raspberry Pi	Connectivity control over devices (camera + servo motor) Perform real-time e-waste object detection
	Particle Electron	Provides connectivity control over devices (sensors + GPS module + DC motor) Forwards sensed data to the cloud server for further processing and analysis via 3-G communication
Actuators	Servo motor	Actuates the opening and closing of the e-waste cap
	Water pump dc motor	Works as a water sprinkler when a fire is detected

(continued)

Table 2. (*continued*)

	Components	Functions
Network	GSM module	A communication technology to perform data transmission to the cloud server
Power	Solar panel-based power bank	Operates the smart bin anywhere
Model	E-waste object detection model	A deep learning model trained on electronic object images dataset using the TensorFlow framework
User Module	LCD display unit	Notifies user of bin status (working/damaged/under maintenance, filling level, and available capacity) If the current bin is full → it directs the user to the next bin that has the required capacity, works properly, and satisfies the shortest path
	Mobile App for collector trucks/ authorizes	Displays the Optimized route for collecting e-waste bins Notifies for any upcoming fires or non-favorable events
	Mobile App for users	Visualizes bin locations on a map and bin status Displays the shortest path to the nearest empty e-waste bin
Cloud Server Module	ThingSpeak Database & web servers	Storing received bins data (location, status) Enables authorities for real-time monitoring Predicting filling levels of bins Forecasting of the future waste generation (i.e., the total volume of e-waste in different areas on a different period basis)

4) Once the container lid is closed, an ultrasonic sensor (HC-SR04) will calculate the filling level of e-waste inside the trash bin (refer to Fig. 4). The level is determined based on the distance between the sensor and the e-waste objects.. In this aspect, the ultrasonic sensor works by emitting eight ultrasonic wave bursts at a frequency of 40 kHz, which are then reflected back to the sensor's receiver. The travel time of the signal is calculated, along with the speed of sound, to determine the filling level of waste inside the bin.

5) The waste status inside the bin is defined into three fill-up levels (low 0–40, medium 40–80, and high 80–100). If the filling level exceeds a certain level (threshold value

Fig. 3. E-waste Object detection results on Mouse, Keyboard, and Smartphone.

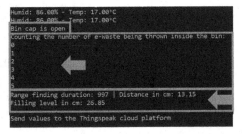

Fig. 4. Number of e-wastes being thrown inside the bin and the bin' filling level.

of 80% full), the system will notify the system administrator through an SMS and an automatic email notification via SMTP. Thus, we can guarantee prompt collection of e-waste when the waste level reaches its maximum fill.

6) Afterward, the load sensor converts the load or force acting on it into an electrical signal representing the actual weight of e-waste.

7) Finally, the e-waste types (i.e., keyboard, mouse, etc.), e-waste count, bin filling level, e-wastes weight, and bins location through the GPS module will be sent to the ThingSpeak cloud platform using HTTP and MQTT protocols over the Internet via a GSM cellular module as a network interface, which is embedded within the Electron Particle kit. These collected pieces of information can be used to predict bins level and forecast total e-waste volume from the specific area on different time bases (i.e., monthly, yearly); this enables municipalities to make smart decisions when planning to handle future waste management for the smart city. Figure 5 presents ThingSpeak Dashboard showing various monitored data, such as e-waste count, filling level, fire indicator, temperature, and humidity.

8) In the background, a flame sensor is utilized to detect heat flame in the range of 760–1100 nm wavelength, with a detection range of up to 100 cm, thus, detecting and preventing any fire that could lead to an explosion. This introduced capability may save significant losses of economy and life. When a heated flame is detected, the system will run water sparkling and send an emergency alert to the system administrator.

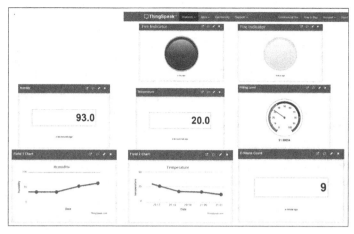

Fig. 5. ThingSpeak Dashboard showing various monitored data, such as e-waste count, filling level, fire indicator, temperature, and humidity.

9) In addition, a temperature and humidity sensor (DH11) is used as a fire prevention mechanism, which helps in predicting an upcoming fire or non-favorable events. When the system notices an increase in temperature, it will send an immediate indication that will be displayed on the ThingSpeak webpage or dashboard. The system will promptly notify the administrator to address the designated e-waste bin (Fig. 5).

The ultrasonic, infrared, and load sensors will only work when e-waste is disposed of. In addition, we will send the values of humidity and temperature sensors to the ThingSpeak platform only when the difference between the current and the last reading increases above a threshold value. The utilized approach mimics an energy-efficient way to operate the smart e-waste bin. Figure 6 and Fig. 7 illustrate the workflow of the proposed smart e-waste bin.

4.4 Prototype Implementation (Hardware)

The smart system was successfully developed as a proof-of-concept in this work, and it could be a promising step toward enhancing e-waste management. Figure 8 shows a schematic diagram for a part of the proposed smart e-waste bin. The diagram presents some hardware used to operate the smart e-waste system, a Particle Electron Kit with four main sensors, namely HC-SR04 ultrasonic sensor, DH11 humidity and temperature sensor, IR Flame module, and Infrared obstacle sensor.

4.5 System Cost

Table 3 outlines the total cost of developing the proposed system. This cost is reasonable given that the system reduces the need for manual labor in traditional waste management practices, resulting in decreased overall waste management costs.

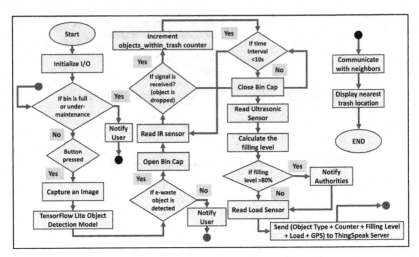

Fig. 6. General workflow of the proposed smart e-waste bin (part 1).

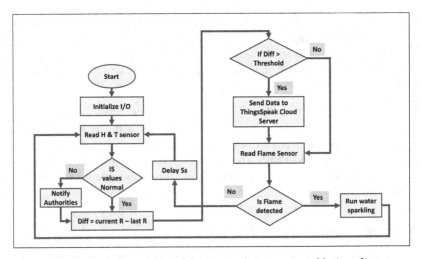

Fig. 7. General workflow of the proposed smart e-waste bin (part 2).

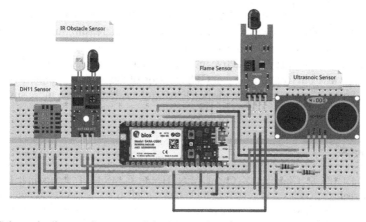

Fig. 8. Schematic diagram for a part of the proposed smart e-waste bin, which shows a Particle Electron Kit with four main sensors.

Table 3. Overall system development cost.

Components (amount = 1)	Cost
Ultrasonic Sensor - HC-SR04	3.95$
IR Obstacle Sensor	2.50$
IR Flame Sensor Module	1.89$
Grove - Temperature & Humidity Sensor (DHT11)	6.50$
GPS Module	11.59$
PARTICLE Electron with Cellular 2G Connectivity Kit	110$
Raspberry Pi 4	60.33$
Solar Panel with power bank	44$
Pi Camera	20$
Servo motor	7.5$
Overall System Cost	~ 270$

5   Conclusion and Future Work

This study proposes a comprehensive smart e-waste management system by integrating various sensors (i.e., ultrasonic sensor, IR sensor, flame sensor, temperature, and humidity sensor, load sensor, etc.) to monitor the current condition of the bin and TensorFlow Lite-based e-waste object detection model that performs real-time e-waste detection and classification. The lightweight nature of the pre-trained model EffiecientDet-Lite4 makes it the perfect match with Raspberry Pi 4. The model successfully identified e-waste objects and classified them according to their respective categories, such as keyboards, monitors, headphones, mouse, and smartphones.

In the future, we aim to improve the e-waste detection model by adding other classes, increasing the number of e-waste images per class, and increasing the training time to improve the model's accuracy and enhance the model's flexibility in identifying waste. Moreover, we aim to build an interactive mobile application that end-users will use to find the nearest e-waste bin from the current GPS location of the user. The implementation of such a system has the potential to lead society toward a safer, greener, more sustainable, and healthier life.

References

1. Ilankoon, I.M.S.K., Ghorbani, Y., Chong, M.N., Herath, G., Moyo, T., Petersen, J.: E-waste in the international context – A review of trade flows, regulations, hazards, waste management strategies and technologies for value recovery. Waste Manage. **82**, 258–275 (2018). https://doi.org/10.1016/j.wasman.2018.10.018
2. Forti, V., , Baldé, C.P., Kuehr, R., Bel, G.: The global E-waste monitor 2020. United Nations University (UNU). In: International Telecommunication Union (ITU) \& International Solid Waste Association (ISWA), Bonn/Geneva/Rotterdam. vol. 120, (2020)
3. International E-Waste Day: 57.4M Tonnes Expected in 2021 | WEEE Forum. https://weee-forum.org/ws_news/international-e-waste-day-2021/
4. Cisco, U.: Cisco annual internet report (2018–2023) white paper. 2020. Acessado em 10 (2021)
5. Cisco, U.: Cisco annual internet report (2018–2023) white paper. Cisco: San Jose, CA, USA, **10**(1), 1–35 (2020)
6. Dorsemaine, B., Gaulier, J.-P., Wary, J.-P., Kheir, N., Urien, P.: Internet of Things: A Definition & Taxonomy. In: 2015 9th International Conference on Next Generation Mobile Applications, Services and Technologies, pp. 72–77. IEEE, Cambridge, United Kingdom (2015)
7. Han, S., Ren, F., Wu, C., Chen, Y., Du, Q., Ye, X.: Using the TensorFlow Deep Neural Network to Classify Mainland China Visitor Behaviours in Hong Kong from Check-in Data. IJGI. **7**, 158 (2018). https://doi.org/10.3390/ijgi7040158
8. Kunst, R., Avila, L., Pignaton, E., Bampi, S., Rochol, J.: Improving network resources allocation in smart cities video surveillance. Comput. Netw. **134**, 228–244 (2018). https://doi.org/10.1016/j.comnet.2018.01.042
9. Kang, K.D., Kang, H., Ilankoon, I.M.S.K., Chong, C.Y.: Electronic waste collection systems using Internet of Things (IoT): Household electronic waste management in Malaysia. J. Clean. Prod. **252**, 119801 (2020). https://doi.org/10.1016/j.jclepro.2019.119801
10. Singh, K., Arora, G., Singh, P., Gupta, A.: IoT-based collection vendor machine (CVM) for E-waste management. J Reliable Intell Environ. **7**, 35–47 (2021). https://doi.org/10.1007/s40860-020-00124-z
11. Ali, N.A.L., Ramly, R., Sajak, A.A.B., Alrawashdeh, R.: IoT E-Waste monitoring system to support smart city initiatives. Int. J. Integr. Eng. **13**, 1–9 (2021)
12. Sampedro, G.A., Kim, R.G.C., Aruan, Y.J., Kim, D.-S., Lee, J.-M.: Smart e-Waste bin development based on YOLOv4 model. In: 2021 1st International Conference in Information and Computing Research (iCORE), pp. 125–128. IEEE, Manila, Philippines (2021)
13. Rani, K.N.A., et al.: Mobile green e-Waste management systems using IoT for smart campus. J. Phys. Conf. Ser. **1962**, 012056 (2021). https://doi.org/10.1088/1742-6596/1962/1/012056
14. Yi, S., Li, C., Li, Q.: A Survey of fog computing: concepts, applications and issues. In: Proceedings of the 2015 Workshop on Mobile Big Data, pp. 37–42. ACM, Hangzhou China (2015)

15. Sauter, M.: 3G, 4G and Beyond: Bringing Networks, Devices and the Web Together. Wiley (2013)
16. File Download/Data Transfer Time Calculator. https://www.meridianoutpost.com/resources/etools/calculators/calculator-file-download-time.php
17. Nguyen, G., et al.: Machine Learning and Deep Learning frameworks and libraries for large-scale data mining: a survey. Artif. Intell. Rev. **52**, 77–124 (2019). https://doi.org/10.1007/s10462-018-09679-z
18. Liang, T., Glossner, J., Wang, L., Shi, S., Zhang, X.: Pruning and quantization for deep neural network acceleration: a survey. Neurocomputing **461**, 370–403 (2021). https://doi.org/10.1016/j.neucom.2021.07.045
19. Huang, Y., Hu, H., Chen, C.: Robustness of on-device models: adversarial attack to deep learning models on android apps. In: 2021 IEEE/ACM 43rd International Conference on Software Engineering: Software Engineering in Practice (ICSE-SEIP), pp. 101–110. IEEE, Madrid, ES (2021)
20. Tan, M., Pang, R., Le, Q.V.: EfficientDet: scalable and efficient object detection. arXiv:1911.09070 (2020)

Data Technologies

Towards a Platform for Higher Education in Virtual Reality of Engineering Sciences

Houda Mouttalib[1,2]([⊠]), Mohamed Tabaa[2], and Mohamed Youssfi[1]

[1] Lab. 2IACS, ENSET, University Hassan II of Casablanca, Casablanca, Morocco
houda.mouttalib-etu@etu.univh2c.ma
[2] Pluridisciplinary Laboratory of Research and Innovation (LPRI), EMSI Casablanca, Casablanca, Morocco

Abstract. Innovative pedagogy is more oriented towards the use of new technology in future education. Virtual and augmented realities, as well as the Metaverse, are today the catalysts for the development of future teaching tools. They allow students to discover, via their smartphones or headsets, destinations around the world while remaining in their classrooms or even from their homes. These technologies are also used to put into practice, especially for the engineering sciences, lessons, and practical work by creating immersive experiences for users. This will significantly change the role of the teacher and the student in digital spaces. The realization of VR or AR learning platforms requires multidisciplinary skills ranging from 3D modeling to web and mobile platforms. In this paper, we present a method for creating a teaching platform for engineering sciences based on WebXR. We have created in our virtual environment a lesson about the Arduino board to train STEM students.

Keywords: education · virtual reality · VR · augmented reality · AR · WebXR · Metaverse

1 Introduction

One of the objectives of higher education is to prepare STEM students for the industry by teaching them engineering, mathematics, science, and technology. These skills are essential for students to succeed in the workforce, where technology is used in various fields, including production and management.

The popularity of 2D technologies increased after the COVID-19 pandemic, which led to worldwide restrictions on social activities, including schools, work, and entertainment. As a result, people relied heavily on technologies like Zoom and Teams for meetings and classes. Researchers saw this as an opportunity to prove that physical presence is not always necessary as long as communication and data sharing can be achieved.

The next revolution after 2D technologies are 3D technologies, which provide more realistic methods that mimic the behavior of objects in real life. These solutions have several advantages, such as increasing student motivation and self-learning skills, building necessary skills, and reducing teaching duration. However, there are also challenges, including controlling the duration, dependence on internet connectivity, and impacts on human social life and security.

In this paper, we present the first version of a teaching platform using virtual reality. We have created two profiles: teacher and student. The teacher can create content by integrating a 3D model, annotations, text, audio, and video. The student can participate in the course and access information about the course. We used the WebXR platform and implemented it on an Arduino UNO board.

The paper will be organized as follows: the second part will discuss the state-of-the-art concerning education in digital spaces. Part three will present a discussion of the implementation and use of the platform. Finally, we will conclude and provide some perspectives on this work.

2 Digital Transformation in Higher Education: State of Art

2.1 Virtual Reality

Abbreviated as VR, it allows a person to feel as though they have been transported to another place without physically changing their position or environment. The first VR experience was created in 1962 and allowed users to take a tour of the streets of New York [1]. Today, people seek to enrich their environment and experiences without traveling or making a lot of effort. This is inspired by the way the human brain can believe in dreams subconsciously while sleeping.

To convince the brain that a human is transported to another place, it requires several elements. These include completely changing the visual elements in front of the eyes at a specific angle and distance [2], adding sound effects to the objects in the virtual environment, and enabling interaction with the virtual elements around the user.

Currently, VR is being used in a wide range of sectors, from gaming to commerce to education. The use cases can vary from employees using it in their work to end-users using it as a marketing solution or as a product to purchase.

2.2 Augmented Reality

Abbreviated as AR, is when a human sees objects that are not really in front of their eyes. AR is mainly used on mobile and tablets that are equipped with cameras. AR is different from VR as the objects need to be added to the real environment [3].

AR technically requires a camera and sensors to detect space and calculate the measurements, detect the light type and direction, and predict user interactions. As an example, we can consider ARCore (Google) and ARKit (Apple) which work on almost all modern mobile operating systems.

2.3 Metaverse

The word Metaverse was first mentioned in the novel Snow Crash in 1992 [4]. With the development of technology, metaverse experiments are in the building stage regarding some problems to solve, but a lot of mini metaverses exist and are accessible [5].

Some of the reasons why we are still building the metaverse are because it needs to be: one metaverse, accessible anytime with the possibility to continue on the last status, real-time, multi-user [6], the freedom to change from one metaverse platform to another, and more [7].

2.4 Virtual 3D Technologies in STEM Higher Education

STEM stands for science, technology, engineering, and mathematics education for students after obtaining a bachelor's degree, which takes an average of 12 years of study. The objective from the students' perspective is to learn skills that will make them ready to join the industry [8].

The use of technology is becoming mandatory for many industries to boost their production. For example, technology is used for the training process of new employees, retrieving data in real-time, using AI and ML to predict trends and solutions, and communicating with fewer boundaries. The list is too long to mention here.

An example that we can elaborate on is using virtual reality for safety training in industries that involve working with hazardous materials or chemicals [9].

2.5 Students' Perspectives on Using AR and VR

Learning can vary based on many factors, such as prior experience with technology, learning preferences, and the specific context in which the use of AR and VR [10]. However, some common perspectives that students liked the experience and find it very useful (see Table 1).

Overall, Many find it to be a valuable and engaging approach to education. By understanding these perspectives, educators and instructional designers can better design AR and VR experiences that meet students' needs and support their learning [11].

2.6 Teachers' Perspectives on Using AR and VR

Teaching can also vary based on several factors, such as prior experience with technology, pedagogical approach, and the specific context in which they are using AR and VR. However, some common perspectives that teachers find it a promising technology (see Table 2).

Overall, while teachers' perspectives on using AR and VR to teach can vary, many find these technologies to be a valuable and innovative approach to education. By understanding these perspectives, educators and instructional designers can better design AR and VR experiences that support teaching and learning. However, there is a lack of pedagogy implementation in this kind of high technology for higher education or specifically for STEM education. The key solution to move forward is to provide easy-to-use, user-friendly interfaces that can be used by teachers of any age or familiarity with technology.

Table 1. Student's feedback on using AR and VR in education.

Feedback	Explanation
Increased engagement	Many students find that using AR and VR technology makes learning more engaging and interactive. By immersing themselves in a virtual environment, students may feel more connected to the material and more motivated to learn [13]
Improved understanding	Using AR and VR technology can also help students better understand complex concepts and ideas. By visualizing abstract concepts in a three-dimensional space, students can gain a more intuitive understanding of the material
Enhanced collaboration	AR and VR technology can also facilitate collaboration and teamwork among students. By allowing students to work together in a shared virtual environment, they can develop communication and problem-solving skills that are valuable in both academic and professional settings
Technical challenges	While many students may enjoy using AR and VR for learning, some may also encounter technical challenges such as hardware limitations or software compatibility issues. These challenges can be frustrating and may hinder students' ability to fully engage with the material
Access and equity	It's important to consider issues of access and equity when using AR and VR technology for learning. Not all students may have equal access to these technologies, which can create disparities in learning outcomes. Additionally, some students may have disabilities or other challenges that make it difficult to use AR and VR technology effectively

2.7 Pedagogy of Learning in STEM Higher Education

Bloom's taxonomy is the most popular and widely used taxonomy based on the research benchmarks used in popular MOOCs.

The objective is to help teachers adapt to technological changes and provide them with tools to have a successful teaching journey [12] (Fig. 1).

2.8 Supporting Different Resource Types for Learning

Having a limited choice to use multiple types of resources like videos, images, and audio... can be useful only in some specific cases as it depends on the objective to achieve.

AR and VR are not the only technologies named so far since we have extended reality that include interaction level and behavioral statuses like the case of assistance and 360 images or videos. In addition to AR and VR, XR (Extended Reality) technology can also be used to teach STEM subjects in higher education. XR is an umbrella term that encompasses AR, VR, and other immersive technologies such as mixed reality (MR) and haptic feedback (Table 3).

Table 2. Teachers' feedback on using AR and VR in education.

Feedback	Explanation
Increased engagement	Teachers may find that using AR and VR technology makes lessons more engaging and interactive for their students. By immersing students in a virtual environment or overlaying digital information in the real world, teachers can capture their students' attention and motivate them to learn
Improved learning outcomes	AR and VR technology can also help teachers achieve better student learning outcomes. By providing students with an interactive and immersive learning experience, teachers can help them develop a deeper understanding of complex concepts and ideas
Enhanced collaboration	AR and VR technology can also facilitate collaboration and teamwork among students. Teachers can use these technologies to create shared virtual spaces where students can collaborate on projects or solve problems
Technical challenges	While many teachers may find AR and VR technology to be valuable tools for teaching, some may also encounter technical challenges such as hardware limitations or software compatibility issues. These challenges can be frustrating and may require additional training or support
Integration with Curriculum	Teachers may also have concerns about integrating AR and VR technology with their curriculum. They may worry about whether these technologies align with their learning objectives or whether they have the necessary resources to effectively use them in the classroom

Overall, AR, VR, and XR technology can provide various types of support to teach STEM subjects in higher education, which can enhance students' learning experiences and improve learning outcomes.

2.9 WebXR

WebXR is a term used to describe the use of extended reality (XR) technology on the web. It is an open standard that allows developers to create and publish AR and VR experiences that can be accessed through a web browser, without the need for users to download and install additional software [14]. WebXR is supported by major web browsers like Chrome, Firefox, and Safari, and it enables users to access immersive experiences on a variety of devices, including smartphones, tablets, and head-mounted displays (HMDs). WebXR can support a wide range of use cases, including education, entertainment, e-commerce, and more.

In the context of education, WebXR can offer several benefits for teaching and learning. For example, educators can use WebXR to create interactive and immersive educational content that can engage students and help them visualize and understand

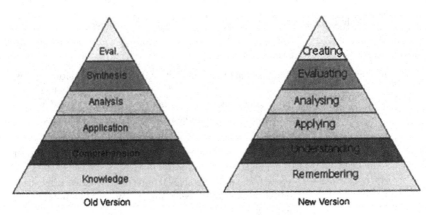

Caption: **Terminology changes** *"The graphic is a representation of the NEW verbage associated with the long familiar Bloom's Taxonomy. Note the change from Nouns to Verbs [e.g., Application to Applying] to describe the different levels of the taxonomy. Note that the top two levels are essentially exchanged from the Old to the New version." (Schultz, 2005) (Evaluation moved from the top to Evaluating in the second from the top, Synthesis moved from second on top to the top as Creating.) Source: http://www.odu.edu/educ/llschult/blooms_taxonomy.htm*

Fig. 1. Bloom's taxonomy levels.

complex concepts. Students can access this content through their web browser, without needing to install any additional software.

WebXR can also enable collaborative learning experiences, allowing students to work together on projects and experiments in a shared virtual space. This can be especially useful for students who are studying in different locations or who are unable to attend in-person classes. In addition, WebXR can provide access to educational content for students who may not have access to expensive hardware or software. By accessing WebXR experiences through a web browser, students can use affordable devices to access high-quality educational content [15] (Fig. 2).

The goal is to have access whenever you have a browser that supports the XR features [16]. The benchmark report on WebXR technologies as of 11 November 2022 (Table 1) provides an idea of the current state of WebXR, based on research Three.js is widely used for research purposes because of the available learning resources (Table 4).

Table 3. Types of support that AR, VR, and XR technology can offer to teach STEM subjects in higher education

Feature	About
Immersive learning environments	AR, VR, and XR technology can provide students with immersive and interactive learning environments that allow them to explore and interact with STEM concepts more engagingly. For example, using MR technology, students can visualize 3D models of complex molecules or physics concepts, and manipulate them with hand gestures
Collaboration	AR, VR, and XR technology can facilitate collaboration and teamwork among students, regardless of their physical location. This can be especially useful for STEM fields that require group projects and experiments. Using VR technology, students can meet in a virtual classroom or lab to work together on projects or solve problems
Simulations and virtual labs	AR, VR, and XR technology can provide students with access to simulations and virtual labs that allow them to experiment with STEM concepts in a safe and controlled environment. This can be especially useful for STEM fields that involve hazardous or expensive experiments
Personalization and adaptive learning	AR, VR, and XR technology can also be used to personalize learning experiences and adapt to students' individual needs and learning styles. For example, using VR technology, teachers can create simulations that adjust the difficulty level of a task based on a student's performance
Real-world applications	AR, VR, and XR technology can provide students with real-world applications of STEM concepts, which can help them understand how the concepts they are learning in class relate to their future careers. For example, using AR technology, students can overlay digital information onto real-world environments to see how a construction project might look before it is built

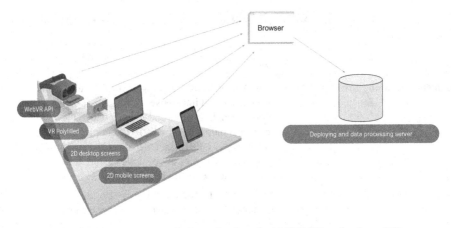

Fig. 2. How to access a platform developed with WebXR technology [20]

3 Discussion

Teachers may need to use technology as a support for their courses, but most of the tools are for assistance only or a fully virtual experience in the 2D format. Our objective is to simplify the tool so teachers can create their courses following their pedagogy in a fully immersive experience [17].

3.1 The Implementation

After choosing the technology that can be used to develop our platform, tests were taken to figure out the limits of WebXR compared to the features that can be found in a native application. The result was very promising; almost everything can be developed in browsers supporting XR.

These features are very similar to what we can have in a native app for any headset brand for VR or AR. Three.js supports more than 50 3D object formats, but the most popular is glTF (glb the binary version for a smaller size). It gives access to the object meshes and materials so we can change, for example, the color or position. WebXR is a complex technology with many cinematic, mathematical, and philosophical complications. In the W3C, we can find the most up-to-date features of this technology [18] (Fig. 3).

- RDBMS: Postgresql will be used as a relational database to store all details about the admins, students, teachers, and courses.
- File system: In addition, we need to use a big data file system like Hadoop Distributed File System (HDFS) to store and manage heavy 3D models.
- Backend API: To interact with the database we need an API, Nodejs is an open-source, cross-platform JavaScript runtime environment for developing and also staying in the same language as the front-end which is javascript.
- Front-end: On the official website of WebXR in the section of Frameworks recommendations, ReactXR is listed, as a framework based on the three.js library that facilitates the construction of the front-end and creates the scenes [19].

Table 4. Benchmark between the technologies of WebXR.

Tech name	Category	functionality	Difficulty (learning resources)	Scalability	Open source
A-Frame	Js framework	Building 3D/AR/VR	Easy		yes
Babylon.js	Js framework	Real-time 3D game engine AR and gaze and teleportation support	Difficult	yes	yes
Three.js	Js framework	AR, VR	Easy		yes
AR.js	Tool for Three.js	AR	Medium		yes
Model viewer	HTML element	displaying 3D models in AR	Easy		yes
p5.xr	An add-on for p5.js A Js library	VR/AR/360	Medium		yes
Playcanvas	Game engine	VR	Difficult	yes	yes
react-xr	hooks using threejs for react js the Js framework	VR/AR	Easy		yes
WebXR Export	Unity WebXR extensions	VR/AR	Difficult		no
Verge3D	Creating interactive 3D web with Blender	AR/VR			no
Wonderland Engine	Dev tool for WebXR	VR/AR	Medium		no
Sumerian	Aws tool	VR	Medium		no

- The end users UX/UI: Any teacher can access and manipulate his lessons from any device that has a web browser supporting xr technology which is the case for almost all modern devices.

  The platform is supposed to help the teacher to create good lessons according to recommendations of the well-known methods based on research in education for STEM.

- Development environment: Working with javascript in both back-end and front-end will reduce development time to build the whole platform and focus on developing

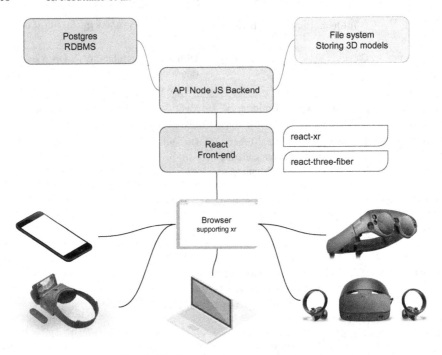

Fig. 3. Platform development ecosystem.

skills in specified areas like VR and AR technologies. Another advantage is that those skills are easy to find for future collaborators and they have a very big and active community of developers.

The 3D manipulation needs to be about:

- Positions
- Rotations
- Hand-controls - in the case of HMD with controllers
- Controls for scene
- Scaling measures - based on the position of the users
- Material texture of the models
- Cursor events - for laptops
- Lights manipulations and interaction - for AR models

  - fog
  - geometry
  - raycaster
  - and more options

- Sound effects
- Models types and formats

  - gltf format

- obj models
- collada models

3.2 How It Works

The first step is for the teacher to log in to the course using their email and password. The second step is for students to join the session using a code sent to their email or shared with them directly. Once everyone is connected, they can all view the same visual information by following the teacher's interactions. In this example, we use a 3D model of an Arduino UNO card (see Fig. 4, Fig. 5, Fig. 6).

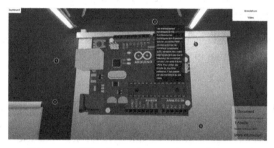

Fig. 4. Annotations on 3D assets. Side view of annotations while moving around the 3D asset in the virtual space. When the teacher login he can add a virtual asset to the environment along with adding annotation for specific points in the 3D object; when we click on the "Annotation" button we can see annotation numbers around the object with the possibility to show/hide details on click.

Fig. 5. The video or audio (the screen's right bottom) features playing in the virtual space. Another feature is to add a video to play in the virtual space, so the students can hide the 3D object and watch the video with all Youtube possibilities like watching in Full screen. In addition, there is another option to add audio as a voice explanation.

Results. The teachers need to easily create their content with minimal effort and time to have a good quality course or training by adding assets; which can be 3D objects and/or 2D items previewed or heard on the browser to the created virtual session. On the other hand, The students can access the shared session by the teacher and get immersed in a multi-user space for real-time interaction.

Fig. 6. A Document preview from the virtual environment. To keep all 2D options and features, we can preview a document with the option to print, full, screen, zoom, scroll, and all others that can be provided by the used browser to preview a PDF document.

One of the objectives is to get analytics of students so the teacher can follow up and be more of a facilitator than an instructor.

4 Conclusion

Covid-19 has accelerated digital transformation in several industries, including education. The use of new immersive technology in education through virtual reality, augmented reality, and through the metaverse is starting to be a reality. In this paper, we present a WebXR-based education platform for engineering. We used a 3D model of an Arduino UNO board to which the teacher added annotations to facilitate access to information for a student participating in this course. As perspectives, we would like to add more courses and 3D models and add the information of the model through text, track, video, file, and a review towards the end of each course.

References

1. Gigante, M.A.: 1 - Virtual reality: definitions, history, and applications. In: Earnshaw, R.A., Gigante, M.A., Jones, H. (eds.) Virtual Reality Systems, pp. 3–14. Academic Press, Boston (1993). https://doi.org/10.1016/B978-0-12-227748-1.50009-3
2. Rzepka, A.M., Hussey, K.J., Maltz, M.V., Babin, K., Wilcox, L.M., Culham, J.C.: Familiar size affects perception differently in virtual reality and the real world. Philos. Trans. R. Soc. B Biol. Sci. **378**, 20210464 (2023). https://doi.org/10.1098/rstb.2021.0464
3. Dunleavy, M.: Design principles for augmented reality learning. TechTrends **58**(1), 28–34 (2013). https://doi.org/10.1007/s11528-013-0717-2
4. Snow Crash. https://www.goodreads.com/book/show/40651883-snow-crash. Accessed 15 Mar 2023
5. Mystakidis, S.: Metaverse. Encyclopedia. **2**, 486–497 (2022). https://doi.org/10.3390/encyclopedia2010031
6. Joshi, S., Pramod, P.J.: A collaborative metaverse based a-la-carte framework for tertiary education (CO-MATE). Heliyon **9**, e13424 (2023). https://doi.org/10.1016/j.heliyon.2023.e13424

7. Park, S.-M., Kim, Y.-G.: A metaverse: taxonomy, components, applications, and open challenges. IEEE Access **10**, 4209–4251 (2022). https://doi.org/10.1109/ACCESS.2021.314 0175
8. Xie, Y., Fang, M., Shauman, K.: STEM education. Annu. Rev. Sociol. **41**, 331–357 (2015). https://doi.org/10.1146/annurev-soc-071312-145659
9. Sanfilippo, F., et al.: A perspective review on integrating VR/AR with haptics into STEM education for multi-sensory learning. Robotics **11**, 41 (2022). https://doi.org/10.3390/roboti cs11020041
10. Marks, B., Thomas, J.: Adoption of virtual reality technology in higher education: an evaluation of five teaching semesters in a purpose-designed laboratory. Educ. Inf. Technol. **27**, 1287–1305 (2022). https://doi.org/10.1007/s10639-021-10653-6
11. Kuhail, M.A., ElSayary, A., Farooq, S., Alghamdi, A.: Exploring immersive learning experiences: a survey. Informatics **9**, 75 (2022). https://doi.org/10.3390/informatics9040075
12. Forehand, M.: Bloom's Taxonomy - Emerging Perspectives on Learning, Teaching and Technology. https://www.d41.org/cms/lib/IL01904672/Centricity/Domain/422/Blooms Taxonomy.pdf. Accessed 31 Mar 2023
13. Coban, M., Bolat, Y.I., Goksu, I.: The potential of immersive virtual reality to enhance learning: a meta-analysis. Educ. Res. Rev. **36**, 100452 (2022). https://doi.org/10.1016/j.edurev. 2022.100452
14. Rodríguez, F.C., Dal Peraro, M., Abriata, L.A.: Democratizing interactive, immersive experiences for science education with WebXR. Nat. Comput. Sci. **1**, 631–632 (2021). https://doi. org/10.1038/s43588-021-00142-8
15. MacIntyre, B., Smith, T.F.: Thoughts on the future of WebXR and the immersive web. In: 2018 IEEE International Symposium on Mixed and Augmented Reality Adjunct (ISMAR-Adjunct), pp. 338–342 (2018). https://doi.org/10.1109/ISMAR-Adjunct.2018.00099
16. Immersive Web Developer WEBXR - Supported Browsers. https://immersiveweb.dev/#sup porttable. Accessed 03 Apr 2023
17. Da Silva, M., Roberto, R.A., Teichrieb, V., Cavalcante, P.S.: Towards the development of guidelines for educational evaluation of augmented reality tools. Presented at the 2016 IEEE Virtual Reality Workshop on K-12 Embodied Learning through Virtual and Augmented Reality, KELVAR 2016 (2016). https://doi.org/10.1109/KELVAR.2016.7563677
18. WebXR Device API. https://www.w3.org/TR/webxr/. Accessed 04 Apr 2023
19. WebXR - Samples Explainer. https://immersive-web.github.io/webxr-samples/explainer. html. Accessed 03 Apr 2023
20. Unboring.net | Workflow.   https://unboring.net/workflows/progressive-enhancement/. Accessed 12 June 2023

Robust Intelligent Control for Two Links Robot Based ACO Technique

Siham Massou[✉] [iD]

LABTIC (Laboratory of Technics of Information and Communication), Abdelmalek Essaadi
University, ENSA Tangier, Tetouan, Morocco
s.massou@uae.ac.ma

Abstract. The optimum neural network combined with sliding mode control
(ONNSMC) introduces the approach as a means of developing a strong controller
for a robot system with two links. Sliding mode control is a strong control method
that has found widespread use in a variety of disciplines and recognized for its
efficiency and easy tuning to solve a wide variety of control issues using nonlinear
dynamics. Nevertheless, the uncertainties in complex nonlinear systems are huge,
the higher switching gain leads to an increase of the chattering amplitude. To mitigate this gain, a neural network (NN) is utilized to predict the uncertain sections of
the system plant with on-line training using the backpropagation (BP) technique.
The learning rate is a hyperparameter of BP algorithm which have an important
effect on results, This parameter controls how much the weights of the network
are updated during each training iteration. Typically, the learning rate is set to a
value ranging from 0.1 to 1. In this study, the Ant Colony Optimization (ACO)
algorithm is employed with the objective of enhancing the network's convergence
speed. Specifically, the ACO algorithm is utilized to optimize this parameter and
enable global search capabilities. "The Lyapunov theory is used to demonstrate
the stability of the proposed approach, while simulations are conducted to evaluate its performance. The control action employed in the approach is observed to
exhibit smooth and continuous behavior, without any signs of chattering.

Keywords: Neural network · backpropagation · Sliding Mode Control · Ant
Colony Optimization · Lyapunov theory

1 Introduction

The design of motion control for robot manipulators has gained significant interest due
to its challenging nature as a complex nonlinear system. Accurate estimation of dynamic
parameters is crucial for the system, but it is difficult to obtain exact dynamic models
due to significant uncertainties, such as payload parameters, internal friction, and external disturbances, which are present in the nominal model of the system. To address
uncertainties in parameters, multiple methods have been suggested. These include neural network-based controls [1–6], neural adaptive PID control [7], fuzzy proportional-
integral-derivative (PID) controller [8], PID controller tuned using the Whale optimizer

© The Author(s), under exclusive license to Springer Nature Switzerland AG 2024
M. Tabaa et al. (Eds.): INTIS 2022/2023, CCIS 1728, pp. 120–128, 2024.
https://doi.org/10.1007/978-3-031-47366-1_9

algorithm [9], ACO controller [10], Nonlinear Model Predictive Control tuned with neural networks [11], as well as the Sliding Mode Control (SMC) [12–16] and fuzzy SMC [17].

The approach known as SMC is highly significant when dealing with systems that possess uncertainties, nonlinearities, and bounded external disturbance. Nonetheless, the control effort may experience unpleasant chattering, and it is necessary to establish bounds on the uncertainties when designing the SMC. The use of boundary layer solutions is a well-known method to eliminate chattering problems in control systems, as described in references [12] and [14]. However, this approach only works effectively for systems with small uncertainties. For systems with large uncertainties, a neural network structure can be employed to estimate the unknown parts of the two-link robot model. As a result, system uncertainties are kept to a minimum, allowing for a lower switching gain to be employed. The backpropagation algorithm (BP) is used to train the neural network weights in real time., as explained in references [19] and [20]. The proposed control method involves incorporating the predicted equivalent control with the robust control term, and the estimated function from the neural network is integrated into the equivalent control component. The learning rate is an important parameter of the BP algorithm, with a recommended value between 0.1 and 1, according to references [18] and [20]. However, choosing a learning rate that is too small or too large can hinder convergence. To address this issue, we utilize the Ant Colony Optimization (ACO) algorithm, which has global search capabilities, to optimize the learning rate and improve training speed.

This paper is structured as follows: Section 2 details the proposed optimal neural network sliding mode control, while Sect. 3 presents the results of simulation that prove the proposed approach's robust control performance. Finally, Sect. 4 provides concluding remarks.

2 Optimal Neural Network Sliding Mode Control Design

2.1 Controller Design

The state space formulation of the dynamic model of the two-link robot is given by [18]:

$$\begin{cases} \dot{x}_1 = x_2 \\ \dot{x}_2 = x_3 \\ \dot{x}_3 = h_{1n}(\underline{x}, \underline{u}) + \xi_1(\underline{x}, t) \\ \dot{x}_4 = x_5 \\ \dot{x}_5 = x_6 \\ \dot{x}_6 = h_{2n}(\underline{x}, \underline{u}) + \xi_2(\underline{x}, t) \end{cases} \tag{1}$$

where $h_{1n}(\underline{x}, \underline{u})$ and $h_{2n}(\underline{x}, \underline{u})$ are referring to the nominal representations of the system and its unknown components $\xi_1(\underline{x}, t)$ and $\xi_2(\underline{x}, t)$. The inputs and outputs of the system are respectively, $\underline{u} = \begin{bmatrix} u_1 & u_2 \end{bmatrix}^T$ and $\underline{x} = \begin{bmatrix} x_1 & x_2 & x_3 & x_4 & x_5 & x_6 \end{bmatrix}^T$. Further information regarding the physical representation and the Lyapunov function can be found in reference [4]. The control law for the robot manipulator is presented in the same source as follows:

$$\underline{u} = g_n^{-1}(\underline{x})\left(-\left(f_n(\underline{x}) + \hat{\xi}(\underline{x}, t)\right) + \begin{pmatrix} \dot{x}_{3d} \\ \dot{x}_{6d} \end{pmatrix} - \gamma \ddot{e} - \beta \dot{e} - ksat(S)\right) \qquad (2)$$

2.2 Neural Network Representation:

This article focuses on a neural network that consists of two layers of adjustable weights. The state input variables are denoted as $\underline{x}$, while the output variables are represented as: $y_1 = \hat{\xi}_1(\underline{x}, t)$ and $y_2 = \hat{\xi}_2(\underline{x}, t)$.

$y_k = W_k^T \sigma(W_j^T \underline{x})$ $k = 1, 2$. The activation function used in the hidden layer is denoted by $\sigma(.)$ and is implemented as a sigmoid function, which can be expressed as: $\sigma(s) = \frac{1}{1+e^{-s}}$.

The connectivity weights between the hidden and output layers, as well as between the input and hidden layers, are specified as: $W_k = [W_{k1} \quad W_{k2} \quad ... \quad W_{kN}]^T$ and $W_j = [W_{j1} \quad W_{j2} \quad ... \quad W_{jN}]^T$. Besides, The actual output $y_{dk}(\underline{x})$, which represents the difference between the actual and nominal functions, can be expressed as:

$$y_{dk}(\underline{x}) = y_k(\underline{x}) + \varepsilon(\underline{x}) \qquad (3)$$

where $\varepsilon(\underline{x})$ is the approximation error of NN.

During the online implementation, the neural network's weights are changed using the gradient descent method (GD), which involves iteratively adjusting the weights to minimize the error function (E). To begin, the GD approach computes the partial derivative of the error function with respect to each weight in the network. This derivative represents the direction in which the error function increases most rapidly. Therefore, the weights are updated in the opposite direction of the partial derivative in order to minimize the error function. The size of the weight update is determined by a learning rate parameter, which is chosen such that the weight update is not too large, in order to avoid overshooting the minimum of the error function, but not too small, in order to avoid slow convergence. The gradient descent method is a popular optimization technique that is widely used in neural network training as follows:

$$\frac{\partial W_{kj}}{\partial t} = -\eta_k \frac{\partial E}{\partial W_{kj}} \qquad (4)$$

where $\eta_k > 0$ is the usual learning rate and the cost function E represents the error between the desired and actual output values and is used as an error index. The least square error criterion is commonly chosen to define the cost function is given by: $E = \frac{1}{2}\sum_{k=1}^{2}\varepsilon_k^2$. The gradient terms $\frac{\partial E}{\partial w_{kj}}$ is the error function's partial derivative with respect to each weight in the network, which are required for the gradient descent method and can be computed using the backpropagation algorithm [19].

2.3 ACO Training Algorithm

Dorigo (1991) invented Ant Colony Optimization (ACO), which is based on actual ant behavior [21, 22]. ACO operates on the principle that, as a collective, ants are capable of finding the most efficient path to their destination through simple communication methods. In the case of real ants, pheromones serve as the communication medium, with ants leaving a trail marker on the ground. Pheromones gradually evaporate over time, unless additional amounts are deposited, indicating that a greater number of ants prefer this path. As a result, the trail with the greatest pheromone levels is considered to be the most optimized path. ACO is typically applied to solve the Traveling Salesman Problem (TSP) and its fundamental concept is as follows: when an ant moves through an edge, it releases pheromone on that edge. The amount of pheromone is proportional to the edge's shortness. The pheromone attracts other ants to follow the same edge. Eventually, all ants choose a unique path, which is the shortest possible path. The ACO methodology is presented in the following manner:

a) *Step 1(initialization):* Randomly place M ants in M cities, and set a maximum number of iterations beforehand. t_{max}; Let $t = 0$, where t denotes the *t_th* iteration step; the amount of pheromone on each edge is set to an initial value.
b) *Step 2 (while $t \leq t_{max}$).*
c) *Step 2.1: Each ant chooses its next city based on the transition probability. The probability of transitioning from the i_th city to the j_th city for the k_th ant is defined as follow:*

$$P_{ij}^k(t) = \begin{cases} \dfrac{\tau_{ij}^\alpha \eta_{ij}^\beta}{\sum\limits_{x \in allowed} \tau_{is}^\alpha(t)\eta_{is}^\beta(t)} & if\ j \in allowed_k \\ 0 & otherwise \end{cases} \tag{5}$$

where $allowed_k$ represents the set of cities that the *k_th* ant can visit; $\tau_{ij}(t)$ is the the value of pheromone on a particular edge. (i, j). The local heuristic function is defined as follows: $\eta_{ij} = \frac{1}{d_{ij}}$

where d_{ij} is the distance between the *i_th* city and the *j_th* city; the parameters α and β establish the degree of influence that trail strength and heuristic information have on each other.

d) *Step 2.2:* Once all ants have completed their tours, the pheromone values are updated using Eq. (6) as shown below:

$$\tau_{ij}(t+1) = (1-\rho)\tau_{ij}(t) + \Delta\tau_{ij}(t) \tag{6}$$

where $\Delta\tau_{ij}(t) = \sum\limits_{k=1}^m \Delta\tau_{ij}^{(k)}(t)$ and

$$\Delta\tau_{ij}^{(k)}(t) = \begin{cases} \dfrac{Q}{L^{(k)}(t)} & if\ the\ k\_th\ ant\ pass\ edge\ (i, j) \\ 0 & otherwise \end{cases}$$

where $L^{(k)}(t)$ refers to the distance traveled by the route taken by the k_th ant during the t_th iteration; is the persistence percentage of the trail (thus, $(1 - \rho)$ corresponds to the evaporation); Q denotes constant quantity of pheromone.

e) *Step 2.3:* Increase the current iteration number $t \leftarrow t + 1$.
f) *Step3:* Terminate the process and choose the shortest path among the routes taken by the ants as the output.

3   Simulation Results

This section of the paper presents the experimental evaluation of the proposed control approach on a two-link robot, which is modeled according to Eq. (1). The primary goal of this control approach is to ensure that the system accurately follows the desired angle trajectory: $x_{1d} = (\pi/3)\cos(t)$ and $x_{4d} = \pi/2 + (\pi/3)\sin(t)$.

The masses are assumed to be $m_1 = 0.6$ $m_1 = 0.6$ and $m_2 = 0.4$ $m_2 = 0.4$. The uncertainties taken into account are in the form of a vector random noise with a magnitude of one. $E = \begin{pmatrix} 5 & 0 \\ 0 & 5 \end{pmatrix}$, $B = \begin{pmatrix} 10 & 0 \\ 0 & 10 \end{pmatrix}$ and $J = \begin{pmatrix} 100 & 0 \\ 0 & 100 \end{pmatrix}$.

The coefficients of the switching functions are given by: $\gamma_{11} = \gamma_{22} = \beta_{11} = \beta_{22} = 4$.

This paper utilizes a population of 40 ants as shown in Table 1.

Table 1. The optimal value of the learning rate η_k that leads to the best global performance.

N° of Iteration	η_k	N° of Iteration	η_k
1	0.8242	11	0.2068
2	0.5533	12	0.2108
3	0.8449	13	0.2097
4	0.5226	14	0.2088
5	0.6521	15	**0.2068**
6	0.3008	16	**0.2068**
7	0.3025	17	**0.2068**
8	0.2085	18	**0.2068**
9	0.2113	19	**0.2068**
10	0.2102	20	**0.2068**

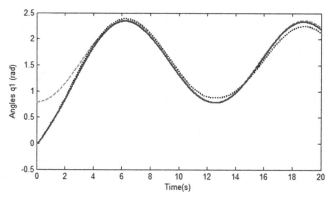

Fig. 1. Angles responses using: the proposed ONNSMC (solid line), NNSMC (…) and desired trajectory (- - -).Displayed equations are centered and set on a separate line.

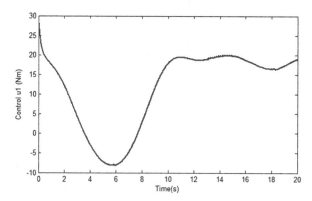

Fig. 2. The control torque signals τ_1 using the proposed ONNSMC

By examining Fig. 1 and Fig. 3, it can be observed that the control approach proposed in this paper achieves accurate tracking of the desired trajectory, even when there are significant uncertainties present, and without any oscillations in the system response. Moreover, Fig. 2 and Fig. 4 demonstrate that the control torque signals are smooth and do not exhibit any oscillatory behavior.

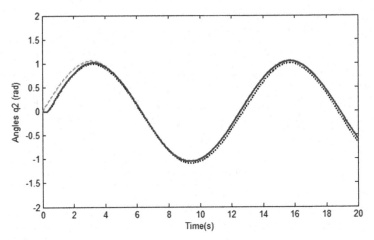

Fig. 3. Angles responses $x_3 = q_2$ using: the proposed ONNSMC (solid line), NNSMC (...) and desired trajectory (- - -).

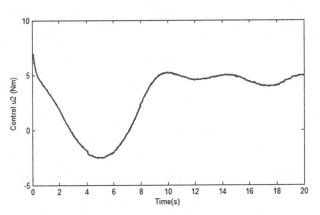

Fig. 4. The control torque signals τ_1 using the proposed ONNSMC

4 Conclusion

This research paper proposes a novel method for robust optimal reference tracking in two-link robot manipulators by combining traditional sliding mode control with neural networks. Utilizing the neural network involves making an estimation of the nonlinear model function that is not known, and its parameters are adapted through the online BP learning algorithm to provide a better description of the plant. This allows for the use of a lower switching gain, even in the presence of large uncertainties. The Ant Colony Optimization (ACO) algorithm is used to optimize the learning rate of the BP algorithm for faster convergence. Simulation results demonstrate the effectiveness of the proposed method in tracking the reference trajectory without any oscillatory behavior. Future research may explore more efficient optimization methods for the sliding additive control gain. The speed of convergence in terms of the tracking performance is depicted in

Figs. 1 and 3, that represent the position tracking for link 1 and link 2. The corresponding control torque signals in Figs. 2 and 4 are smooth and free of oscillatory behavior.

References

1. Patino, H.D., Carelli, R., Kuchen, B.R.: Neural networks for advanced control of robot manipulators. IEEE Trans. Neural Netw. **13**, 343–354 (2002)
2. Hussain, M.A., Ho, P.Y.: Adaptive sliding mode control with neural network based hybrid models. J. Process. Control. **14**, 157–176 (2004)
3. Liu, P.X., Zuo, M.J., Meng, M.Q.H.: Using neural network function approximation for optimal design of continuous-state parallel –series systems. Computers and operations Re-search **30**, 339–352 (2003)
4. Sefreti, S., Boumhidi, J., Naoual, R., Boumhidi, I.: Adaptive neural network sliding mode control for electrically-driven robot manipulators. Control Eng. Appl. Inform. **14**, 27–32 (2012)
5. Cao, C.Z., Wang, F.Q., Cao, Q.L.: Neural network-based terminal sliding mode applied to position/force adaptive control for constrained robotic manipulators. Adv. Mech. Eng. **10**(6), 1–8 (2018)
6. Zhang, S., YT, D., YC, O.: Adaptive neural control for robotic manipulators with output constraints and uncertainties. IEEE Trans. Neural Netw. Learn. **29**(11), 5554–5564 (2018)
7. Rahimi, H., Nohooji: Constrained neural adaptive PID control for robot manipulators. J. Franklin Inst. **357**(7), 3907–3923 (2020). https://doi.org/10.1016/j.jfranklin.2019.12.042
8. Van, M., Do, X.P., Mavrovouniotis, M.: Self-tuning fuzzy PID-nonsingular fast terminal sliding mode control for robust fault tolerant control of robot manipulators. ISA Trans. (2019). https://doi.org/10.1016/j.isatra.2019.06.017
9. Loucif, F., Kechida, S., Sebbagh, A.: Whale optimizer algorithm to tune PID controller for the trajectory tracking control of robot manipulator. J. Braz. Soc. Mech. Sci. Eng. (2020). https://doi.org/10.1007/s40430-019-2074-32074
10. Baghli, F.Z., El Bakkali, L., Lakhal, Y.: Optimization of arm manipulator trajectory planning in the presence of obstacles by ant colony algorithm. Procedia Eng. **181**, 560–567 (2017)
11. Rong, H.J., Wei, J.T., Bai, J.M., Zhao, G.S., Liang, Y.Q.: Adaptive neural control for a class of MIMO nonlinear systems with extreme learning machine. Neurocomputing **149**, 405–414 (2015)
12. Slotine, J.J.: Sliding controller design for non-linear systems. Int. J. Control. **40**, 421–434 (1984)
13. Utkin, V.I.: Sliding modes in control optimization. Springer-Verlag, Heidelberg (1992). https://doi.org/10.1007/978-3-642-84379-2
14. Slotine, J.J., Sastry, S.S.: Tracking control of nonlinear systems using sliding surfaces with applications to robot manipulators. Int. J. Control. **39**, 465–492 (1983)
15. Shi, H., Liang, Y.B.Y.B., Liu, Z.H.: An approach to the dynamic modeling and sliding mode control of the constrained robot. Adv. Mech. Eng. **9**(2), 1–10 (2017)
16. Li, H., Shi, P., Yao, D., Wu, L.: Observer-based adaptive sliding mode control of nonlinear markovian jump. Syst. Automatica **64**, 133–142 (2016)
17. Yin, X., Pan, L., Cai, S.: Robust adaptive fuzzy sliding mode trajectory tracking control for serial robotic manipulators. Robot. Comput. Integr. Manuf. **72**, 101884 (2021)
18. Massou, S., Boufounas, E.M., Boumhidi, I.: Optimized neural network sliding mode control for two links robot using PSO technique. In: Proceedings of the Mediterranean Conference on Information & Communication Technologies (2015)

19. internal Representations by Error Propagation, Cambridge: Parallel Distributed Processing, vol. 1, MIT Press (1986)
20. Fu, l.: Neural Networks in Computer Intelligence, New York: McGraw-Hill (1995)
21. Dorigo, M.: Optimization Learning and Natural Algorithms, PhD thesis, Dipartimento di Elettronica, Politecnico di Milano, Milan, Italy (1992)
22. Maniezzo, V., Dorigo, M., Colorni, A.: The Ant System: optimization by a colony of cooperating agents. IEEE Trans. Syst. Man Cybern. Part B Cybern. **26**(1), 29–41 (1996)

Multimodal Learning for Road Safety Using Vision Transformer ViT

Asmae Rhanizar[ID] and Zineb El Akkaoui[✉]

National Institute of Posts and Telecommunications, Rabat, Morocco
{rhanizar,elakkaoui}@inpt.ac.ma
http://www.inpt.ac.ma

Abstract. This paper proposes a novel approach for multimodal learning that combines visual information from images with structured data from a multi-column dataset. The approach leverages the power of vision transformer (ViT) models, which are based on self-attention layers, to extract high-quality visual features from images. The proposed approach was evaluated on a road safety problem, specifically the identification of high-risk areas for road accidents. The experiment was conducted on a dataset of road sections in Morocco and demonstrated the effectiveness of the proposed approach in improving the accuracy of the classification task. The results show that the multimodal approach outperformed unimodal approaches that relied solely on either visual data or structured data. The proposed approach can be applied to various domains beyond road safety, such as healthcare, finance, and social media analysis, where multimodal data is abundant and complex relationships between different data modalities need to be captured. The contribution of this work is the development of a multimodal classification model that combines visual and structured data leveraging the power of vision transformer (ViT) for image encoding, resulting in high-quality visual features. This approach is a departure from classical convolutional models, which lack self-attention layers, making it suitable for a wide range of applications.

Keywords: Multimodal learning · Vision transformer (ViT) · Road safety · Smart camera locations

1 Introduction

Multimodal learning has become increasingly important in various fields, including computer vision, natural language processing, and machine learning [4,9,10, 24]. By integrating multiple sources of data, such as text, images, and audio, multimodal approaches provide a more comprehensive view of the problem at hand, leading to better performance and more informed decision-making.

Our study introduces a novel approach to multimodal learning that merges visual features obtained from images utilizing a vision transformer (ViT) with structured data present in a multi-column dataset. Our proposed technique exploits the strength of ViT models, which are dependent on self-attention layers, to extract visually meaningful features with better quality than classical convolutional models [4]. Furthermore, our proposed approach employs a late fusion

M. Tabaa et al. (Eds.): INTIS 2022/2023, CCIS 1728, pp. 129–140, 2024.
https://doi.org/10.1007/978-3-031-47366-1_10

strategy, which permits a productive combination of modalities, increasing its applicability to various domains.

As a case study, we apply our proposed approach to the problem of identifying high-risk areas for road accidents. Our approach utilizes snapshots of maps to define road features with greater accuracy and detail, allowing for more precise predictions of high-risk areas that can benefit from smart camera placement. This multimodal predictive framework combines structural data and images to determine the most suitable locations for smart cameras, enabling more effective and efficient traffic management. The experiment was conducted on a dataset of road sections in Morocco and demonstrated the effectiveness of the proposed approach in improving the accuracy of the classification task.

The main contribution of this research is the creation of a novel multimodal classification model using images and tabular data that utilizes vision transformer (ViT) for image encoding to generate superior quality visual features. In contrast to conventional convolutional models that do not incorporate self-attention layers, this approach has immense potential for application in diverse domains, including healthcare, finance, and social media analysis, where there is an abundance of multimodal data and intricate relationships between different data modalities need to be captured.

2   Litterature Review

Multimodal learning has gained significant attention in recent years due to its potential to improve performance in various applications. Multimodal learning refers to the integration of multiple sources of information, such as text, audio, image, and video data, to learn from different modalities and obtain a more comprehensive understanding of the problem. Deep multimodal learning, an extension of traditional multimodal learning, has gained significant attention in recent years [22,23]. It combines deep learning techniques with multiple modalities of data to learn representations that capture the complex relationships between the modalities. In particular, fusion is a key component in multimodal learning, and refers to the process of combining multiple sources of information, such as text, images, audio, or other structured data, into a single representation or decision. There are three main types of methods to represent multimodal fusion. First, the joint representation, which integrates unimodal representations through mapping them together into a unified space [28]. The second category is coordinated representation, which takes advantages of cross-modal similarity models to represent unimodal in a coordinated space separately [27]. The last one is the encoder-decoder model, which aims to acquire intermediate layers that project one modality to another [8,9,18,26]. In multimodal learning, a prevalent approach is to limit the initial layers of a network to unimodal processing and introduce connections between modalities in later layers.

Multimodal learning has been successfully applied in various fields, including computer vision, natural language processing, and speech recognition. In computer vision, deep multimodal learning has been used for tasks such as image captioning [4,9] and visual question answering [10,24]. The ability of deep multimodal learning to effectively integrate multiple sources of information makes it a powerful tool for real-world applications in fields such as healthcare, finance, and transportation. For example, in healthcare domain, multimodal learning has been used to combine different medical data, such as medical imaging (MRI, CT, PET, X-ray and others), electronic health records, and genomics, to improve disease diagnosis and treatment [6,7]. For instance, [19] proposes a multi-modal learning approach, TabVisionNet, that integrates tabular and image data with a novel attention mechanism called Sequential Decision Attention, achieving significantly better performance than single-modal and other multi-modal learning approaches in a real case scenario of Thin-Film Transistor Liquid-Crystal Display (TFT-LCD) manufacturing.

Multimodal learning has been also applied in various areas of intelligent transportation systems (ITS) to enhance the performance of traditional unimodal approaches. For instance, in the field of traffic prediction [11,12], multimodal models can incorporate data from diverse sources such as traffic cameras, road sensors, weather reports, and social media to improve the accuracy and robustness of traffic flow estimation. In addition, multimodal learning has been used for activity recognition in intelligent vehicles [13,14], where the fusion of vision, audio, and sensor data can help identify the behavior of drivers and passengers, leading to safer driving and personalized in-car services. Moreover, multimodal approaches have been applied to road safety, including crash analysis [25] and prediction [15], driver behaviour analysis [16,17] to improve traffic flow and reduce the likelihood of accidents.

In summary, multimodal learning has shown great potential in various real-world applications, including intelligent transportation systems. The use of deep learning techniques has enabled the development of sophisticated models that can effectively learn from and integrate multiple modalities of data. Previous works have utilized various models to extract features from different modalities, such as deep neural networks like CNN [16,17] or DCNN [25]. However, recently, transformers have become increasingly popular due to their ability to capture complex relationships between elements in a sequence, resulting in better performance on tasks such as machine translation and sentiment analysis. Pretrained transformers are now available for each modality and are widely used such as BERT for text encoding [12] and ViT for vision encoding [4]. In particular, combining images and tabular data has been shown to provide better performance in machine learning tasks [19,20]. While the use of both tabular data and images in machine learning models is common, their fusion through transformers is relatively unusual, yet it has shown to significantly improve performance in various tasks such as object recognition and prediction, making it a promising approach to explore. In this study, we propose a novel approach for multimodal fusion of images and tabular data using a vision transformer ViT [4], which can leverage the complementary information from both images and structured data modalities. Our approach has the potential to provide a more accurate and comprehensive understanding of complex real-world problems, such as identifying high-risk areas in road networks for improving road safety. Our contribution is two-fold:

1. we introduce a new approach for multimodal learning that combines tabular and image data using a vision transformer (ViT);
2. we demonstrate the effectiveness of this approach in a real-world case study in Morocco, where we use it to identify locations with a high risk of traffic accidents and recommend placement of speed cameras to improve road safety.

3   Problem Definition

Many multimodal studies have focused on the fusion of modalities such as text, images, audio, or video, with applications ranging from Visual Question Answering (VQA) to text-to-image generation and generating high-quality images. However, few studies have explored the fusion of images and structured data modalities using a vision transformer (ViT) based model.

In this paper, we propose a novel multimodal learning approach that combines visual features extracted from images using a vision transformer with structured data in a multi-column dataset. The goal is to leverage the strengths of both modalities and achieve a more comprehensive understanding of the data. To the best of our knowledge, our proposed approach is among the first to fuse images and structured data modalities using a vision transformer (ViT).

3.1   Vision Transformer (ViT)

Vision Transformer (ViT) is a type of deep neural network architecture used in computer vision tasks such as image classification, object detection, and segmentation. It was first introduced by Dosovitskiy & al. at 2020 [4]. ViT is based on the Transformer architecture, which was originally proposed for natural language processing tasks.

The input to ViT is a sequence of image patches, which are obtained by dividing the original image into non-overlapping patches of equal size. The image patches are then flattened and transformed into a sequence of tokens, which are fed into the Transformer encoder. ViT has been shown to achieve excellent performance on image classification tasks, even surpassing the performance of traditional CNNs on some datasets. In our case, by incorporating snapshots of the maps into the ViT model in a patch-wise manner, we were able to extract rich visual features that capture the nuances of road characteristics and conditions (See Fig. 1).

3.2   Model Architecture

Our proposed multimodal learning approach combines two types of modalities: snapshots of maps and structured data representing road features. The images

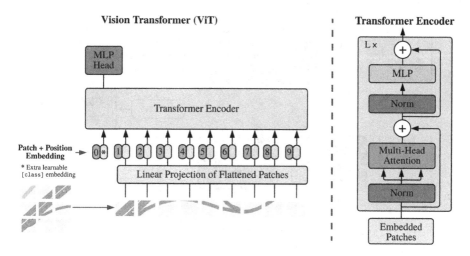

Fig. 1. ViT applied to high-risk areas identifying problem

are encoded using the vision transformer model, as described in the previous subsection. The ViT model encodes each image patch separately before the patches are fused together.

After the images are encoded, they are combined with the structured data in a cross-model attention manner. This process allows the model to attend to the most informative parts of the input data from both modalities. The fusion of the modalities occurs in a late fusion manner, allowing for the independent processing of both modalities before combining them in the final stage of the model architecture (See Fig. 2).

The proposed multimodal model architecture can be easily extended to other domains with different types of data modalities. The incorporation of the ViT model in our model architecture makes it possible to extract high-quality visual features from images, which is crucial for many computer vision tasks.

4   Model Application: The Identification of High-Risk Areas for Smart Camera Locations

The problem we aim to solve is identifying high-risk areas in road networks to improve road safety. To our knowledge, existing approaches have been limited to single-source data, such as road features or accident data, which can be inaccurate and incomplete. To overcome this limitation, we propose a novel multimodal learning approach that combines two modalities: snapshots of maps and a dataset of road features. Our approach utilizes the complementary information from both modalities to provide a more accurate and comprehensive understanding of the risk factors in road networks. By leveraging the visual features extracted from the snapshots of maps using a vision transformer and the

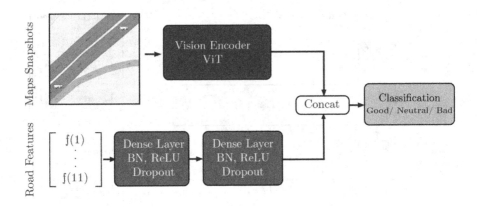

Fig. 2. Model architecture

structured data in the road features dataset, our proposed model can identify high-risk areas with higher accuracy and detail as demonstrated in later sections.

4.1 Dataset

In our case study, we define road features as characteristics that have an impact on road safety, such as speed limits, traffic density, and road surface condition. In a previous study [1], we proposed a predictive framework that utilized road features (as shown in Table 1) as predictors for a classifier algorithm. For our first modality, we used the same dataset as in the previous study, which includes information gathered from various sources. The road features were extracted from this dataset using the available characteristics, including data on speed limit violations, annual traffic volumes, and geographical maps published by the Moroccan authorities.

In addition, a dataset of map snapshots representing different road segments was prepared. To maintain consistency across all images, we designed a tool to automatically capture snapshots of the maps for the chosen road sections (as show in Fig. 3). The tool, built in JavaScript, utilizes HERE Javascript-based API with maps from the HERE location platform [29]. This ensures uniformity in size and scale among all the images. We collected data from various georeferenced parts of the Moroccan road network for use in our study (as shown in Fig. 4). To test the model's generalization ability, we also created a separate test dataset. To ensure reliable model training, we divided our dataset into 80% training and 20% testing sets, using a cross-validation method.

4.2 Experimental Setup

To implement our proposed multimodal ViT model, we utilized the Hugging Face library, an open-source software library that offers state-of-the-art machine learning models and pre-trained models. This library is built on top of PyTorch and

Fig. 3. Location capture tool

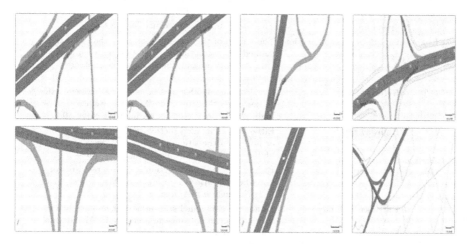

Fig. 4. Snapshots of maps of Morrocan road sections

TensorFlow and offers various multimodal models that can process and extract features from different modalities such as text, images, and audio. Hugging Face library also includes vision transformers that are particularly useful for image processing. For our study, we used a pre-trained ViT model (google/vit-base-patch16-224-in21k) that was trained on ImageNet-21k, consisting of 14 million images and 21,843 classes. By using transfer learning, we could better tune our multimodal model and improve its performance on our specific task.

We used the FastAI and "image_tabular" libraries to combine images with tabular data and train a joint model using the integrated data. The FastAI library allowed us to easily load both image and tabular data and package them into fastai LabelLists. Tabular data, which represents road features, contains useful information [1]. By combining tabular data with images, we aimed to provide our model with more comprehensive input that can result in better predictions.

Table 1. Features description

Code	Feature	Description
$AADT$	AADT	Annual average of the daily traffic in the controlled section
N_{lanes}	Number of lanes	The number of lanes of the controlled section
LM	Line marking	Either the line is continuous or broken on the controlled section. Continuous line = 1; Broken line = 0
MS	Median strip	Either the controlled section has a median strip or not, knowing that a median strip is a separation between opposing traffic lanes. Has a median strip = 1; Has not a median strip = 0
SL	Speed limit	The speed limit on the controlled section
L_{ss}	Length of straight section	The length of the straight section of the road. It's defined by calculating the distance between two curves upstream and downstream the controlled section
HE	Highway exit	Either the controlled section is near a highway exit or not when the site is in a highway. Near a highway exit = 1; Not near a highway exit = 0
HT	Highway toll	Either the controlled section is near a highway toll or not when the site is in a highway. Near a highway toll = 1; Not near a highway toll = 0
RA	Rest area	Either the controlled section is near a rest area or not when the site is in a highway. Near a rest area = 1; Not near a rest area = 0
UA	Entrance to a city	Either the controlled section is near an entrance to a city. Near an entrance to a city = 1; Not near an entrance to a city = 0
D_{ua}	Distance from urban area	Road distance from the nearest urban area

Our approach involved creating a ViT model as a vision transformer and building a tabular model with categorical features represented using embeddings. We then customized the fully connected layers as a last step.

During fine-tuning, we experimented with different hyperparameters, such as learning rates and batch sizes, to optimize the performance of our model. We also used various data augmentation techniques to increase the size of our dataset and improve the generalization capability of our model. These techniques included random rotations, flips, and brightness adjustments to the images, as well as adding noise to the structured data.

4.3   Results

Extensive experiments were conducted to assess the effectiveness of the proposed multimodal transformer model, and to compare it with both traditional and state-of-the-art methods. The evaluation included traditional unimodal classifiers such as KNN, RF, and SVM which were previously evaluated [1] on the same structured dataset but with single modal usage. After fine-tuning our ViT model for multimodal fusion, we observed a significant improvement in performance compared to the traditional unimodal classifiers. Our model achieved an accuracy of 96.7% and a ROC AUC score of 0.85 on the validation set after training for 10 epochs, outperforming the other methods tested (as presented in Table 2).

Table 2. Accuracy %

Model	Accuracy
Support Vector Machine	58
Random Forest	95
Gaussian Naive Bayes	81
Multimodal-ViT	96.7

Furthermore, we conducted ablation experiments to investigate the impact of different components of the proposed multimodal transformer model on the overall performance. The results demonstrate that the inclusion of the ViT model for image encoding and the cross-modal attention fusion strategy were the key factors contributing to the superior performance of the proposed model. Overall, the experimental results provide strong evidence for the effectiveness and potential of the proposed multimodal transformer model for road safety applications. The model not only outperforms traditional and classical methods but also offers a flexible and extensible framework for integrating different modalities of data in other domains beyond road safety.

5 Conclusion

In this paper, we have reviewed the potential of multimodal learning for improving performance in various real-world applications, including intelligent transportation systems. We have proposed a novel approach using a vision transformer ViT that can leverage the complementary information from both images and structured data modalities. Our approach has the potential to provide a more accurate and comprehensive understanding of complex real-world problems, such as identifying high-risk areas in road networks for improving road safety. Also, the proposed approach has great potential for application in a variety of domains beyond road safety, such as healthcare, finance, and social media analysis, where multimodal data is prevalent and complex relationships between different modalities need to be captured.

By incorporating visual information into our multimodal learning, our approach offers a unique perspective on road safety analysis that could enhance the capabilities of intelligent transportation systems. In future work, we plan to conduct further experiments to evaluate the effectiveness of our approach in identifying high-risk areas on road networks. We believe that our work contributes to advancing the field of multimodal learning in the context of road safety and has the potential to lead to more effective and efficient transportation systems.

References

1. Rhanizar, A., Akkaoui, Z.E.: A predictive framework of speed camera locations for road safety. Comput. Inf. Sci. **12**, 92 (2019). https://doi.org/10.5539/cis.v12n3p92
2. Nakamura, S., Komada, M., Matsushita, Y., Ishizaki, K.: Effects of the feature extraction from road surface image for road induced noise prediction using artificial intelligence. Noise Vib. Conf. Exhib. (2019). https://doi.org/10.4271/2019-01-1565
3. Golrizkhatami, Z., Acan, A.: ECG classification using three-level fusion of different feature descriptors. Expert Syst. Appl. **114**(5), 54–64 (2018). https://doi.org/10.1016/j.eswa.2018.07.030
4. Dosovitskiy, A., et al.: An image is worth 16×16 words: transformers for image recognition at scale. arXiv (2020). https://doi.org/10.48550/arXiv.2010.11929
5. Zhang, C., Yang, Z., He, X., Deng, L.: Multimodal intelligence: representation learning, information fusion, and applications. IEEE J. Sel. Topics Signal Process. **14**, 478–493 (2019). https://doi.org/10.1109/JSTSP.2020.2987728
6. Ramachandram, D., Taylor, G.W.: Deep multimodal learning: a survey on recent advances and trends. IEEE Signal Process. Mag. **34**, 96–108 (2017). https://doi.org/10.1109/MSP.2017.2738401
7. Huang, S., Pareek, A., Seyyedi, S., Banerjee, I., Lungren, M.P.: Fusion of medical imaging and electronic health records using deep learning: a systematic review and implementation guidelines. NPJ Digit. Med. **3**, 136 (2020). https://doi.org/10.1038/s41746-020-00341-z
8. Yu, J., Li, J., Yu, Z., Huang, Q.: Multimodal transformer with multi-view visual representation for image captioning. IEEE Trans. Circ. Syst. Video Technol. **30**, 4467–4480 (2020). https://doi.org/10.1109/TCSVT.2019.2947482
9. Chen, J., Zhuge, H.: A news image captioning approach based on multimodal pointer-generator network. Concurr. Comput. Pract. Exp. **34**, e5721 (2022). https://doi.org/10.1002/cpe.57212
10. Sharma, D., Purushotham, S., Reddy, C.K.: MedFuseNet: an attention-based multimodal deep learning model for visual question answering in the medical domain. Sci. Rep. **11**, 19826 (2021). https://doi.org/10.1038/s41598-021-98390-1
11. Min, J.H., Ham, S.W., Kim, D.-K., Lee, E.H.: Deep multimodal learning for traffic speed estimation combining dedicated short-range communication and vehicle detection system data. Transp. Res. Rec. **2677**(5), 247–259 (2022). https://doi.org/10.1177/03611981221130026
12. Zhou, B., Liu, J., Cui, S., Zhao, Y.: Large-scale traffic congestion prediction based on multimodal fusion and representation mapping. arXiv (2022). https://doi.org/10.48550/ARXIV.2208.11061

13. Zhou, B., Liu, J., Cui, S., Zhao, Y.: A multimodality fusion deep neural network and safety test strategy for intelligent vehicles. IEEE Trans. Intell. Veh. **6**, 310–322 (2021). https://doi.org/10.1109/TIV.2020.3027319

14. Feng, D., et al.: Deep multi-modal object detection and semantic segmentation for autonomous driving: datasets, methods, and challenges. IEEE Trans. Intell. Transp. Syst. **22**, 1341–1360 (2021). https://doi.org/10.1109/TITS.2020.2972974

15. Jae, G.C., Chan, W.C., Gyeongho, K., Sunghoon, L.: Car crash detection using ensemble deep learning and multimodal data from dashboard cameras. Expert Syst. Appl. **183**, 115400 (2021). https://doi.org/10.1016/j.eswa.2021.115400

16. Luntian, M., et al.: Driver stress detection via multimodal fusion using attention-based CNN-LSTM. Expert Syst. Appl. **173**, 114693 (2021). https://doi.org/10.1016/j.eswa.2021.114693

17. Mohammad, N.R., Bahareh, N., Frederic, M., Andry, R., Vinod, C.: Automatic driver stress level classification using multimodal deep learning. Expert Syst. Appl. **138**, 114693 (2019). https://doi.org/10.1016/j.eswa.2019.07.010

18. Roy, S.K., Deria, A., Hong, D., Rasti, B., Plaza, A., Chanussot, J.: Multimodal fusion transformer for remote sensing image classification. arXiv (2022). https://doi.org/10.48550/ARXIV.2203.16952

19. Liu, Y., Lu, H.P., Lai, C.H.: A novel attention-based multi-modal modeling technique on mixed type data for improving TFT-LCD repair process. IEEE Access **10**, 33026–33036 (2022). https://doi.org/10.1109/ACCESS.2022.315895

20. Gessert, N., Nielsen, M., Shaikh, M., Werner, R., Schlaefer, A.: Skin lesion classification using ensembles of multi-resolution EfficientNets with meta data. MethodsX **7**, 100864 (2020). 2215-0161. https://doi.org/10.1016/j.mex.2020.100864

21. Kannojia, S.P., Jaiswal, G.: Ensemble of hybrid CNN-ELM model for image classification. In: 2018 5th International Conference on Signal Processing and Integrated Networks (SPIN), Noida, India, pp. 538–541 (2018). https://doi.org/10.1109/SPIN.2018.8474196

22. Ngiam, J., Khosla, A., Kim, M., Nam, J., Lee, H., Ng, A.: Multimodal deep learning. In: Proceedings of the 28th International Conference on Machine Learning, ICML 2011, pp. 689–696 (2011). https://doi.org/10.1109/SPIN.2018.8474196

23. Srivastava, N., Salakhutdinov, R.R.: Multimodal learning with Deep Boltzmann Machines. In: Advances in Neural Information Processing Systems (NIPS 2012), vol. 25, pp. 2222–2230 (2012). https://doi.org/10.1109/SPIN.2018.8474196

24. Cadene, R., Ben-younes, H., Cord, M., Thome, N.: MUREL: multimodal relational reasoning for visual question answering. In: 2019 IEEE/CVF Conference on Computer Vision and Pattern Recognition (CVPR), pp. 1989–1998 (2019). https://doi.org/10.1109/CVPR.2019.00209

25. Gao, Z., Liu, Z., Zheng, J.Y., Yu, R., Wang, X., Sun, P.: Predicting hazardous driving events using multi-modal deep learning based on video motion profile and kinematics data. In: 2018 21st International Conference on Intelligent Transportation Systems (ITSC), pp. 3352–3357 (2021). https://doi.org/10.1109/ITSC.2018.8569659

26. Shukor, M., Couairon, G., Grechka, A., Cord, M.: Transformer decoders with MultiModal regularization for cross-modal food retrieval. In: 2022 IEEE/CVF Conference on Computer Vision and Pattern Recognition Workshops (CVPRW), pp. 4566–4577 (2022). https://doi.org/10.1109/CVPRW56347.2022.00503

27. Nojavanasghari, B., Gopinath, D., Koushik, J., Baltrusaitis, T., Morency, L.P.: Deep multimodal fusion for persuasiveness prediction. In: International Conference on Multimodal Interfaces (ICMI), pp. 284–288 (2016). https://doi.org/10.1145/2993148.2993176

28. Poria, S., Cambria, E., Gelbukh, A.: Deep convolutional neural network textual features and multiple kernel learning for utterance. In: Proceedings of the 2015 Conference on Empirical Methods in Natural Language Processing, pp. 2539–2544 (2015). https://doi.org/10.18653/v1/D15-1303
29. HERE location platform. https://www.here.com/

Intelligent Multi-agent Distributed System for Improving and Secure Travel Procedures: Al-Karama-King Hussein Bridge Study Case

Amjad Rattrout[(⊠)] [iD] and Hussein Younis[iD]

Department of Natural, Engineering and Technology Sciences, Arab American University, Jenin, Palestine
{amjad.rattrout,Hussein.Younis}@aaup.edu

Abstract. Passports and other types of identification can take advantage of advanced technologies. Many national and international organizations are developing machine-readable solutions for biometric data. However, the selection of technologies remains questionable due to privacy and security concerns. The State of Palestine has recently started issuing biometric passports, and therefore such techniques had to be highlighted in depth to be employed at border bridges, especially et al.-Karama-King Hussein Bridge. This paper proposes an intelligent multi-agent distributed system for improving and securing travel procedures based on RFID technology and blockchain, replacing manual procedures et al.-Karama-King Hussein Bridge, and making travel mobility more secure. We implement agent-based and discrete event simulation for the proposed system and design an experimentation framework where we can reliably vary several parameters. The result from the experiments shows that the number of agents involved in the travel procedures, particularly in the early and last stages, and the optimal situation to decrease passenger overcrowding at the bridge and travel time demand a rapid reaction in the number of agents corresponding with the crossing's capacity and available resources.

Keywords: Electronic Passport · Biometrics · RFID

1 Introduction

Digital transformation is a strategic goal for any government. Thus, many governments seek to employ technologies such as Radio-frequency identification (RFID) and blockchain to close the service gap between government and citizens. Digital transformation helps achieve sustainable development effectively, as the digitization of various areas makes its performance much better [1]. With the developments in many techniques, it has become possible to use these technologies for orderly, safe, systematic and responsible people mobility. The State of Palestine seeks to achieve the goals of sustainable development by digitizing many logistics services in travelling and mobility for Palestinian citizens and modernizing its border document infrastructure, the latest of which was the launch of a biometric passport in 2022 [2].

© The Author(s), under exclusive license to Springer Nature Switzerland AG 2024
M. Tabaa et al. (Eds.): INTIS 2022/2023, CCIS 1728, pp. 141–152, 2024.
https://doi.org/10.1007/978-3-031-47366-1_11

A biometric passport also known as "ePassport" is defined as a traditional passport that holds an embedded RFID chip which contains users' personal information and other biometric information like photos, fingerprints, or iris scans, this information is used to confirm that the passport belongs to the same user holding it [3]. RFID technology works on radio frequency of radio waves to automatically identify objects which contain RFID tags without the need to place the tracking object in a straight line with the reader [4]. The core elements of RFID technology consist of RFID Reader for reading and writing data from/into an RFID tag, an antenna for better readable consistently and the RFID tag which contains the data. There are two basic types of RFID tags which are active and passive RFID tags and the main distinction between them is that passive tags are cheaper and use the radio energy transmitted by the RFID reader to be read without a need for a power source, Therefore, passive tags are used with Biometric passport [5]. The main principle of how RFID technology works are that when the RFID tag is in the communication range of the RFID reader, the readers can access the database of the RFID tag and carry out the Identification process.

Although RFID technology has special advantages in designing "ePassport", such as verification of biometric and biographic information to confirm the identity of travellers, there are several concerns are arising, the main of which is the level of security and privacy protection and how to protect data from penetration and intrusion. It requires the integration of RFID with different protection mechanisms to maintain the privacy of the individual, allow travellers to control their data and enable the protection of data against manipulation [6].

A possible solution that could be used is blockchain technology that relies on presenting the distributed database as interconnected copies where data is linked into a continuous chain of blocks that contains information in a way that each new data block refers to the previous one. blockchains use cryptographic methods such as hashing to protect data. The main advantage of using blockchain is that when data is recorded inside a chain, it becomes very difficult to change it [7]. Each block in the blockchain has data which depends on the action that has been performed, the hash code which is always unique and it's calculated once the block is created. The third element inside each block is the hash of the previous block to make the blockchain more secure.

Through extensive discussions with the Palestinian authorities in charge of the Al-Karama bridge We can conclude that the current problems stem from the current procedures, which include various manual and paper procedures carried out and monitored by the bridge's human resources, such as checking procedures, checking bags, travel booking, and so on. In addition, the passenger manually fills out many paper documents utilized in the Al Karama bridge. There is also an obvious problem in the overcrowding of travellers at the crossing, thus travellers waiting too long at the bridge, which leads to many issues. The latest statistics published by the Palestinian police indicate that the average number of passengers per week in 2023 was about 32 thousand travellers [8].

The main objective of this study is to lay new foundations in terms of procedures et al. Karama bridge in the state of Palestine based on distributed identification system concerning RFID technology, blockchain and biometric passport to replace manual procedures used in it, to make travels mobility more secure and to limit the use of fraudulent documents by more accurate identification of individuals. The secondary objectives for the proposed system are:

1. Utilizing RFID technology in electronic passports.
2. Ensure the security and safety of passengers' data from hacking and modification.
3. Reduce passenger time and effort by improving travel procedures.
4. Disposal of paper documents used in travelling and digitalize all necessary documents for travel completion.
5. Reduce the cost of travel for both passengers and operators.

The following sections are the system architecture presented in Sect. 2. The logical data structure for the proposed system is presented in Sect. 3. The characteristics of the proposed system as distributed system and the database architecture are discussed in Sect. 4 and Sect. 5. The state diagram for the proposed system is presented in Sect. 6. An agent-based simulation for the proposed algorithm is presented in Sect. 7. The final section concludes this paper.

2 System Architecture

The proposed system is an Intelligent RFID Multi-agent Distributed system (IRMADS) that consists of multi-agents that perform a specific task, work together in a distributed way and are connected through a fully protected network to achieve the desired goal. IRMADS provides different services like biometric identification process, inspect travellers' luggage, Check-in and exit of travellers...etc. The term Intelligent reflects the ability of system agents to take decisions individually [9].

IRMADS consists of multi-agents as shown in Fig. 1 as follows:

1. **RFID reader agent:** It is used to gather information from an RFID tag attached to the passport or packages.
2. **Checker agent:** each checker agent is connected with RFID readers or other devices to get input data; depending on these data and predefined roles it performs a specific task and obtains a result that is positive or negative.
3. **Payment Agent:** The responsibility of this agent is to carry out the financial transactions for travel Such as payments through a Visa card.
4. **RFID tags generator agent:** responsible for printing RFID tags depending on user's inputs such as the number of packages.
5. **Recognition agent:** responsible for identification process based on Biometric data such as iris recognition and fingerprint.
6. **Entry/ Exit gate Agent:** it's an intermediate between different states of travel that allow the traveller to pass based on his/her current state.

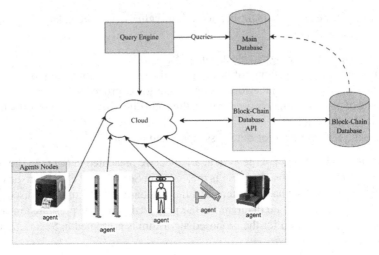

Fig. 1 IRMADS System Architecture

3 Logical Data Structure

The International Civil Aviation Organization (ICAO) which is a specialized agency of the United Nations issued a standardized data structure for travel documents that can be used to organize RFID tags contents [10]. There are sixteen data groups as described in Table 1. These data are stored once in E-passport when it's issued.

Table 1 Mandatory and optimal standardized data groups featured for E-passport

Data group number	Data group type	Data group contents
DG1	mandatory	Document details
DG2	mandatory	Encoded identification features such as the encoded face
DG3	optional	Encoded identification features such as encoded fingerprints
DG4	optional	Encoded identification features such as encoded irises
DG5	optional	Displayed portrait
DG6	optional	Reserved for future use
DG7	optional	Displayed signature mark
DG8	optional	Encoded data features
DG9 and DG10	optional	Encoded structure features
DG11, DG12, DG13, G14, DG15 and DG16	optional	Miscellaneous

In addition, all data for travel procedures in the al Karama bridge is stored as a block in the blockchain database where each blockchain block in the system contains a unique hash, previous block hash, datetime stamp, stage, the status of each stage and other data (TX) which is created in the blockchain by a transaction made by each agent as shown in Fig. 2.

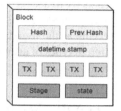

Fig. 2 System blockchain block structure

The hash value is calculated based on (SHA-256) Cryptographic to verify data integrity in each block [11]. Thus, this philosophy of data storage provides a secure way to know each passenger's condition while maintaining a lack of manipulation of the data entered.

4 IRMADS as Distributed System

As the system consists of multi-agents working in a distributed way to achieve the desired goal, it has the following characteristics:

4.1 Scalability

IRMADS is a scalable system if it can handle the increased number of its user and resources with time due to changes in system demands without affecting the performance of the system or increasing the administrative domain complexity [12]. This feature is reflected in the proposed system through the system's ability to cope with the increasing number of passengers through the multi-distrusted RFID readers with the ability to read multiple tags simultaneously and share the processed data between them in a degree of privacy [13]. In addition, the number of agents in the system can be increased in proportion to the requirements without affecting the existing system or redesigning the system each time it scales in size. Furthermore, the distribution of the system supports the additional hardware and computing bandwidth and distribute the tasks to the different agent during high-usage periods.

4.2 Openness

IRMADS is an Openness system if it can extend its hardware and software components without effect the integrity of existing components. This feature is reflected in how data are presented using international standards for biometric data and procedure transactions.

Also, the design of the proposed system allows to extend of its stages, reimplemented and integrated variously without generating any compatibility difficulties, while being viewed as an integrated whole by the user [14].

4.3 Resource Sharing

Resource sharing refers to a user's capacity to access and interact with resources across many agents in the system. This should include access to hardware, software, and data throughout the system, as well as serving as the foundation for consistent and synchronized information sharing across different types of agents within the distributed network [15].

5 IRMADS Database Based on Blockchain Data Architecture

IRMADS consists of the main distributed database as shown in Fig. 3 that contains the latest state for any transaction related to the passenger that is derived from the blockchain. The latest state is computed by traversing the entire blockchain from the first to the last block while considering every transaction within a block. Through the Query engine, any agent can inquire about the required data to perform related tasks [16].

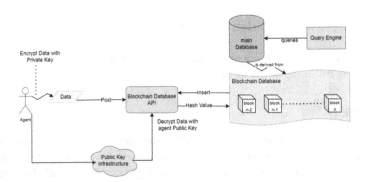

Fig. 3 IRMADS database architecture based on Blockchain

The data flow between IRMADS components is summarized in:

1. The agent creates a transaction record and encrypts data with the related private key.
2. Agent posts the encrypted data to blockchain database API.
3. blockchain database API decrypt data using the agent public key.
4. blockchain database API calculates the hash value and inserts the transaction into the database.

Only authorized agents can interact with blockchain database API, thus guaranteeing the accountability, confidentially and integrity of data. In addition, agents can interact with the main database using a query engine (read-only queries) [17].

6 State Diagram Distribution for IRMADS

The philosophy of the proposed system is to divide the desired target into several states for both entry and exit. Each state involves multi-agents to work together to be completed by performing predefined tasks (state events). user can move from one state to another sequentially if the state event is satisfied. Each state represents part of the travel procedures followed.

Figure 4 illustrates the state diagram of travel procedures where the end state means that the traveller has satisfied all the conditions of the previous state and therefore, he/she can travel and the end failure state means that the traveller has not achieved all the necessary conditions of travel and therefore he/she cannot travel.

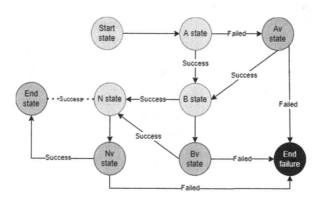

Fig. 4 State diagrams for travel procedures

In each state, the event is satisfied if all sub-events for involved agents in that state are satisfied. The user can reach the end state if

$$\bigwedge_{i=0}^{N} E_i = true \tag{1}$$

where N is the number of states in travel procedures and E is the intersection of all sub-events.

Table 2 describes the travellers' stages with all conditions for each state and the agents concerned [18].

Table 2 The proposed system states and their events are based on Fig. 4

state	conditions	Verification steps on event failure	Agents involved
Start state			
State A	• If the traveller has been identified • If the traveller is allowed to travel • If the Passport belongs to the traveller • If the Traveler's age exceeds the legal age of travel	Manual intervention is required by the operators of the bridge to examine the conditions and obstacles. The outputs of this case are either the completion of the stage that caused this event or moving to the end failure state	RFID reader agent, Checker agent, Recognition agent
State B	• If the number of bags entered by the traveller • If travel fees are paid	Manual intervention is required by the operators of the bridge to examine the conditions and obstacles. The outputs of this case are either the completion of the stage that caused this event or moving to the end failure state	RFID tags generator agent, Payment Agent
State C	• If the bags are checked • If the bags belong to the traveller	Manual intervention is required by the operators of the bridge to examine the conditions and obstacles. The outputs of this case are either the completion of the stage that caused this event or moving to the end failure state	Checker agent
State D	• If the traveller is satisfied with all previous events	Manual intervention is required by the operators of the bridge to examine the conditions and obstacles. The outputs of this case are either the completion of the stage that caused this event or moving to the end failure state	Checker agent, RFID reader agent
End state			

7 Agent-Based and Discrete Event Simulation for IRMADS

The efficiency of the proposed system in handling the current problem must be determined by implementing a simulation for the proposed system. A JavaScript programing language and farmwork called "p5js" is used in implementing the simulation. "P5.js" is a tool used for creating interactive visuals with code in the web browser [19]. The distributed conceptualization of the IRMADS in the simulation involves all stages, agents and interactions. Based on the state diagram explained in Table 2 of the IRMADS, the whole system in the simulation consists of six stages and each stage represents a state of the system. Each stage consists of N agents with different types and can be adjusted by the user. The agent in the simulation is represented as a yellow box if it's idle or a red box if it's busy as illustrated in Fig. 5.

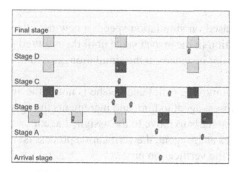

Fig. 5 Distributed conceptualization of agents in the simulation

7.1 Agent and Traveler Data Structure

Each agent instance in the system has the following attributes:

(1) Xcord: represents the x coordinate for the agent in the simulation canvas.
(2) Ycord: represents the y coordinate for the agent in the simulation canvas.
(3) State: represents the state of the agent either idle or busy.
(4) max capacity: the maximum number of travellers can handle at the same time.
(5) current user count: the current number of travellers being handled.

Each traveller in the system has the following attributes:

(1) Xcord: represents the x coordinate for the traveller in the simulation canvas.
(2) Ycord: represents the y coordinate for the traveller in the simulation canvas.
(3) arrival-time: represent the time and date when the traveller arrives arrival stage.
(4) travelTime: represent the time and date when the traveller has completed all stages events.
(5) state: the current state of the traveller.
(6) is verified: indicate whether the traveller has been verified in the current stage or not.
  5. verificationProcess: indicate whether the traveller is in the verification process or not.

7.2 Simulation Work Flow

There are four main functions in the simulation, (1) the generation function which is responsible for generating the population every tick until the population reached the required population number. (2) the pick traveller function which is responsible for choosing travellers based on its attributes to assign a task to him which is moving to the next state. (3) the pick agent function which is responsible for choosing the closest agent to the traveller in the next stage concern the agent state and the number of current travellers being handled.

The main steps to run the simulation are as follows:

(1) Adjust the simulation parameters including the number of travellers, the number of agent instances in each stage and the simulation speed.
(2) Start the simulation.
(3) In every tick and based on simulation speed, a new traveller instance is generated with a random position in the arrival stage until the required population is satisfied.
(4) For all current traveller instances in the simulation, an action is taken based on their state as follows:
  i. if the traveller is not moving (idle) and he/she is not in the verification process, the system picks the closest agent to him, and increments the agent's current user count by one. The traveller starts to move to the assigned agent.
  ii. If the traveller arrives at the agent, the verification process is starting for the traveller.
  iii. If the traveller is in the verification process:
(a) Once the traveller is satisfied with the current stage verification process, the state of the traveller increment by one, he/she is ready to move to the next stage and the current agent travellers count decrement by one.
(b) If the traveller failed in satisfying the current stage verification process, he/she is moved to the manual check phase to be handled and the current agent travellers count decrement by one.
(5) if the traveller completes all stages and the verification process successfully, he/she assigns as he/she can travel.

7.3 Simulation Results and Analysis

Many experiments were conducted with a population equal to 1000 using a different number of agents in each stage as follows (Table 3):

The result revealed that the number of agents, particularly in the early and last stages, is so critical that it must be proportionate to the number of current travellers. The rise in the number of agents must be disciplined rather than static so that it is mostly determined by the number of travellers. Access to optimal status to decrease passenger overcrowding at the bridge and travel time demands a rapid reaction in the number of agents corresponding with the crossing's capacity and available resources.

Table 3 Simulation Results

Ex. number	Number of agents in each stage	population	Number of ticks until all travellers satisfied all states
1	Stage A: 2, Stage B, C and D: 3	1000	7937
2	Stage A: 3, Stage B, C and D: 3	1000	6209
3	Stage A: 4, Stage B, C and D: 3	1000	5903
4	Stage A: 5, Stage B, C and D: 3	1000	5935
5	Stage D: 2, Stage B, C and A: 3	1000	8301
6	Stage D: 3, Stage B, C and A: 3	1000	5783
7	Stage D: 4, Stage B, C and A: 3	1000	6153
8	Stage D: 5, Stage B, C and A: 3	1000	5553

8 Conclusion

The use of digitization and modern technologies plays an essential role in improving the services provided to citizens. The paper proposed distributed identification system concerning RFID technology, blockchain and biometric passport to replace manual procedures et al.-Karama-King Hussein Bridge and make travel mobility more secure. A simulation of the proposed system was also implemented to seriously identify the problem and a serious attempt to reach the strengths offered by this system, which highlighted the time factor and how to distribute various types of agents to reduce the waiting time for travellers. Here it should be noted that the cost of applying this system on the ground needs a real financial study and this is what can be done in the future.

References

1. Mondejar, M.E., et al.: Digitalization to achieve sustainable development goals: steps towards a Smart Green Planet. Sci. Total. Environ. **794**, 148539 (2021)
2. P.C.O. Ministers: Decisions taken by the Palestinian Cabinet during its session No. 92, Palestinian Council of Ministers, 18 January 2021. http://www.palestinecabinet.gov.ps/portal/Decree/DetailsEn/de2818be-b1ac-4d9e-a770-827067039930. Accessed 13 Dec 2022
3. Khairnar, S.K., Bhamare, P.P., Hire, A.S.: E-Passport Using RFID Tag and Fingerprint Sensor. Int. J. Sci. Res. Eng. Dev. **2**(5), 302–306 (2019)
4. Wang, Y.: Optimization of material flow by lean tools and RFID integration into a vendor-involved eKanban system, PhD Thesis. Massachusetts Institute of Technology (2021)
5. Marquardt, N., Taylor, A.S., Villar, N., Greenberg, S.: Visible and controllable RFID tags. pp. 3057–3062 (2010)
6. Ari, J., Molnar, D., Wagner, D.: Security and privacy issues in e-passports. In: First International Conference on Security and Privacy for Emerging Areas in Communications Networks (SECURECOMM'05) (2006)
7. Aleksandr, L., Nickolay, V., Arturas, K.: logistics of construction materials. In: Matec Web of Conferences. EDP Sciences (2018)

8. P. police, ألف07 مسافر تنقلوا عبر معبر الكرامة الإسبوع الماضي January 2023. https://www.palpol ice.ps/content/491380.html. Accessed 30 Jan 2023

9. Amjad, R., AbuRob, F., Badir, H.: Distributed RFID multi-agent system for healthcare hospitals. Bus. Intell. Big Data, **B-14**, 291–302 (2018)

10. Elfita, A., Kareng, Y., Argo Victoria, O.: The role of ICAO (international civil aviation organization) in implementing international flight safety standards. KnE Soc. Sci. (2021)

11. Velmurugadass, P., Dhanasekaran, S., Anand, S.S., Vasudevan, V.: Enhancing Blockchain security in cloud computing with IoT environment using ECIES and cryptography hash algorithm. Mat. Today Proc. **37**, 2653–2659 (2021)

12. Hopkins, A.B.T., McDonald-Maier, K.D.: Debug support for complex systems on-chip: a review. IEE Proc. Comput. Digital Tech. **153**(4), 197 (2006). https://doi.org/10.1049/ip-cdt: 20050194

13. Basel, A., Andrew, C., Jorge, C., Radha, P.: Scalable RFID Systems: a Privacy-Preserving Protocol with Constant-Time Identification. In: IEEE Transactions on Parallel and Distributed Systems (2010)

14. Tanenbaum, A.S., Van Steen, M.: Distributed Systems: Principles and Paradigms. Prentice-Hall (2007)

15. Vladyko, A., Khakimov, A., Muthanna, A., Ateya, A.A., Koucheryavy, A.: Distributed edge computing to assist ultra-low-latency VANET applications. Future Internet **11**(6), 128 (2019)

16. Androulaki, E., et al.: Hyperledger fabric: a distributed operating system for permissioned blockchains. In: Proceedings of the Thirteenth EuroSys Conference (2018)

17. Narendira Kumar, V.K., Srinivasan, B.: Biometric passport validation scheme using radio frequency identification. Int. J. Comput. Netw. Inf. Secur. **5**(5), 30–39 (2013)

18. "ارشادات السفر على معبر الكرامة في أريحا," Palestinian Police, 05 August 2012. https://www.pal police.ps/content/298803.html. Accessed 26 Dec 2021

19. Sandberg, E.: Creative Coding on the Web in p5.js : a Library Where JavaScript Meets Processing. Blekinge Institute of Technology, Faculty of Computing, Department of Software Engineering, Sandberg1 (2019)

A New Approach for the Analysis of Resistance to Change in the Digital Transformation Context

Bachira Abou El Karam[1]([✉]), Rabia Marghoubi[1], Fadoua Khanboubi[2], and Driss Allaki[3]

[1] InnovatiVE REsearch on Software, Systems, and data, INPT, Rabat, Morocco
{abouelkaram.bachira,m.rabia}@inpt.ac.ma
[2] LIM Lab. IOS team, Department of Computer Science, FSTM, Casablanca, Morocco
[3] Smart, Embedded, Enterprise and Distributed Systems, INPT, Rabat, Morocco
d.allaki@inpt.ac.ma

Abstract. In a context marked by the rapid evolution of technologies and the omnipresence of IT at the heart of all activities, the digital transformation of companies is no longer a luxury but an absolute necessity. This technological transformation can lead to resistance from the employees affected by the change. In order to properly conduct the change management process, it is necessary to ensure the involvement of employees from the beginning of this process, which is composed of three phases: the change management strategy, the diagnosis, and the actions implementation. This paper focuses on the diagnostic phase and more specifically on the evaluation stage. This evaluation measures the employees' hesitation to express their degree of resistance toward the digital initiatives launched in the company. However, this assessment is usually done subjectively, and employees express their hesitation in non-uniform manners. In this work, we propose a weighted generalized hesitating fuzzy approach based on the fusion of theoretical concepts of generalized hesitant fuzzy sets and formal concept analysis (FCA), to formalize the measurement of degree hesitation in change resistance. This approach is flexible and allows the top management of each organizational unit to correctly measure the resistance to change of their teams and then evaluate that measure at the global organizational level.

Keywords: Decision-Making · Hesitant Fuzzy Sets · Weighted Generalized Hesitating Fuzzy Sets · Galois lattices · Digital Transformation · Resistance to Change

1 Introduction

Increasing competitiveness and ensuring sustainable development by providing intelligent products and services that meet the needs of customers: these are the main guidelines for every company to maintain its position in the market. Indeed, with the advent of Industry 4.0, no company can avoid rethinking its business model to keep up with this new technological revolution. However, in the business world, this technological change commonly called "Digital Transformation" is not always considered in the same way. Some see it as a threat, while others see it as an opportunity.

M. Tabaa et al. (Eds.): INTIS 2022/2023, CCIS 1728, pp. 153–167, 2024.
https://doi.org/10.1007/978-3-031-47366-1_12

In a digital transformation context, the introduction of digital initiatives in the company is mandatory to achieve its strategic objectives. This technological mutation of the company is not always positively perceived by employees, who are focused on the fear of change in their work and role, the fear of losing their job or acquiring new skills using new technologies and working differently.

In this situation, the resistance to change of the team deserves a thoughtful analysis to better appreciate resistance at the overall company level. However, when team members want to express their rate of resistance to change concerning a digital initiative, they are usually hesitant, making it difficult to reach a final agreement. For example, two members want to express their rate of resistance to change relative to a given digital initiative, the first announces 0.6 but the second prefers to express himself in the interval between [0.4; 0.6], and subsequently, the difficulty of establishing a common degree of adhesion. In this sense, and to ensure the involvement of the actors, from the beginning of the process, it is crucial to provide them with diverse evaluation modes that cater to their individual needs: interval of numbers, decimal or binary. This paper, which is a continuity of our work [1], aims at developing a structural analytical approach based on the fusion of the theoretical concepts of Formal Concept Analysis (FCA) [2–6] and Generalized Hesitant Fuzzy Sets [7–13]. This proposal allows the analysis of the different forms of evaluation expressed by the company's teams. This variety of evaluation methods take different forms (values in [0, 1], net values, an interval of values, etc.) while considering the parameter of the heterogeneity of the teams' profiles in the analysis, by proposing a weighting vector expressing the weights of the company's teams according to their profiles and their expertise. This contribution also allows the generation of potentially interesting groupings between actors and digital initiatives thanks to the Formal Concept Analysis, for leading good change management. All these methods combined lead to more realistic results as shown by an illustrative example. The rest of the article is structured as follows. Section 2 presents related work. Section 3 presents the literature review on formal concept analysis, hesitant fuzzy sets, and their extensions. Section 4 introduces the proposed methodological solution. Section 5 presents an example to illustrate the different steps of our approach. Section 6 presents the obtained results. The last section concludes the paper and discusses future work.

2 Related Work

For decision-makers, choosing the most optimal grouping from a set of alternatives based on different attributes can be a challenging task. This is because the information available may be vague, uncertain, and subject to hesitation, which makes the decision-making process more complex in the real world. This work is an expansion of our previous proposal, which involved integrating the concept of fuzzy set theory and formal concept analysis theory. On one hand, the aim of that work was to model vague and uncertain data in an evaluation process. On the other hand, the other objective was to generate potentially interesting groupings of vague and imprecise data using the Galois lattice. Indeed, the integration of formal concept analysis (FCA) with fuzzy logic to deal with ambiguous and imperfect data, has been widely addressed in the literature in several domains such as information retrieval [14, 15] knowledge discovery [16–18], text mining [19, 20], ontology engineering [21, 22] and assessment [23, 24].

Nevertheless, the said works do not consider the issue of hesitation in the evaluation and decision-making process.

To deal with hesitation, Torra [8] introduced the concept of hesitant fuzzy sets (HFS), which allows the assignment of a degree of membership of an element to a set presented by several possible values. Unlike fuzzy set theory, the concept of HFS can more accurately reflect the phenomenon of hesitancy in the representation of preferences over items and can more adequately describe human hesitancy than other common extensions of fuzzy sets. In the last few years, there have been several publications in the literature that address the application of HFS to the decision-making process. For example, XUE AND ZESHUI [13] proposed a decision-making method based on the extension of the theory of classical formal concept analysis using hesitant fuzzy sets, Alfakeeh and Almalaoui [25] used the AHP-TOPSIS technique based on hesitant fuzzy sets to estimate the risks of various web applications, Arunodaya and Shyi-Ming [26] proposed a new multi-attribute decision making (MADM) approach based on Fermatean hesitant fuzzy sets (FHFS) and the VIKOR method. However, all these methods ignore the possibility of expressing the hesitation in different forms in the same hesitant fuzzy element (net value, an interval of values, fuzzy value, and so on).

Our work mainly allows analyzing the various evaluations expressed by the teams of the company, under various forms (values in [0, 1], net values, an interval of values, etc.). This is based on the fusion of the theoretical concepts of the Formal Concept Analysis (FCA) and the generalized hesitant fuzzy sets (GHFS), the said extension also considers the parameter of the heterogeneity of the profiles of the teams in the analysis, by proposing a vector of weighting expressing the teams' weights of the company according to their profiles and their expertise. This approach is intended to better reflect the hesitation exhibited by humans, in contrast to other common extensions of the fuzzy set theory.

3   Background

The theoretical foundation of our analysis for resistance to change concerning a digital transformation initiative combines the concepts of Formal Concept Analysis (FCA) and Generalized Hesitant Fuzzy Sets (GHFS). The rest of this section briefly introduces FCA, Fuzzy FCA, Hesitant Fuzzy Sets, and their extensions in accordance with the needs of our approach.

Formal Concept Analysis (FCA) is a data analysis method introduced by Wille [2], and it aims to identify knowledge called formal concepts, grouping objects having the same attributes called respectively extension and intention. The intention includes the set of maximal properties that all the objects of the extension fulfill, and the extension contains the set of maximum objects satisfying all the properties of the intention and ordered hierarchically in a graph called Galois lattice, and this, starting from the data which are initially presented in the form of a binary table called a formal context. The definition of these concepts is very well described in [2, 4–7]. But in real life, data are not always presented in the form of binary contexts. Indeed, certain relations between objects and properties can be partially known, imprecise, fuzzy, or completely unknown (measurements, observations, judgments, and so on). As a result, Formal Concept Analysis (FCA) is brought to consider formal contexts of varying natures, obtained through measurements, observations, evaluations, and other methods. In this context, the relationship between an object and an attribute is not limited to a Boolean form (0 or 1) but can be characterized by uncertainty, fuzziness, or even imprecision.

Starting from this observation, and based on the theory of fuzzy sets, developed by Lotfi Zadeh in 1965 [2], which states that an element can belong strongly or weakly to a set, several approaches have proposed to extend the Formal Analysis of Classical Concepts to the Formal Analysis of Fuzzy Concepts to mathematically represent the imprecision relative to certain classes of objects, where any attachment of an attribute to an object would be a matter of degree of membership to [0, 1].

Nevertheless, despite the success of the Formal Analysis of Fuzzy Concepts in several domains related to uncertainty, it has limitations in dealing with imprecise and vague information when dealing with different sources of imprecision that appear at the same time. This situation is very common in the decision-making process when a decision maker might consider different degrees of membership of an element x in set A (e.g. {0.45,0.52,0.48}). To deal with such cases, Torra and Narukawa [7] introduced the notion of a Hesitant Fuzzy Set (HFS). The HFS, as one of the extensions of Zadeh's Fuzzy set [27], allows assigning a degree of membership of an element to a set presented by several possible values and can express the hesitating information more completely than other extensions of the fuzzy set. Thus, the hesitant fuzzy set can reflect human hesitancy more objectively than other classical extensions of the fuzzy set.

On the other hand, it is sometimes difficult for experts to express the degrees of membership of an element to a given set only by values between 0 and 1 but also by intervals of values. Different extensions of HFS have been introduced in the literature to overcome this limitation, such as Dual Hesitant Fuzzy Sets (DHFS) [27] which consist of two parts, the membership hesitancy function, and the non-membership hesitancy function; Interval-Valued Hesitant Fuzzy sets (IVHFS) [28] which are a generalization of HFS in which the degrees of membership of an element to a given set is defined by several possible interval values; Generalized Hesitant Fuzzy sets (GHFS) [11] allowing each degree of membership to include several forms of hesitancy: values in [0,1], an interval of values, etc. In other words, membership is the union of certain fuzzy sets or interval-valued fuzzy sets; Hesitant Fuzzy Linguistic term sets (HFLTS) present a model of linguistic decision-making in which decision-makers evaluations are provided through uncertain linguistic variables [29].

4 Proposed Approach

In this section, we describe a generalized hesitant fuzzy model of resistance to change in a digital transformation context for top management of organizational units.

The proposed approach is based on the combination of the theory of generalized hesitant fuzzy sets and the theory of formal concept analysis (FCA). The specificity of this approach is twofold. Firstly, it permits the analysis of various evaluations expressed in different formats (values in [0, 1], net values, an interval of values, etc.) by the company teams, utilizing the Generalized Hesitant Fuzzy Sets. Moreover, it accounts for the diversity in the team's profiles and expertise during analysis, by presenting a weighting vector relative to the team's profile. Secondly, it allows the generation of concepts and the classification of uncertain and imprecise data thanks to the Galois lattice in a group decision making context.

In the following, we give the necessary notations to understand the process of computing the generalized hesitant fuzzy matrices for analysis. Let $A = \{\Theta 1, \Theta 2,..., \Theta m\}$ be the set of teams involved in the organizational units. $\Gamma = \{\gamma 1, \gamma 2,..., \gamma n\}$, a set of digital initiatives. K_{ij} corresponds to the set of estimates (digits between [0, 1], interval values, net value, etc.) of resistance to change expressed by team members (Θi) for a digital initiative (γj). Let $\Psi = (\omega 1,..., \omega m)$ be a vector of numbers in [0, 1] such that $\omega 1 +... + \omega m = 1$, ωi measures the weight of a team Θi according to its profile in the company (technical team, business team, financial team, security team, and so on.).

The flow chart of the process is shown in Fig. 1.

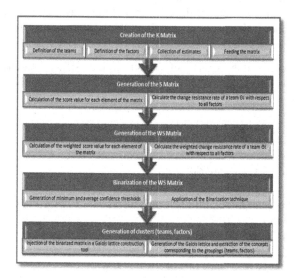

Fig. 1. Flow chart of Generalized Hesitant Fuzzy Galois Lattices' Construction

The proposed method involves the following steps:

Step 1: Construction of the K matrix which corresponds to the generalized hesitant fuzzy context of teams and digital initiatives; this step includes four sub-steps:

- List the participating teams in the evaluation process ($\Theta 1, \Theta 2,..., \Theta m$) where m is the number of teams.
- Identify the digital initiatives ($\gamma 1, \gamma 2,..., \gamma n$) where n is the number of the digital initiatives.
- Assign the set K_{ij} consisting of the estimates of resistance to change expressed by each team member (Θi) relative to the digital initiative (γj). The elements of the set of estimates can take different forms (values in [0, 1], net values, range of values, etc.).

The K matrix is shown in Table 1.

Table 1. Generalized Hesitant Fuzzy Context of Teams and digital initiatives

Matrix K	$\gamma 1$	...	γj	...	γn
$\Theta 1$					
...					
Θi			K_{ij}		
...					
Θm					

Step 2: Generation of the matrix S that corresponds to the context of the score values relative to the sets Kij consisting of the estimates of the resistance to change expressed by each team member (Θi) relative to the digital initiative (γj); this step includes three sub-steps:

- Compute the score values $s(\Theta i)$ j of the set K_{ij} of resistance-to-change estimates expressed by members of the team Θi relative to the digital initiative γj, where:

$$K_{ij} = U_{k=1}^{\text{card }\Theta i} \{r_k\}j \; ;$$
$$s=0 \; ;$$
$$\text{for } (k=1; k= \text{card } \Theta i; k{+}{+})$$
$$\text{if } r_k \in [0,1] \text{ then } s= s+r_k \; ;$$
$$\text{if } r_k \text{ is an interval like } [\gamma_k, \eta_k] \text{ then } s= s+ 1/2 \, (\gamma_k +\eta_k);$$
$$\text{end for } ;$$
$$s(\Theta i) \, j= s/ \text{card } \Theta i \; ;$$

- Calculate the change resistance rate of a team Θi with respect to all digital initiatives γj, where: $\Phi(\Theta i) = 1 / |\Gamma| \times \Sigma j \, s(\Theta i)j$ and $|\Gamma|$ is the cardinal of all digital initiatives $\Gamma = \{\gamma 1, \gamma 2,...,\gamma n\}$.
- Calculate The overall rate of resistance to change in the company where: $H(\Theta) = 1/|A| \times \Sigma i \, \Phi(\Theta i)$ and $|A|$ is the cardinal of $A = \{\Theta 1, \Theta 2,..., \Theta m\}$

The S matrix is shown in Table 2.

Step 3: Generation of the WS matrix that corresponds to the context of the weighted score values of the Kij sets consisting of the estimates of resistance to change expressed by each team member (Θi) with respect to the digital initiative (γj); this step includes three sub-steps:

- Compute the weighted score values s ωi (Θi) j of the set Kij of resistance-to-change estimates expressed by members of the team Θi with respect to the digital initiative γj, where: s ωi $(\Theta i)j = \omega i \, s(\Theta i)j$ and ωi measures the weight of a team Θi according to its profile.
- Calculate the weighted change resistance rate of a team Θi with respect to all digital initiatives γj, where: $\Phi \, \omega i(\Theta i) = \omega i \, \Phi(\Theta i)$ and ωi measures the weight of a team Θi according to its profile.

Table 2. Values of the score function related to the context of Table 1

Matrix S	$\gamma 1$	...	γj	...	γn	Hesitant Fuzzy Digital Initiative Aggregator for teams: $\Phi(\Theta i)$
$\Theta 1$						
...						
Θi			$s(\Theta i)j$			$\Phi(\Theta i) = 1/n \times \Sigma j\, s(\Theta i)j$
...						
Θm						
$\odot i = 1m(\Theta i)$	$H(\Theta) = 1/\mid A \mid \times \Sigma i\, \Phi(\Theta i)$					

- Calculate the overall weighted rate of resistance to change in the company where: $H\omega(\Theta) = 1/\mid A \mid \times \Sigma i\, \Phi\omega(\Theta i)$ and $\mid A \mid$ is the cardinal of $A = \{\Theta 1, \Theta 2, ..., \Theta m\}$.

The WS matrix is shown in Table 3.

Table 3. Values of the weight-score function related to the context of Table 1

Matrix WS	$\gamma 1$	...	γj	...	γn	Weighted Hesitant Fuzzy Digital Initiative Aggregator for teams: $\Phi^{\omega}(\Theta i)$
$\Theta 1$						
...						
Θi			$s^{\omega i}(\Theta i)j = \omega i.s(\Theta i)j$			$\Phi^{\omega}(\Theta i) = \omega i.\Phi(\Theta i)$
...						
Θm						
$\odot_{i=1}{}^{m}(\Theta i)$	$H^{\omega}(\Theta) = 1/\mid A \mid \times \Sigma i\, \Phi^{\omega}(\Theta i)$					

Step 4: Binarization of the WS matrix with well-defined confidence thresholds; this step includes two sub-steps:

- Compute the average and minimum confidence thresholds Tavg, Tmin corresponding to the average and minimum values of resistance to change by digital initiative.
- Apply the binarization technique which consists of comparing the weight score function value of the hesitant fuzzy element with the threshold value. If the value of the weight score function of the hesitant fuzzy element h is greater than or equal to the confidence threshold of the attribute, then the hesitant fuzzy element will take the value 1. Otherwise, it is reduced to 0.

Step 5: Generation of concepts (teams, digital initiatives); this step includes two sub-steps:

- Injection of the binarized matrix in a Galois lattice construction tool.

- Generation of the Galois lattice and extraction of the concepts corresponding to the groupings (teams, digital initiatives).

The calculation path is provided in Fig. 2. The decision-maker selects the generalized hesitant fuzzy matrix as input to the process: the matrix K (Table 1) which corresponds to the generalized hesitant fuzzy context of teams and digital initiatives; the matrix S (Table 2) which corresponds to the context of score's values of teams and digital initiatives; the matrix WS (Table 3) which corresponds to the context of weighted score's values of teams and digital initiatives. The decision-maker can have an overall assessment of the resistance to change in the enterprise given by: $H(\Theta) = 1/|A| \times \Sigma i\, \Phi\,(\Theta i)$ and an overall weighted assessment of the resistance to change given by:

$H^{\omega}\,(\Theta) = 1/|A| \times \Sigma_i \Phi^{\omega}\,(\Theta i)$.

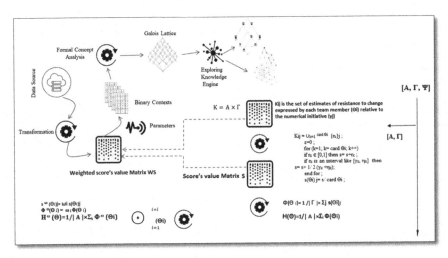

Fig. 2. Generalized Hesitant Fuzzy Formal Concepts exploration process.

5   Illustrative Example

To illustrate the formal analysis of generalized hesitant fuzzy contexts, we propose an illustrative example.

Let A be the set of teams involved in the organizational units and Γ the set of digital initiatives in a digital transformation project:

A = {$\Theta1$: Functional team, $\Theta2$: Technical team, $\Theta3$: Financial team, $\Theta4$: Security team}.

Γ = {$\gamma1$: Big data, $\gamma2$: IoT, $\gamma3$: Blockchain, $\gamma4$: Cloud Computing}.

Let ω = (0.2, 0.25, 0.3, 0.25) be a vector of numbers, such that ωi measures the weight of a team Θi relative to all teams in the firm.

Table 4 illustrates the case of a Generalized Fuzzy Hesitant Context.

The score function values related to the context in Table 4 are computed using the algorithm above and illustrated in Table 5.

Table 4. Generalized Hesitant Fuzzy Context of Teams and digital initiatives

$K = A \times \Gamma$	Big Data $\gamma 1$	IOT $\gamma 2$	Blockchain $\gamma 3$	Cloud Computing $\gamma 4$
Functional team $\Theta 1$	{0.5,0.4,0.7,[0.2,0.4],0.6}	{0.3,[0.3,0.5],0.5,0.3,0.6}	{0.3,0.5,0,0}	{0.1,[0.2,0.4],0.2,0.3,0.4}
Technical team $\Theta 2$	{0.2,0.5,0.2}	{0.2,0.5,[0.1,0.3]}	{0,0,0}	{0.2,0.1, [0.1,0.3]}
Financial team $\Theta 3$	{[0.5,0.7],0.7}	{0.8,0.7}	{0.6,0.5}	{[0.3,0.5],0.2}
Security team $\Theta 4$	{0.5,0.6}	{0.8,0.6}	{0, 0}	{0.5,0.4}

Table 5. Values of the score function related to the context of Table 4

S	Big Data $\gamma 1$	IOT $\gamma 2$	BlockChain $\gamma 3$	Cloud Computing $\gamma 4$	Hesitant Fuzzy Digital Initiative Aggregator for teams: $\Phi(\Theta i)$
Functional team $\Theta 1$	0.5	0.42	0.2	0.26	0.34
Technical team $\Theta 2$	0.3	0.3	0	0.16	0.19
Financial team $\Theta 3$	0.65	0.75	0.55	0.3	0.56
Security team $\Theta 4$	0.55	0.7	0	0.45	0.42
$\odot_{i=1}{}^4(\Theta_i)$	$H(\Theta) = 1/l\ A\ \vert \times \Sigma_i\ \Phi(\Theta i) = 0.377$				

Table 6 describes the values of the weight score function, calculated by using the function in step 3.

Once the generalized hesitant fuzzy context is fixed, a threshold binarization technique is positioned to generate the associated concept lattices. For this, we used the following confidence thresholds: $T_{avg} = \{0.51, 0.56, 0.2, 0.29\}$ and $T_{min} = \{0.3, 0.3, 0.16, 0.16\}$. T_{avg} represents the average values of resistance to change per digital initiative, and T_{min} indicates the minimum values of resistance to change per digital initiative. The binarized contexts and Galois lattices generated using the T_{avg} and T_{min} confidence thresholds are as follows (Tables 7, 8 and 9) :

The closed concepts generated from the confidence threshold T_{avg} shown in Fig. 3 are as follows:{($\Theta 3$), ($\gamma 1$, $\gamma 2$, $\gamma 3$, $\gamma 4$)},{($\Theta 3$, $\Theta 4$), ($\gamma 1,\gamma 2$, $\gamma 4$)},{($\Theta 1$, $\Theta 2$, $\Theta 3$, $\Theta 4$), ($\emptyset$)}.

The closed concepts generated from the confidence threshold T_{min} shown in Fig. 4 are as follows:{($\Theta 1$, $\Theta 3$),($\gamma 1,\gamma 2$, $\gamma 3$, $\gamma 4$)}, {($\Theta 1$, $\Theta 2$, $\Theta 3$, $\Theta 4$),($\gamma 1,\gamma 2$, $\gamma 4$)}.

Table 6. Values of the weighted score function related to the context of Table 4

WS	Big Data $\gamma 1$	IOT $\gamma 2$	Blockchain $\gamma 3$	Cloud Computing $\gamma 4$	Weighted Hesitant Fuzzy Digital Initiative Aggregator for teams: $\Phi^{\omega} (\Theta i)$
Functional team $\Theta 1$	0.4	0.336	0.16	0.208	0.27
Technical team $\Theta 2$	0.3	0.3	0	0.16	0.19
Financial team $\Theta 3$	0.78	0.9	0.66	0.36	0.67
Security team $\Theta 4$	0.55	0.7	0	0.45	0.42
$\odot_{i=1}{}^{4}(\Theta_i)$	$H^{\omega} (\Theta) = 1/\mid A \mid \times \Sigma_i\ \Phi^{\omega} (\Theta i) = 0.387$				

Table 7. Binary context with the threshold T_{avg}

	Big Data $\gamma 1$	IOT $\gamma 2$	Blockchain $\gamma 3$	Cloud Computing $\gamma 4$
Functional team $\Theta 1$	0	0	0	0
Technical team $\Theta 2$	0	0	0	0
Financial team $\Theta 3$	1	1	1	1
Security team $\Theta 4$	1	1	0	1

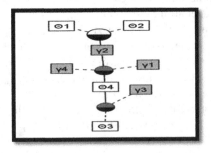

Fig. 3. Galois Lattice, threshold $= T_{avg}$

Table 8. Binary context with the threshold T_{min}

	Big Data $\gamma 1$	IOT $\gamma 2$	Blockchain $\gamma 3$	Cloud Computing $\gamma 4$
Functional team $\Theta 1$	1	1	1	1
Technical team $\Theta 2$	1	1	0	1
Financial team $\Theta 3$	1	1	1	1
Security team $\Theta 4$	1	1	0	1

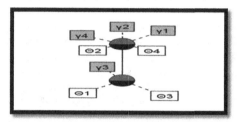

Fig. 4. Galois Lattice, threshold $= T_{min}$

6   Results and Discussion

The figures quoted above show the navigation through the concept lattices. The exploration practice is conducted to better determine the optimal grouping of digital initiatives and company teams involved in the digital transformation project (closed concepts). For example, the closed concept $\{(\Theta 3, \Theta 4), (\gamma 1, \gamma 2, \gamma 4)\}$, generated from the T_{avg} (threshold average) means that the Financial team and the Security team, both resist to change with respect to the digital initiatives (Big Data, IoT, Cloud Computing). We can also see that the overall weighted rate of resistance to change in the company is different (higher in this case) from the overall classical rate of resistance to change in the same company. This reflects the importance of taking into account the weight of the teams in the evaluation, thus allowing to provide the results that are most adapted to the company's strategy. Also, we notice that the intentions (the set of digital initiatives) and the extensions (the set of teams) of the concepts generated from the average threshold are subsets included in the intentions and the extensions of the concepts generated from the minimal threshold. We can interpret this inclusion by choosing a minimum value threshold that covers more teams in the treatment of resistance to change.

The concepts generated thanks to the Galois lattice, allow the company to identify the optimal combinations between the digital initiatives and the company's teams involved in the digital transformation project (to increase the chance of optimizing the actions to be planned in terms of change management). For example, the concept $\{(\Theta 3, \Theta 4), (\gamma 1, \gamma 2, \gamma 4)\}$, generated from the threshold $= \{0.51, 0.56, 0.2, 0.29\}$ indicates that both teams 3 and 4 are impacted by the resistance to change of digital initiatives 1, 2 and 4, and subsequently the company can consider including both teams in the training cycles related to digital initiatives 1, 2, and 4 for change management.

All teams are impacted by the resistance to change of digital initiatives; the choice of a threshold is defined according to the context of the company, considering the budgetary aspects and the availability of resources.

Without any doubt, setting a threshold level means excluding teams whose score is below the threshold defined in the Galois context. Nevertheless, they are indeed concerned by the resistance to change, but in the second place.

Table 9. Analytics and navigation dashboard

Company's overall resistance to change rate	$H(\Theta)=1/\|A\|\times\Sigma_i \Phi(\Theta i) = 0.377$		
Company's overall weighted resistance to change rate	$H^\omega(\Theta)=1/\|A\|\times\Sigma_i \Phi^\omega(\Theta i) = 0.387$		
Teams	Team's weighted change resistance rate $\Phi^{\omega i}(\Theta i)= \omega i \Phi(\Theta i)$	Team's max weighted change resistance rate $max(\omega i \Phi(\Theta i))$	Team's min weighted change resistance rate $min(\omega i \Phi(\Theta i))$
$\Theta 1$	0.27	0.4	0.16
$\Theta 2$	0.19	0.3	0
$\Theta 3$	0.67	0.9	0.36
$\Theta 4$	0.42	0.7	0
Generalized Hesitant Fuzzy Galois Lattice Navigator			
Thresholds	T_{avg}		T_{min}
Galois Lattice	**Figure 3**		**Figure 4**
Generalized Hesitant Fuzzy Formal Concepts	$\{(\Theta 3), (\gamma 1, \gamma 2, \gamma 3, \gamma 4)\}$ $\{(\Theta 3, \Theta 4), (\gamma 1, \gamma 2, \gamma 4)\}$ $\{(\Theta 1, \Theta 2, \Theta 3, \Theta 4), (\emptyset)\}$		$\{(\Theta 1, \Theta 3), (\gamma 1, \gamma 2, \gamma 3, \gamma 4)\}$ $\{(\Theta 1, \Theta 2, \Theta 3, \Theta 4), (\gamma 1, \gamma 2, \gamma 4)\}$

By the end, it can be concluded that the objective of our approach is:

- To take into consideration the hesitations of the actors according to different forms during a decision-making process.
- To take into consideration the weights of the company's teams according to their profiles and their expertise by proposing a vector of weighting during the assessment.
- To select the digital initiatives to be prioritized.
- To classify the teams to be grouped according to their degrees of resistance to carry out good change management.
- To ensure an optimization in the actions to be planned in terms of change management.

7 Conclusion

The modeling of uncertainty in an evaluation and decision-making process is necessary to obtain satisfactory and unbiased results that reflect human hesitation more objectively. This paper proposes an analytical approach to handle and analyze imprecise and vague information when various sources of imprecision occur concurrently during an evaluation process. Our approach combines the theoretical concepts of generalized fuzzy hesitant sets, which are useful for dealing with decision-making problems involving fuzzy hesitant information, with Formal Concept Analysis (FCA) theory. The FCA theory is adept at generating potentially valuable groupings based on observations and the classification of vague and imprecise data utilizing the Galois lattice. Our approach is well-suited for situations where decision-makers have uncertainty in various forms and are hesitant between multiple potential memberships.

This proposed approach was modeled for the measurement of the resistance to change of the company's teams in a digital transformation context, we also proposed a weighting of the evaluation degrees of the teams according to their profiles, through the score function used to express the average opinion of the different team members. We also used a threshold binarization technique to generate the concepts determining the optimal grouping of the digital initiatives and the company's teams involved in the digital transformation project. The proposed model is then illustrated with a simple example to prove the accuracy and validity of the methods proposed in this paper.

However, the choice of a particular threshold is a trade-off between loss of data accuracy, loss of data relationships, and increase in context size. In this case, this method excludes teams whose score is lower than the threshold defined in the Galois context, which can be considered a threat to the validity of this work.

The limitations of our approach suggest some research perspectives. There is a need for the development of a repository of digital initiatives that can address resistance to change in a manner that is tailored to the organization's context and scale. The application of our approach on real case studies related to group decision making problems defined with uncertainty, where decision makers will be able to provide their evaluations in different forms using GHFS. And also, the development of a software solution to automate the developed approach and provide decision makers with analytical dashboards to monitor the transformation driven by resistance to change.

References

1. Boulmakoul, A., Khanboubi, F., El karam, B.A., Marghoubi, R.: Distributed Microservices Architecture for Fuzzy Risk-Based Structural Analysis of Resistance to Change in Digital Transformation Practice. In: Braubach, L., Jander, K., Bădică, C. (eds.) Intelligent Distributed Computing XV. IDC 2022. Studies in Computational Intelligence, vol. 1089. Springer, Cham (2023). https://doi.org/10.1007/978-3-031-29104-3_9
2. Wille, R.: Restructuring Lattice Theory: an approach based on hierarchies of concepts. In: Rival, I. (ed.) Ordered Sets. NATO Advanced Study Institutes Series, vol. 83. Springer, Dordrecht (1982). https://doi.org/10.1007/978-94-009-7798-3_15

3. Aswani Kumar, C., Chandra Mouliswaran, S., Amriteya, P., Arun, S.R.: Fuzzy formal concept analysis approach for information retrieval. In: Ravi, V., Panigrahi, B., Das, S., Suganthan, P. (eds.) Proceedings of the Fifth International Conference on Fuzzy and Neuro Computing (FANCCO - 2015). Advances in Intelligent Systems and Computing, vol. 415. Springer, Cham (2015). https://doi.org/10.1007/978-3-319-27212-2_20

4. Wu, X., Wang, J., Shi, L., Gao, Y., Liu, Y.: A fuzzy formal concept analysis-based approach to uncovering spatial hierarchies among vague places extracted from user-generated data. Int. J. Geogr. Inf. Sci. **33**(5), 991–1016 (2019)

5. Rocco, C.M., Hernandez-Perdomo, E., Mun, J.: Introduction to formal concept analysis and its applications in reliability engineering. Reliab. Eng. Syst. Saf. **202**, 107002 (2020)

6. Alwersh, M.: Integration of FCA with Fuzzy logic : a survey. MDT. **11**(5), 373–385 (2021)

7. Torra, V., Narukawa, Y.: On hesitant fuzzy sets and decision. In: 2009 IEEE International Conference on Fuzzy Systems [Internet]. Jeju Island, South Korea: IEEE, pp. 1378–82 (2009) [cited 2022 Dec 25]. http://ieeexplore.ieee.org/document/5276884/

8. Torra, V.: Hesitant fuzzy sets. Int. J. Intell. Syst. **25**(6), 529–539 (2010)

9. Xia, M., Xu, Z.: Hesitant fuzzy information aggregation in decision making. Int. J. Approximate Reasoning **52**(3), 395–407 (2011)

10. Liao, H., Xu, Z.: A VIKOR-based method for hesitant fuzzy multi-criteria decision making. Fuzzy Optim. Decis. Making **12**(4), 373–392 (2013)

11. Qian, G., Wang, H., Feng, X.: Generalized hesitant fuzzy sets and their application in decision support system. Knowl. Based Syst. **37**, 357–365 (2013)

12. Farhadinia, B.: Hesitant fuzzy set lexicographical ordering and its application to multi-attribute decision making. Inf. Sci. **327**, 233–245 (2016)

13. Yang, X., Xu, Z.: Hesitant fuzzy concept lattice and its application. IEEE Access **8**, 59774–59786 (2020)

14. Zou, C., Deng, H.: Using fuzzy concept lattice for intelligent disease diagnosis. IEEE Access **5**, 236–242 (2017)

15. Hao, S., Shi, C., Niu, Z., Cao, L.: Concept coupling learning for improving concept lattice-based document retrieval. Eng. Appl. Artif. Intell. **69**, 65–75 (2018)

16. Martin, T., Majidian, A.: Finding fuzzy concepts for creative knowledge discovery. Int. J. Intell. Syst. **28**(1), 93–114 (2013)

17. Tang, P., Hui, S.C., Fong, A.C.M.: A lattice-based approach for chemical structural retrieval. Eng. Appl. Artif. Intell. **39**, 215–222 (2015)

18. Singh, P.K., Aswani Kumar, C., Gani, A.: A comprehensive survey on formal concept analysis, its research trends and applications. Int. J. Appl. Math. Comput. Sci. **26**(2), 495–516 (2016)

19. De Maio, C., Fenza, G., Gallo, M., Loia, V., Senatore, S.: Formal and relational concept analysis for fuzzy-based automatic semantic annotation. Appl. Intell. **40**(1), 154–177 (2014)

20. Chen, X., Qi, J., Zhu, X., Wang, X., Wang, Z.: Unlabelled text mining methods based on two extension models of concept lattices. Int. J. Mach. Learn Cyber. **11**(2), 475–490 (2020)

21. Sheeba, T., Krishnan, R.: Semantic predictive model of student dynamic profile using fuzzy concept. Procedia Comput. Sci. **132**, 1592–1601 (2018)

22. Jain, S., Seeja, K.R., Jindal, R.: A New methodology for computing semantic relatedness: modified latent semantic analysis by fuzzy formal concept analysis. Procedia Comput. Sci. **167**, 1102–1109 (2020)

23. Liu, P., Cui, H., Cao, Y., Hou, X., Zou, L.: A method of multimedia teaching evaluation based on fuzzy linguistic concept lattice. Multimedia Tools Appl. **78**(21), 30975–31001 (2019)

24. Lyu, H.M., Shen, S.L., Zhou, A., Zhou, W.H.: Data in flood risk assessment of metro systems in a subsiding environment using the interval FAHP–FCA approach. Data Brief **26**, 104468 (2019)

25. Alfakeeh, A., Almalawi, A., Alsolami, F., Abushark, Y., Khan, A., Bahaddad, A., et al.: Hesitant fuzzy-sets based decision-making model for security risk assessment. CMC - Tech Sci. Press **27**(70), 2297–2317 (2021)
26. Raj Mishra, A., Chen, S.M., Rani, P.: Multiattribute decision making based on Fermatean hesitant fuzzy sets and modified VIKOR method. Inf. Sci. **1**(607), 1532–1549 (2022)
27. Zhu, B., Xu, Z., Xia, M.: Dual hesitant fuzzy sets. J. Appl. Math. **2012**, 1–13 (2012)
28. Zerarga, L., Djouadi, Y.: Interval-valued fuzzy extension of formal concept analysis for information retrieval. In: Huang, T., Zeng, Z., Li, C., Leung, C.S. (eds.) Neural Information Processing. ICONIP 2012. Lecture Notes in Computer Science, vol. 7663. Springer, Berlin, Heidelberg (2012). https://doi.org/10.1007/978-3-642-34475-6_73
29. Rodríguez, R., Martinez, L., Herrera, F.: Hesitant fuzzy linguistic term sets for decision making. IEEE Trans. Fuzzy Syst. **1**(20), 109–119 (2012)

Augmented Data Warehouses for Value Capture

Nabila Berkani[1(✉)] and Ladjel Bellatreche[2]

[1] Ecole Nationale Supérieure d'Informatique (ESI), Algiers, Algeria
n_berkani@esi.dz
[2] LIAS/ISAE-ENSMA, Poitiers, France
bellatreche@ensma.fr

Abstract. Nobody can deny the monumental impact of Big Data on Data Warehouse ($\mathcal{DW}$) technology. This impact has been materialized by the spectacular adaptation of Big Data solutions, initially developed to deal with the different Big Data V's (Volume, Variety, Velocity, Veracity), to the context of DW. This gives raise to the concept of augmented DW. The usage of MapReduce and Spark to manage volume, stream processing systems for deploying stream DW, and multimodel DW to handle data variety, are examples of these adaptations. By deeply analyzing these adaptations, we figure out that the V corresponding to Big Data Value did not get the same attention as the other Vs. DWs are built to capture value, otherwise, they will have a marginal utility. One of the major problems of the value capturing in DW concerns the lack of data when performing the warehouse exploration through OLAP queries. This situation is caused by the absence of concepts/hierarchies/instances satisfying these queries in the initial sources used to build the target DW. To increase the utility of a DW in terms of value capture, the selection of alternative resources is recommended. In this paper, we first illustrate the different scenarios requiring concept and data enrichment and focus on the usage of external resources such as Linked Open Data and ontologies to deal with the absence of data. Secondly, we propose a technique to value capturing by revisiting the $\mathcal{DW}$ life cycle phases. Value metrics are given based on the value-capturing requirements. Finally, experiments are conducted to show the effectiveness of our proposal.

1 Introduction

Traditional $\mathcal{DW}$ contributes to collecting, cleaning, and integrating data from diverse sources into a repository for analysis purposes using BI tools such as data mining, OLAP queries, and exploratory techniques. An important characteristic of $\mathcal{DW}$ is its adaptability over time in considering new types of data sources and adapting its models, methods, techniques, methodologies, tools, and platforms to consider the dimensions and the aspects of the new connected world [20] and different V's of Big Data (Volume, Variety, Veracity, and Velocity). The Big Data processing frameworks like MapReduce and Spark have been successfully reused

© The Author(s), under exclusive license to Springer Nature Switzerland AG 2024
M. Tabaa et al. (Eds.): INTIS 2022/2023, CCIS 1728, pp. 168–182, 2024.
https://doi.org/10.1007/978-3-031-47366-1_13

in the context of DW [6] to deal with data volume. Existing stream processing systems such as Apache Kafka have been also reproduced to deploy stream DW^1. The notion of multi-model DW has been used to address the problem of data variety [10]. These reproductions efforts gave rise to the augmented DW [9].

The adaptation efforts from Big Data solutions to DW concern mainly volume, Variety, and Velocity. These efforts ignore an important V of Big Data related to Value. The success of any $\mathcal{DW}$ strongly depends on value capture. Generally speaking, five important pillars are required to make valuable decisions [30]. (1) company's requirement collection and understanding. Several studies showed that 1/3 of $\mathcal{DW}$ projects fail to meet their initial objectives [28]. This is due to the absence of data for timely decision-making and poor project management. (2) Usage of data-enabled solutions. It is important to note that $\mathcal{DW}$ is one of these solutions. It is associated with a well-known life cycle including phases for selecting data sources, extracting, transforming, and loading the data into a repository, and selecting its appropriate deployment infrastructure [18]. (3) The expertise of the studied domain. The true power of any exploitation of the data resident in a $\mathcal{DW}$ can be harnessed only when we have some form of domain knowledge [26]. The recent large body of $\mathcal{DW}$ exploitation tools developed for more specific domains (such as Transportation and Finance)^2 attests the crucial role of domain knowledge in the exploitation tasks. (4) Easy-use and flexible exploration tools. Reaching valuable decisions strongly depends on the OLAP queries performed on $\mathcal{DW}s$. The success of these queries has become a crucial issue for reaching valuable strategic decisions, and the survival of $\mathcal{DW}$ projects. The user has to be able to formulate her/his queries and handle their failures which may directly impact decision-making. (5) The degree of risk when working with data and queries. The risk is usually associated with value [27]. A recent type of risk that companies face regarding $\mathcal{DW}s$ is their augmentation by external resources such as Linked Open Data [22].

In traditional $\mathcal{DW}s$ projects, value capture has been *implicitly* studied without naming it in their exploitation phase. With the explosion of Web data and domain ontologies, a company owning $\mathcal{DW}s$ is either looking to build $\mathcal{DW}$ from ontology-based data sources [2], or to augment its $\mathcal{DW}$ with external semantic sources such as LOD [22] by adding some risk. This situation increases requirement satisfaction and automatically augments value capture. By analyzing the existing studies, we identify that they focus on their internal sources to answer their requirements. Instead of considering only internal sources that are not rich enough to capture valuable data, we focus in this paper, on the external sources that may bring added value. Once identified, we propose a comprehensive and generic methodology that handles this issue by zig-zagging between data sources (semantic $\mathcal{DW}$, global ontology, and Linked Open Data). A set of metrics quantifying this value capture is given.

The rest of the paper is structured as follows. Section 2 presents our related work. In Sect. 3, we present the hints of our proposal associated with a

---

^{1} https://www.alibabacloud.com/blog/599340.

^{2} https://www.cubus.eu/sites/default/files/fileupload/the_bi_survey_17_-_the_results.pdf.

motivating example. Our approach is presented in Sect. 4. An experimental study is conducted in Sect. 5. Section 6 concludes our paper and outlines future work.

2   Related Work

Data Warehouse Design Lifecycle Maturity. The design of traditional $\mathcal{DW}$ passes through two main generations: *traditional* design and *semantic* design. The first generation has been characterized by the presence of a well-defined life cycle [16]: requirements definition, conceptual design, logical design, Extract-Transform-Load (ETL) design, and physical design. The requirements definition phase allows for analyzing user requirements and business processes. The conceptual design phase offers an abstract view of the application and facilitates communication between users and designers. It performs a transformation of the data sources schemes and the user requirements specification into a formalized conceptual multidimensional schema. The formalization results comprise the fact schemata with their related measures and dimension hierarchies. Multidimensional modeling has attracted the attention of several researchers. Most of the conceptual multidimensional models proposed in the literature are similar as demonstrated in [4]. The obtained multidimensional schema is represented using ad hoc models [15], extended ER [21], or UML models [24]. The logical design phase converts the conceptual schema to a logical one with respect to the target logical data model (mostly relational or multidimensional). The logical schemes are generated according to transformation rules and applied with a given algorithm. The ETL phase allows to the extraction of data from sources, it populates the target schema with integrated data. These data have also to be transformed to match the $\mathcal{DW}$ schema [31]. The physical design phase implements $\mathcal{DW}$ system and eventually defines some relevant optimization structures. Figure 1 illustrates the design life cycle phases.

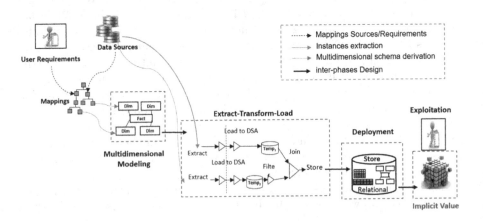

Fig. 1. Data Warehouse Design Lifecycle Maturity

Contrary to the first generation, the semantic design incorporates ontologies in all phases of the life cycle of $\mathcal{DW}$ design [3]: user requirements formalization and semantics elicitation [13,23], the definition of multidimensional concepts (facts and dimensions) [25], the data integration [11] and the automation of ETL process [8,29]. Ontologies have shown their contribution to conceptual design, because of their similarity with conceptual models. They also deal with semantic heterogeneity, considered the main difficulty during the integration process. Nobody can deny the large contribution of ontologies in designing $\mathcal{DW}$ systems requiring one domain ontology, with reduced size of data and few restrictions. However, building $\mathcal{DW}$ only from traditional relational database sources may penalize its value. To deal with the value risk, recent studies proposed augmenting traditional $\mathcal{DW}s$ with external sources such as LOD and knowledge graphs [19].

Data Augmentation/Enrichment. In the context of $\mathcal{DW}s$, the absence of concepts/hierarchies/instances may penalize value capturing. Among the works in the literature, we are interested in those dealing with $\mathcal{DW}$ augmentation by integrating external sources such as LOD. By examining traditional $\mathcal{DW}s$, we realized that they do not fulfill all decision-maker requirements since data sources alimenting a target $\mathcal{DW}$ are not rich enough to capture required knowledge for decision making. External sources (LOD) represent an interesting asset for this purpose [19]. A couple of research efforts have considered LOD in the construction of $\mathcal{DW}s$ [1,12,17]. However, by deeply analyzing studies integrating LOD, we notice that they were not proposed with the spirit to promote the added value that may be brought by LOD. We believe that the LOD environment represents a nice opportunity to be the *elected model*. This situation strongly positively affects the $\mathcal{DW}$ design process with the purpose to create the added *value* for decision-makers.

3   Motivating Example

In this section, we present a motivating example that will be used in our case study. Let us assume the existence of $\mathcal{DW}$ created by the Federal Aviation Administration[3] (FAA) of the United States. Its main role is to regulate all aspects of civil aviation in order to perform analyses of air traffic. Let us consider the existence of a global ontology (GO) atmonto[4] shared by existing internal data sources. The MD schema of $\mathcal{DW}$ was derived from the projection of user requirements on *GO* and populated using real datasets provided by the historical flight data from the U.S. Department of Transportation[5]. Figure 2 presents the MD schema obtained (in a light color).

Example 1. We want to analyze the delays of air transport along the states and cities for the last three years using respectively the dimensions Dim:Geo

---

[3] https://www.faa.gov/.

[4] https://data.nasa.gov/ontologies/atmonto/.

[5] https://www.bts.gov/topics/airlines-and-airports-0.

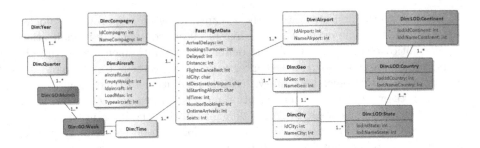

Fig. 2. Multidimensional Schema.

and Dim:Time. To this end, we define a cube, denoted delaySC using a SUM aggregation on delays of the different airports of a city (if many).

The OLAP query Drill-down (delaySC, Dim:Time, month) returns an empty answer. Face such a situation, we propose to the user different services to handle the problem as shown in Fig. 3. They are (1) the $\mathcal{DW}$ augmented by its global ontology GO ($DW\_Augmentation(GO)$) (no risk), and (2) the $\mathcal{DW}$ augmented by the LOD ($DW\_Augmentation(LOD)$) (taking a risk of using external resources). The user has also the ability to compose these services. Figure 3 gives a zigzag options: Z_1 : $DW\_Augmentation(GO)$ and Z_2 : $DW\_Augmentation(GO)$ ∘ $DW\_Augmentation(LOD)$.

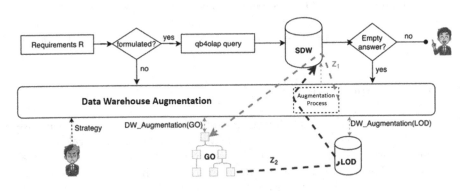

Fig. 3. Data Warehouses Services.

4 $\mathcal{DW}$ Augmentation for Value Capture

In this section, we give an overview of our proposal presented in Fig. 4. Given a set of inputs, namely: (i) a shared global ontology (GO), (ii) an existing internal data source (S_i), and (iii) a set of user requirements ($\mathcal{R}$). We assume that our target $\mathcal{DW}$ is being built based on shared domain ontology and that the set of internal data sources (S_i) considered are semantic sources defined by their local ontologies (LO_i) and instances part. The LO_i references the GO which is annotated with the mappings of those concepts and properties.

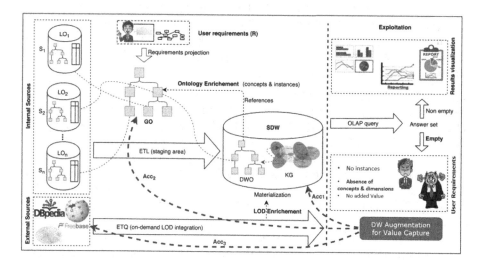

Fig. 4. Our proposal

During the creation of $\mathcal{DW}$ from scratch, requirements are represented using the goal model and projected on the GO to derive the MD schema meeting user needs. In the end, we produce a conceptual, MD schema represented as an ontology, called DWO, annotated with MD concepts. Previous work [5] details the following steps and used algorithms. Once the $\mathcal{DW}$ is built, some new needs may arise which leads to several problems corresponding to two major situations: (1) the expressed OLAP queries return an empty set of answers and (2) the expressed OLAP queries may not be written because of the absence of some MD concepts. All of these situations often affect decision-making, which may be extremely severe with regard to the urgency and importance of quick results. In order to manage these problems, we propose in this work an approach called $\mathcal{DW}$ *Augmentation for Value Capture*. It offers the user two services, that may be combined to achieve the expected solution and thus augment value capture.

4.1 GO Augmented-$\mathcal{DW}$

On the basis of new needs, the user invokes the GO *augmented-$\mathcal{DW}$ service*. The following steps are done:

Requirements Analysis. This step allows to the identification of the relevant concepts and properties according to the user's requirements. This is in order to build a dictionary that will serve to translate his/her needs to a requirement model. As the ontology describes the majority of concepts and properties of a given domain, a projection of requirements on resources (concepts and roles) of the *GO* is done. The most relevant ontological concepts and properties to express requirements are identified. Note that only the new concepts and properties that do not exist in the current MD scheme are kept and used to enrich it. For example, the requirement (Aircraft with the lowest rate of delay at given airports per month and year.) is specified using the following resources of the atmonto ontology (Aircraft, rate, delay, airport, year, and month). Only the (year and month) concepts are retained.

Conceptual Design. The *DWO* (viewed as a conceptual abstraction model of the *DW*) is extended with the concepts/properties identified in the previous step. This is done by extracting the fragment of *GO* corresponding to requirements. Two scenarios are identified: (i) *DWO* ⊂ *GO*: *GO* satisfies all requirements. Here *DWO* is extracted from the *GO* and (ii) *DWO* ⊃ *GO*: *GO* does not fulfill all requirements. The user is informed about the situation. The solution returns the list of unsatisfied requirements and invites the user to choose another service (LOD augmented *DW* or combined services). Afterward, we exploit the automatic reasoning capabilities to correct all inconsistencies of *DWO*. Then, we identify the multidimensional structure of the *DW* model where we consider fact concepts as central concepts and dimensions as concepts influencing them. The proposed algorithm in [7] is used to annotate the *DWO* with MD concepts annotations. Figure 2 illustrates the MD schema obtained where *year* and *month* dimensions are derived from *GO*.

Logical and Physical Design. This step enables to derive the logical *DW* model by translating the *DWO* to RDF logical model. Several works in the literature proposed methods for translating ontologies described in a given formalism (PLIB, OWL, RDF). Here, the logical model becomes the RDF data model that covers many of the MD components which could be expressed by: QB, QB4OLAP, or IGOLAP vocabularies. The RDF QB is the current W3C standard. The QB4OLAP vocabulary is the extension of QB that allows implementing of the main OLAP operations, such as rollup, slice, and dice, using standard SPARQL queries. We adopt the QB4OLAP vocabulary where two sets of RDF triples are derived: (i) *cube schema* that defines the structure of the cube, in terms of dimension levels, measures, and hierarchies, and (ii) *cube instances* that defines level members, facts and measured values. These meta-data are used to automatically produce SPARQL queries that implement OLAP operations as defined in [14]. Once triple cubes are defined they are deployed on the current *DW* according to the physical storage.

ETL Process. Since the *DW* is operational and keeps integrating data from internal data sources. The ETL process is enriched and consolidated using jobs implemented according to the new MD schema and requirements. We formalize the problem of consolidation as follows: (i) Current flow: existing ETL flows satisfying the n current information requirements at time t and (ii) New flow (jobs): ETL flow satisfying the upcoming requirement at $t+1$. A new ETL flow is derived by synchronizing both flows. Using operations commonly encountered in workflow management: (i) AND-Join: identify both ETL flows, apply potential deadlocks, and perform the join operation between concepts, (ii) OR-Join: corresponds to a merger operation of concepts and properties done using Merge operator and (iii) Clean: performs a data cleaning, checks null values and deletes duplicate data before loading in the target $\mathcal{DW}$.

4.2   On-Demand $\mathcal{DW}$ Augmentation

In order to explicit value capture, we offer a service that allows satisfying new needs by integrating LOD sources. This service incurs risk as to the quality and availability of external sources. Note that the amount of MD data published is constantly increasing, due to initiatives such as Open Data and Open Government Data, among others ones. Our aim is to integrate statistical Linked Data (LOSD) using common OLAP operations defined with QB4OLAP vocabulary.

OLAP Queries Derivation. Usually, the ETL process loads all available data in the $\mathcal{DW}$ before the user starts querying them. In some cases, this may be impossible especially when this process does not ensure the availability of required data since they are not found in the data sources. The alternative investigated in this paper is fetching and storing data once new requirements arise during the analysis process. These requirements are translated into OLAP queries using QB4OLAP vocabulary. This is the only effort provided by the user since he/she has to write the OLAP query on the LOD dataset.

Discover and Pre-process LOD Cube. In order to feed an MD cube, *On-demand LOD augmented $\mathcal{DW}$ service* fetch facts and dimensions from LOD, and load them into the cube only when they are needed to answer some OLAP queries. QB4OLAP metadata helps the user to browse statistical LOD and discover the fragment satisfying his/her requirements. Useful concepts/instances about a Cube can be found by resolving URIs of entities related to the Cube. OLAP queries are executed to extract the LOD fragment where classes and properties of QB4OLAP vocabulary are used to derive the LOD Cube. For instance, to fetch the cube that contains Facts and their statistical data, the qb:Observation and qb:DataSet classes liked via the property qb:dataset are extracted and their instances. Similarly for observations linked to a member dimension via the class qb:DimensionProperty and associated to measure values via the class qb:MeasureProperty. As a result, the LOD cube is extracted in the form of a virtual cube where URIs are identified and then used to integrate them in the $\mathcal{DW}$ cube.

Suppose a new requirement arises (delay of Flights by city and state and country) that may become a problem since the data cube lacks the dimensions state and country. Here, the user invokes the service and selects the LOD fragment (Geo statistical LOD[6]). The following QB4OLAP query is used to derive the LOD cube.

---

[6] http://statistics.data.gov.uk/home.

```
## Data structure definition and dimensions
dw:Flight a qb:DataStructureDefinition ;
rdf:type dw:geo .
## Dimensions
qb:component qb:dimension dw:city .
qb:component qb:dimension dw:lod:state .
qb:component qb:dimension dw:lod:country .
## Definition of measures
qb:component qb:measure dw:Runtime .
## Attributes
qb:component qb:attribute dw:Flight
```

QETL Process for Augmented $\mathcal{DW}$. QB4OLAP allows operation over already published observations without the need of rewriting the existing one. Note that in a typical MD schema, observations are the largest part of the data while dimensions are usually orders of magnitude smaller. Thus, we avoid rewriting the observations and we enrich the existing cube with MD concepts (dimensions, hierarchies ...) and their instances. The following algorithm describes the Query ETL process that feeds an MD cube with statistical LOD fragment using the QB4OLAP vocabulary.

4.3 Value Metrics for $\mathcal{DW}$ Augmentation

In this section, we describe the metrics that we use to evaluate the proposed approach. Our ultimate goal is to evaluate value capture by augmented $\mathcal{DW}$ and show the effectiveness of our proposal. For that reason, we propose three metrics that measure: (i) satisfied/unsatisfied user requirements, (ii) availability of analysis axes for the expression of OLAP queries, and (iii) rate of available instances in augmented $\mathcal{DW}$. It should be mentioned that the value capture metric is a percentage belonging to the interval $[0, 1]$, where the metric value approaches 1 is the best case (increase value), and 1 in the worst (decrease value).

Requirement Satisfaction. Our predominant evaluation metric is requirement satisfaction. This metric tells us how well, the rate of satisfied OLAP queries makes value increase.

$$ValueReq(DW) = \frac{NumberUnsatisfiedReq(DW)}{NumberAllReq(DW)} \tag{1}$$

Where $NumberUnsatisfiedReq(DW)$ indicates the number of unsatisfied requirements on $\mathcal{DW}$ and $NumberAllReq(DW)$ represents the number of all requirements expressed on the target $\mathcal{DW}$. Value approaches 1 is the best case where value is increased.

Algorithm 1. the QETL process for LOD augmented DW.

Input: Current DW_{cube}, Set of user requirements R
Output: Target LOD DW_cube Augmented
Require: d: dimension, hl : hierarchy level, lm level member, f: fact, m: measure;
1: R formulated as an OLAP queries Q_{OLAP} using qb4olap vocabulary;
2: $cube_{LOD} = \emptyset$;
3: **for all** (Q_{OLAP}) **do**
4:    $cube_{LOD} = $ Discover(qb4olap.Q_{OLAP});
5: **end for**
6: **for all** dimensions ?d $\subset$ (?d a qb:DimensionProperty)$_{LOD}$ **do**
7:    Create new dimension d in DW_{cube} where d $\subset$ (?d a qb:DimensionProperty)$_{LOD}$;

8:    **for all** Hierarchy levels hl $\subset$ (?hl a qb4o:LevelProperty)$_{LOD}$ **do**
9:        AddTriples$_{DW}$ (?hl a qb4o:LevelProperty) and (?hl qb4o:inDimension ?d);
10:       AddTriple$_{DW}$ (?lm qb4o:inLevel ?hl) to dimension d;
11:       **for all** (li , lj) $\in$ hl of (qb4o:hasHierarchy ?hl)$_{LOD}$ and (li $\rightarrow$ lj) **do**
12:           AddTriple$_{DW}$ (li qb:parentLevel lj) to dimension d;
13:       **end for**
14:    **end for**
15: **end for**
16: **for all** measure m : (?f qb:component [qb:measure ?m])$_{LOD}$ and ?f $\in DW_{cube}$ **do**
17:    AddTriple$_{DW}$ (?f qb:component [qb:measure m; qb:hasAggregateFunction qb4o:AggFun]);
18: **end for**

Source Self-efficacy. Value is not only related to requirements satisfaction but may be correlated to the $\mathcal{DW}$ environment, such as data sources. Here we measure the efficacy of a data source in increasing/decreasing the value by evaluating provided instances to satisfy requirements. This is crucial in selecting external sources. Metric value approaches 1 is the best case.

$$ValueData(S_i) = \frac{NumberIntegInstances(S_i)}{NumberTotalInstances(DW)} \tag{2}$$

Where $NumberIntegInstances(S_i)$ and $NumberTotalInstances(DW)$ represent the number of instances of $\mathcal{DW}$ by integrating the source S_i and the total number of instances of the $\mathcal{DW}$.

Availability of Analysis Axes. This metric is strongly related to MD concepts provided by sources. This information provides some hints to the user about the choice of external sources to be queried. It measures the percentage of comfort provided by the source in terms of MD concepts integrated.

$$ValueAnalysis(S_i) = \frac{Number\_Concepts(S_i)}{TotalNumber\_Concepts(DW)} \tag{3}$$

Where $Number\_Concepts(S_i)$ is the number of MD concepts of the DW schema by integrating the source S_i and $TotalNumber\_Concepts(DW)$) describes the total number of MD concepts of $\mathcal{DW}$.

5   Experiments

In this section, we carry out a set of experiments to show the effectiveness of our proposal in terms of user requirement satisfaction (OLAP query answers) and value capture by $\mathcal{DW}$ augmentation.

5.1   Experimental Setup

Let's consider the case study presented in our motivating example. Our $\mathcal{DW}$ used for analyzing Air Traffic was created by the integration of four internal data sources relating to US Airlines and implemented on Oracle semantic DBMS using N-Triple format. We considered statistical LOD of Air Traffic[7] and Statistical Linked Geo Data[8] as external LOD sources. We also considered a set of (17) analytical requirements collected from NASA Benchmark queries (e.g. The carrier with the lowest rate of delay at given airports.). Figure 2 illustrates the MD schema obtained. We run the experiment on an HP ProLiant DL385 server Gen10 Intel Xeon E5-2620V3(2.4 GHz) with 16 cores and 128 GB of RAM. All components were implemented in Java. The Jena 2.13.0 library is used to manipulate RDF. QB and QB4OLAP graphs are stored and run on Triple store Virtuoso 7.

5.2   Obtained Results

In this section, we describe the obtained results.

Query Response Cases. In this evaluation, we aim to show the importance of our study in a real case. The evaluation was conducted on $\mathcal{DW}$ integrating internal sources where the analyst starts to write the queries (set of 17 analytical requirements). She/he notices that a set of queries cannot be written with the current $\mathcal{DW}$ schema. Among those written, some have an empty answer. Table 1 describes the rate according to each case. Finding, over time, the new requirement corresponds to more than half of the requirements already met.

Table 1. Query response Cases

Cases	Positive Answer	Empty Answer	Impossible to write
Rate of queries	41%	24%	35%

---

[7] https://catalog.data.gov/dataset/air-traffic-passenger-statistics.
[8] http://statistics.data.gov.uk/home.

Value Capture Evaluation. The second evaluation was conducted on the basis of the same sample of queries, in particular, the 9 unanswered ones. We have invoked the $\mathcal{DW}$ augmentation services on different versions of the $\mathcal{DW}$ (Internal sources, GO augmented, and LOD augmented). The execution of the OLAP queries was carried out in four-time stages (t0, t1, t2, and t3) to estimate the rate of requirement satisfaction. Recall that relationship between unmet requirements and value capture is an inverse one where a high rate of requirement unsatisfaction corresponds to a decrease in Value Capture. Figure 5b illustrates the rates of unmet requirements obtained. We notice that as the augmentation process progresses, unmet requirements decrease because the availability of MD concepts and instances can satisfy the needs which means increased Value Capture.

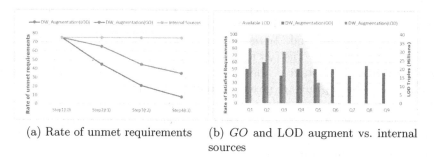

(a) Rate of unmet requirements   (b) *GO* and LOD augment vs. internal sources

Fig. 5. Value Capture Evaluation.

Assume that LOD was accessible at the beginning. From the Q5 query, a network problem occurred and LOD became inaccessible. Figure 5 describes the results obtained. We can notice that the LOD augmented approach provides good results for Q1–Q4 queries (high rate of satisfied requirements which means Value Capture has significantly increased). However, the absence of LOD has resulted in a high decrease in value. Finding, each solution could satisfy all/some requirements according to the environment. The user has to choose his/her most relevant solution for the decision-making process.

Table 2 provides more details about obtained results. Value Capture is calculated according to user requirements satisfaction. It clearly indicates that the consideration of LOD brings some comfort in decision-making in terms of the final number of dimensions (Dim) and measures (Meas) and rates of satisfied requirements. Having comfort actually augments Value Capture.

Table 2. Value Capture Evaluation

Augmentation Services	Dim/Meas	Input Size	Rate needs	Value Capture
Internal Sources	6/1	550×10^3	45%	35%
GO Augmented-DW	8/4	4.1×10^5	65%	48%
LOD Augmented-DW	12/8	2.9×10^6	92%	65%

6　Conclusion

In this paper, we attempt to federate the $\mathcal{DW}$ research community around the crucial problem that touches decision-makers in their day-to-day work live representing the Value Capture and its impact on decision-making. To study this problem, we consider the case of augmented semantic $\mathcal{DW}$. This augmentation is performed by considering internal and external resources. Due to the originality of our proposal, we propose a motivating example related to aviation analysis to illustrate our main ideas. We claim that to deal with Value Capture, a *deep understanding* of the environment of the studied $\mathcal{DW}$ (an augmented semantic $\mathcal{DW}$ in this proposal) is required. Understanding this environment contributes to defining an extended Common Warehouse Model including all elements of an augmented semantic DW. To increase a $\mathcal{DW}$ Value Capture, different services are proposed: (1) semantic $\mathcal{DW}$ augmentation by the global ontology GO owed by a company (no risk) and (2) semantic $\mathcal{DW}$ augmentation by the LOD (taking an externalization risk). The fact that the augmentation brings new multidimensional patterns and instances, the value of the $\mathcal{DW}$ augments. Various metrics quantifying value capture are given. A proof of concept is given.

Actually, we are developing a tool supporting our augmentation approach, and defining other metrics issued from real scenarios. We are also envisaging to move beyond relational DBMSs, by exploring non-relational big data systems to manage the integration of external sources.

References

1. Abelló, A., Gallinucci, E., Golfarelli, M., Rizzi Bach, S., Romero Moral, O.: Towards exploratory OLAP on linked data. In: SEBD, pp. 86–93 (2016)
2. Abelló, A., et al.: Using semantic web technologies for exploratory OLAP: a survey. IEEE Trans. Knowl. Data Eng. **27**(2), 571–588 (2015)
3. Abelló, A., Romero, O., Pedersen, T.B., Llavori, R.B., Nebot, V., Cabo, M.J.A., Simitsis, A.: Using semantic web technologies for exploratory OLAP: a survey. IEEE TKDE **27**(2), 571–588 (2015)
4. Abelló, A., Samos, J., Saltor, F.: YAM^2: a multidimensional conceptual model extending UML. Inf. Syst. **31**(6), 541–567 (2006)
5. Bellatreche, L., Khouri, S., Berkani, N.: Semantic data warehouse design: from ETL to deployment à la carte. In: DASFAA, pp. 64–83 (2013)
6. Benkrid, S., Bellatreche, L., Mestoui, Y., Ordonez, C.: PROADAPT: proactive framework for adaptive partitioning for big data warehouses. Data Knowl. Eng. **142**, 102102 (2022)
7. Berkani, N., Bellatreche, L., Benatallah, B.: A value-added approach to design BI applications. In: Madria, S., Hara, T. (eds.) DaWaK 2016. LNCS, vol. 9829, pp. 361–375. Springer, Cham (2016). https://doi.org/10.1007/978-3-319-43946-4_24
8. Berkani, N., Bellatreche, L., Khouri, S.: Towards a conceptualization of ETL and physical storage of semantic data warehouses as a service. Clust. Comput. **16**(4), 915–931 (2013)
9. Berkani, N., Bellatreche, L., Khouri, S., Ordonez, C.: The contribution of linked open data to augment a traditional data warehouse. J. Intell. Inf. Syst. **55**(3), 397–421 (2020)

10. Bimonte, S., Gallinucci, E., Marcel, P., Rizzi, S.: Data variety, come as you are in multi-model data warehouses. Inf. Syst. **104**, 101734 (2022)
11. Calvanese, D., Lenzerini, M., Nardi, D.: Description logics for conceptual data modeling. In: Chomicki, J., Saake, G. (eds.) Logics for Databases and Information Systems. The Springer International Series in Engineering and Computer Science, vol. 436, pp. 229–263. Springer, Boston (1998). https://doi.org/10.1007/978-1-4615-5643-5_8
12. Deb Nath, R.P., Hose, K., Pedersen, T.B.: Towards a programmable semantic extract-transform-load framework for semantic data warehouses. In: DOLAP, pp. 15–24 (2015)
13. Djilani, Z., Khouri, S.: Understanding user requirements iceberg: semantic based approach. In: Proceedings of the 5th International Conference on Model and Data Engineering (MEDI), pp. 297–310 (2015)
14. Etcheverry, L., Vaisman, A.A.: QB4OLAP: a new vocabulary for OLAP cubes on the semantic web. In: CLOD, vol. 905, pp. 27–38 (2012)
15. Golfarelli, M., Maio, D., Rizzi, S.: The dimensional fact model: a conceptual model for data warehouses. Int. J. Coop. Inf. Syst. **7**(2–3), 215–247 (1998)
16. Golfarelli, M., Rizzi, S.: A survey on temporal data warehousing. Int. J. Data Warehouse. Min. (IJDWM) **5**(1), 1–17 (2009)
17. Kämpgen, B., O'Riain, S., Harth, A.: Interacting with statistical linked data via OLAP operations. In: Simperl, E., et al. (eds.) ESWC 2012. LNCS, vol. 7540, pp. 87–101. Springer, Heidelberg (2015). https://doi.org/10.1007/978-3-662-46641-4_7
18. Khouri, S., Semassel, K., Bellatreche, L.: Managing data warehouse traceability: a life-cycle driven approach. In: Zdravkovic, J., Kirikova, M., Johannesson, P. (eds.) CAiSE 2015. LNCS, vol. 9097, pp. 199–213. Springer, Cham (2015). https://doi.org/10.1007/978-3-319-19069-3_13
19. Konstantinou, N., et al.: The VADA architecture for cost-effective data wrangling. In: SIGMOD, pp. 1599–1602 (2017)
20. Meehan, J., Aslantas, C., Zdonik, S., Tatbul, N., Du, J.: Data ingestion for the connected world. In: CIDR (2017)
21. Moody, D.L., Kortink, M.A.: From enterprise models to dimensional models: a methodology for data warehouse and data mart design. In: DMDW, p. 5 (2000)
22. Nebot, V., Berlanga, R.: Statistically-driven generation of multidimensional analytical schemas from linked data. Knowl. Based Syst. **110**, 15–29 (2016)
23. Nebot, V., Llavori, R.B.: Building data warehouses with semantic web data. Decis. Support Syst. **52**(4), 853–868 (2012)
24. Prat, N., Akoka, J., Comyn-Wattiau, I.: A UML-based data warehouse design method. Decis. Support Syst. **42**(3), 1449–1473 (2006)
25. Romero, O., Simitsis, A., Abelló, A.: *GEM*: requirement-driven generation of ETL and multidimensional conceptual designs. In: Cuzzocrea, A., Dayal, U. (eds.) DaWaK 2011. LNCS, vol. 6862, pp. 80–95. Springer, Heidelberg (2011). https://doi.org/10.1007/978-3-642-23544-3_7
26. Salakhutdinov, R.: Integrating domain-knowledge into deep learning. In: SIGKDD, p. 3176 (2019)
27. Sales, T.P., Baião, F., Guizzardi, G., Almeida, J.P.A., Guarino, N., Mylopoulos, J.: The common ontology of value and risk. In: Trujillo, J.C., et al. (eds.) ER 2018. LNCS, vol. 11157, pp. 121–135. Springer, Cham (2018). https://doi.org/10.1007/978-3-030-00847-5_11
28. Salinesi, C., Gam, I.: A requirement-driven approach for designing data warehouses. In: REFSQ (2006)

29. Simitsis, A., Skoutas, D., Castellanos, M.: Natural language reporting for ETL processes. In: ACM DOLAP, pp. 65–72 (2008)
30. Urbinati, A., Bogers, M., Chiesa, V., Frattini, F.: Creating and capturing value from big data: a multiple-case study analysis of provider companies. Technovation **84**, 21–36 (2019)
31. Vassiliadis, P.: A survey of extract-transform-load technology. IJDWM **5**(3), 1–27 (2009)

A Parallel Processing Architecture for Querying Distributed and Heterogeneous Data Sources

Ahmed Rabhi$^{(\boxtimes)}$ and Rachida Fissoune

Data Engineering and system Team (IDS) - National School of Applied Sciences, Abdelmalek Essaadi University, Tangier, Morocco
`ahmed.rabhi@etu.uae.ac.ma`, `rfissoune@uae.ac.ma`

Abstract. Collecting information from distributed data sources in the web of data is a topic of great interest since the number of data sources is eloquently increasing. The general objective of our work is to set up an aggregated search engine able to integrate an answer for a SPARQL query, and this, by collecting data from web accessible data sources alongside local databases via a single query interface. Runtime optimization is an essential task in such search engines, for this purpose, we present a general view on different processing steps in aggregated search engines to highlight the costliest step in terms of runtime, then, we propose an efficient parallel processing architecture to optimize runtime. The proposed parallel processing architecture allows collecting intermediate results from each data source independently, thus, this architecture supports answers integration from heterogeneous data sources, in this context, we present the ontology-based data access paradigm and its importance to query heterogeneous data sources in our aggregated search engine.

Keywords: Aggregated search · SPARQL · Distributed queries · Heterogeneous datasets · OBDA

1 Introduction

Optimizing runtime is a crucial goal in aggregated search engines, it is necessary to adopt a solution allowing to minimize the waiting time to the user and to return results in an optimal duration. The work of this paper is the enhancement of our last work [1], our main goal is designing and setting up a search system that is able to answer a SPARQL query by aggregating intermediate data from independent and heterogeneous data sources. Therefore, runtime optimization is a major focus in our work, besides, the system must collect pieces of data from each source independently to enrich the variety of collected data. We propose in this paper a parallel processing architecture to minimize runtime in our aggregated search system, this architecture is based on multithreading so that the execution will be carried out in a parallel way using several threads.

© The Author(s), under exclusive license to Springer Nature Switzerland AG 2024
M. Tabaa et al. (Eds.): INTIS 2022/2023, CCIS 1728, pp. 183–194, 2024.
https://doi.org/10.1007/978-3-031-47366-1_14

This paper presents our proposed architecture for parallel processing in our aggregated search system. First, we present a general view on query execution's workflow in our system to highlight the sequence of tasks, and to identify phases that must be executed parallelly. Then, we present our parallelized architecture, the aim of this architecture is to optimize runtime, besides, this architecture improves the intermediate data collection phase by considering the heterogeneity of data sources.

Additionally, we present the usefulness of "ontology-based data access" paradigm to query heterogeneous data. Indeed, since our objective is to design a system allowing querying heterogeneous data sources, we propose to adopt the paradigm named *"ontology-based data access"* (OBDA) so that the system can collect intermediate data from heterogeneous data sources (data sources of different formats). Beside, the parallel processing architecture plays a key role to optimize the heterogeneous data collection phase seen the complexity of the process.

The rest of this paper is organized as follows: Sect. 2 presents related work. In Sect. 3, we present our proposed parallel processing architecture for our system. We present in Sect. 4 the usefulness and importance of Ontology-Based Data Access in our system to allow querying heterogeneous data. Section 4 presents experimental evaluation to test the efficacy of efficiency of the parallel processing architecture in terms of runtime optimization and intermediate data collection. Finally, we present a conclusion of this work in Sect. 5.

2   Related Work

According to S. Sushmita et al. [2], aggregated search is an approach allowing access to distributed information which aims is producing responses to queries by collecting pieces of data from separate sources and creating associations between them to generate a complete answer. G. Echbarthi and H. Kheddouci [3] proposed a solution for aggregated search called LaSaS allowing the user to query multiple RDF graphs without needing to know the structure of datasets.

Many solutions exist to look for response to a SPARQL query in independent data sources of the web of data. DARQ [4] is a federated search engine providing access to multiple SPARQL endpoints to respond to a query transparently, according to the authors, independence of data sources usually leads to significant network traffic overhead. Saleem et al. [5] presented a solution that is based on indexing to optimise runtime in federated SPARQL queries, their proposed solution uses statistics about sources quality and yield to set up an execution plan. Indeed, referring to sources statistics is a strategy used by many aggregate search systems to minimize execution time. Among these systems, we cite Avalanche [7] and SPLENDID [6].

X. Wang et al. [8] affirm that by adopting a parallel processing architeture aggregated search systems can improve the exploitation of the potential to connect to multiple SPARQL endpoints which may optimize runtime during data collection. A. Schätzle et al. [9] propose a solution based on data partitioning, their system query large-scale RDF data based on Hadoop technologies to return real-time answers for a SPARQL query. The solution presented by M. Hassan et al. [10] aims to minimize execution time in distributed queries and this by adopting a relational partitioning strategy for RDF data. PRoST is a solution proposed by M. Cossu et al. [11] to optimize RDF data access in aggregated search, Their solution involves partitioning partitioning RDF data using Apache Spark.

Ontology-Based Data Access (OBDA) is an approach allowing access to data by providing a conceptual layer (T. Bagosi et al. [12]). According to E. Kharlamov et al. [13] thanks to OBDA aproach, users can query multiple data sources via a single conceptual view, it then allows the integration of data of different structures and formats. Hence, the major feature of OBDA is answering a query by integrating heterogeneous databases. The basis of idea of this paradigm is using an ontology that represents the mediator between the queried databases and the user. According to F. Baader et al. [14] the ontology layer in OBDA systems describes the knowledge that can be extracted from databases as well as the domain and vocabulary needed to reformulate queries. Thus, the user will be able to get semantic access to the databases of his interest, as cited by M. R. Kogalovsky [15]. According to D. Calvanese et al. [16], thanks to this paradigm, the user should only know the structure of the ontology layer in order to look for an information over multiple databases without needing to know the precise location of the data. As asserted by G. De Giacomo et al. [17], an important advantage of OBDA paradigm ensuring the independence between data layer and the ontology layer, communication between the two layers is done using a mapping mappings.

3   A Parallel Processing Architecture for Aggregated Search in the Web of Data

In our system, the process of a query goes through for main of steps that are query preparing, execution planning, clusters execution and results preparing. The graph in Fig. 1 presents an overview on the succession of tasks to process a SPARQL query, according to this graph, sub-queries clusters can be executed independently since each cluster is intended to be run in a different data source, the system creates a cluster that contains a set of sub-queries for each data source (see our previous article [18] for more details), thus, the clusters execution phase is candidate to be executed in a parallel architecture. In the next part we evaluate runtime in each step phase to identify the step that worth to be optimized.

Figure 2 is a histogram showing the variation in terms of runtime for each step of the process. By observing the results, we notice that the runtime of query preparing is negligible, it represents 0.079% of the global runtime. The execution planning step and the results processing step cannot be executed in parallel, moreover, these two steps are not too expensive compared to the global runtime. Consequently, according to these observations, we obviously deduce that the greediest step in terms of runtime is "clusters execution".

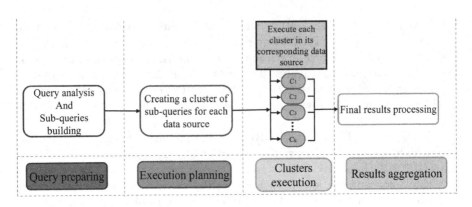

Fig. 1. Overview on the process workflow and the synchronization between tasks

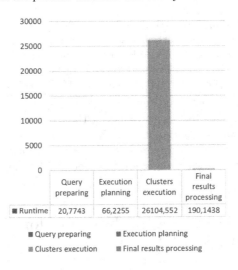

	Query preparing	Execution planning	Clusters execution	Final results processing
■ Runtime	20,7743	66,2255	26104,552	190,1438

■ Query preparing   ■ Execution planning
■ Clusters execution   ■ Final results processing

Fig. 2. The distribution of runtime over steps of the process in (ms)

According to this study, we propose an architecture that focuses on clusters execution steps, the main idea of this architecture is based on multithreading where the system executes clusters parallelly. Multithreading allows executing several tasks parallelly where each task is executed via a set of threads that we call thread pool.

As illustrated in Fig. 3, the parallel processing architecture of our system contains two levels of parallelization, the first level allows the system to connect with several data sources in parallel. The second level allows several sub-queries to be executed in a parallel way.

In this work we focus on two advantages of this parallel processing architecture: optimize execution time and ensure independence between sub-queries during their execution. In fact, the second level of parallelization consists in collecting the necessary intermediate data for each sub-query independently of the other sub-queries, thus, this architecture enriches the diversity of intermediate results which increases the chance of finding the answer to the user's query even if the data sources are of different formats and structures.

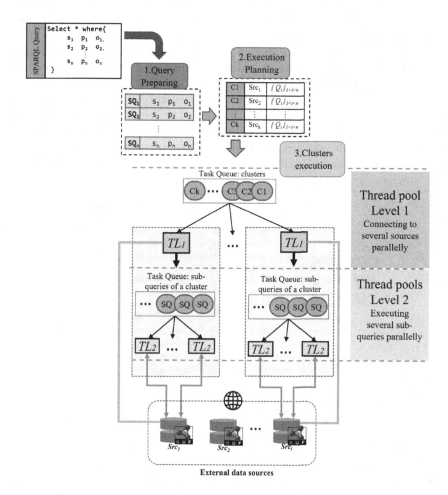

Fig. 3. System architecture using the parallel processing solution

4   Querying Heterogeneous Sources with Our Search Engine

Besides integrating information from distributed data sources, our system is designed to be able to integrate information from heterogeneous data sources. In fact, one of the main objectives of this work is to query data sources with different data formats via a single SPARQL query interface. For this purpose, we introduce the paradigm named"Ontology-based data access (OBDA)".

The ontology-based data access paradigm (OBDA) is adopted to enrich querying data having different formats and structures through an ontology, this ontology presents a semantic structure of the data as well as a vocabulary describing the different concepts provided by data sources and the relationships between these concepts. Thus, the OBDA makes it possible to query several distributed and heterogeneous sources (having different formats) via a single SPARQL query interface providing a unified view of these data sources. Hence, thanks to OBDA, our system can use data on the web of data and integrate it with a local database. The basic structure of an OBDA system is illustrated in Fig. 4, it is composed of three layers, the ontology layer presents the semantic structure of heterogeneous data source, the data layer contains different data sources with different formats, finally, the mapping layer rewrites SPARQL queries to make them compatible with the different data sources' format.

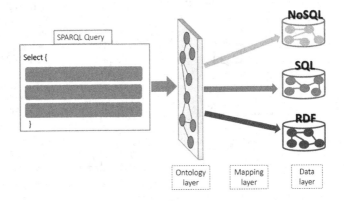

Fig. 4. Example of an OBDA system's architecture

To explain the need of this paradigm in our work, we rely on an example, where we use two external RDF datasets and a local SQL database. The two RDF datasets that are accessible via SPARQL endpoints in the web, the first dataset contains musical data about artists and songs [19], the second data set is GeoNames that contains geographical data (areas of country, population, etc.,) [20], the content of these two datasets is briefly described in Table 1, the local database used in this example is an SQL database containing data about members of a certain laboratory, a short description of the database is presented in Table 1. Assuming that we want to look for the following information: "the musical groups having the same origins of the members of our laboratory, as well as the location of their countries of origin", according to each dataset's content, this information can only be found if we decompose it into three parts and look for each one in a different data source (see Fig. 5).

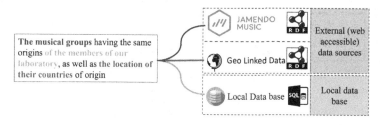

Fig. 5. Example of a query that needs collecting data from external RDF data sources alongside a local database

Table 1. Short description of data sources' content

Data source	Local	External	Format	Description
Jamendo		X	RDF	Is an open access RDF data source that contains general information about musical artists as their cities, their music genre...
GeoNames		X	RDF	Is an open access RDF data source that contains geographic information about cities and countries as their localisation, area...
Our Data base	X		SQL	Is a local SQL data base that contains information about members of a research laboratory

Our objective is to design a solution for our system to be able to collect data from web accessible RDF data sources and local database via a single SPARQL query interface, since our system already processes SPARQL queries over distributed data sources, then, it is theoretically enough to set up an OBDA system for the local SQL database so that we can query it with SPARQL, in fact, the ontology layer of the OBDA system recognizes SPARQL queries, thus, thanks to the OBDA paradigm, our aggregated search system will consider the SQL database as a local data source allowing SPARQL queries alongside external SPARQL endpoints (Fig. 6), and using the parallel processing architecture (presented in previous section), the system creates a thread pool level 1 to be in charge of the connection with the local database as if it was an external SPARQL endpoint, this parallel processing architecture also ensures independence between data sources and the local database during the execution. Therefore, our system will be able to integrate information from heterogeneous data sources.

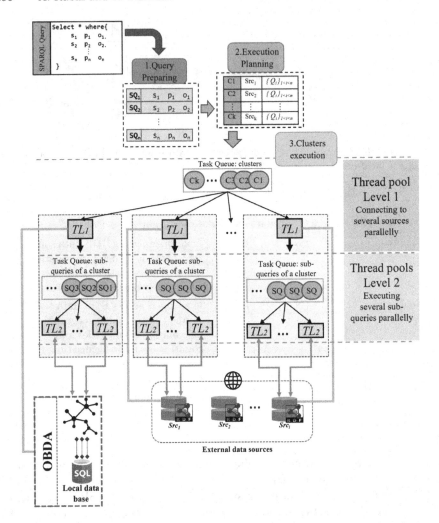

Fig. 6. The usefulness of OBDA to query heterogeneous data sources with our system

5   Demonstration and Results

In this section we present a demonstration of the efficiency of our system to integrate a local database with external RDF data sources of the web of data.

5.1   Data Sources and the Query

Datasets: In this experiment, we evaluated the efficiency of our solution using three RDF datasets that are available on the web and accessible via SPARQL Endpoints (see Table 2) and a local SQL database whose relational schema is shown in Fig. 7.

Table 2. The RDF data sources used

Datasource	Endpoint URL
Jamendo	http://dbtune.org/jamendo/sparql/
GeoNames	http://linkeddata.fh-htwchur.ch/lodestar/sparql/

To summarize the content of our local database, it allows to manage the researchers in a laboratory, the projects to which they are assigned, the material used in each project and the technicians responsible for the maintenance of each equipment. For the evaluation, we focus on the "hometown" (see Fig. 7) attribute of the researcher table, this attribute designates the original city of researchers in our laboratory.

We have created an ontology equivalent to the relational schema presented in Fig. 7, this ontology describes the concepts extracted from our local database, Fig. 8 describes the 4 classes of the ontology as well as data properties and object properties of each class.

The Query: We used the SPARQL query in Fig. 9 to evaluate and demonstrate the efficiency of our system to integrate data from heterogeneous data sources. This query looks for "The musical artists whose city is the hometown of researchers of our laboratory who are involved in projects, as well as the location of their cities". This query requires aggregating data from *Jamendo* and *GeoNames* data sources besides our local database.

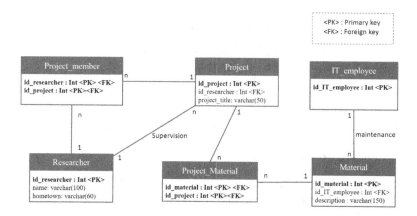

Fig. 7. Tables and Relationships our relational laboratory database

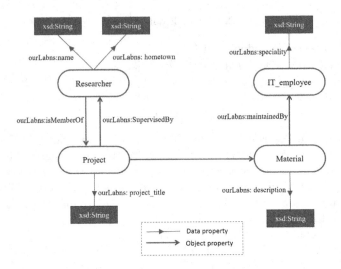

Fig. 8. Ontology generated from the relational schema of our local database

```
PREFIX foaf: <http://xmlns.com/foaf/0.1/>
PREFIX geonames:<http://www.geonames.org/ontology#>
PREFIX wgs: <http://www.w3.org/2003/01/geo/wgs84_pos#>
PREFIX mo:<http://purl.org/ontology/mo/>
PREFIX ourLabns: <http://localhost/ourLabDB#>
SELECT   ?cityName ?member   ?an ?lat ?long
WHERE
{
        ?a a mo:MusicArtist.
        ?a   foaf:based_near ?place.              ├ Jamendo
        ?a   foaf:name ?an.
        ?place     geonames:name ?cityName.
        ?place   wgs:lat ?lat.                     ├ GeoNames
        ?place   wgs:long ?long.
        ?member    ourLabns:isMemberOf   ?project. ├ Our Database
        ?member    ourLabns:hometown  ?cityName.
}
```

Fig. 9. Query for the simulation

5.2   Execution Results

As illustrated in the Fig. 9 The first three triple patterns of the query are found in Jamendo, the next three are found in Geonames and the last two triple patterns are executed on our ontology presented in Fig. 8.

After executing triple patterns and collecting the necessary intermediate results for the query from each data source, our system integrated data into a final answer and the results are presented in Table 3, the table shows the URI of the found member, the name of the artist as well as the information sought on the city.

Table 3. Results of the query

cityName	member	an	lat	long
Kanton Aargau	ourLabns:resPedro	Zerfall	47.39557	8.17214

6 Conclusion

We presented in this paper our system as a solution for aggregated search. The aim of this work is to set up a parallel processing architecture able to optimize runtime and improve data aggregation from heterogeneous data sources. Our system is an aggregated search engine capable of responding to a SPARQL query by collecting the necessary data from independent data sources, the system decomposes the initial query into several parts forming sub-queries, then, the system collects intermediate results of each sub-query independently.

According to the analytical study presented in Sect. 3, *sub-queries execution* is the most expensive phase in terms of execution time, during this step the system interacts with external data sources and retrieves intermediate data, which makes it dependent on the flow of data transfer and the sources quality.

To optimize runtime, we presented in this paper parallel processing architecture that allows the system to connect to several sources simultaneously and execute several sub-queries in a parallel way, this architecture optimizes data transfer time without any data loss. Another important feature of this architecture is to ensure independence between sub-queries which enhances the variety of intermediate data.

We also presented the usefulness of the ontology-based data access paradigm in order to allow querying heterogeneous data source thanks to our system. This paradigm can work very well with our system so that the user may query not only RDF data sources but also SQL data bases. According to the demonstration presented in Sect. 5, our solution makes it possible to exploit data from the web of data and integrate them with local databases.

We intend to the evaluate the effectiveness of our solution by querying other data formats. We will also experimentally compare our system with existing systems. We will improve the functionalities of the OBDA part so that the user can add more databases to it.

References

1. Rabhi, A., Fissoune, R., Tabaa, M., Badir, H.: Intermediate results processing for aggregated SPARQL queries. In 2021 IEEE/ACS 18th International Conference on Computer Systems and Applications (AICCSA), pp. 1–8. IEEE (2021)
2. Sushmita, S., Joho, H., Lalmas, M., Villa, R.: Factors affecting click-through behavior in aggregated search interfaces. In Proceedings of the 19th ACM International Conference on Information and Knowledge Management, pp. 519–528 (2010)
3. Echbarthi, G., Kheddouci, H.: A graph matching approach based on aggregated search. In 2017 13th International Conference on Signal-Image Technology & Internet-Based Systems (SITIS), pp. 376–379. IEEE (2017)

4. Quilitz, B., Leser, U.: Querying distributed RDF data sources with SPARQL. In: Bechhofer, S., Hauswirth, M., Hoffmann, J., Koubarakis, M. (eds.) ESWC 2008. LNCS, vol. 5021, pp. 524–538. Springer, Heidelberg (2008). https://doi.org/10. 1007/978-3-540-68234-9_39

5. Saleem, M., Potocki, A., Soru, T., Hartig, O., Ngomo, A.C.N.: CostFed: cost-based query optimization for SPARQL endpoint federation. Procedia Comput. Sci. **137**, 163–174 (2018)

6. Görlitz, O., Staab, S.: SPLENDID: SPARQL endpoint federation exploiting void descriptions. In: Proceedings of the Second International Conference on Consuming Linked Data, vol. 782, pp. 3–24 (2011)

7. Başca, C., Bernstein, A.: Querying a messy web of data with avalanche. J. Web Semant. **26**, 1–28 (2014)

8. Wang, X., Tiropanis, T., Davis, H.C.: LHD: optimising linked data query processing using parallelisation. In LDOW (2013)

9. Schätzle, A., Przyjaciel-Zablocki, M., Skilevic, S., Lausen, G.: S2RDF: RDF querying with SPARQL on spark. arXiv preprint arXiv:1512.07021. (2015)

10. Hassan, M., Bansal, S.K.: Data partitioning scheme for efficient distributed RDF querying using apache spark. In 2019 IEEE 13th International Conference on Semantic Computing (ICSC), pp. 24–31. IEEE (2019)

11. Cossu, M., Färber, M., Lausen, G.: Prost: distributed execution of SPARQL queries using mixed partitioning strategies. arXiv preprint arXiv:1802.05898 (2018)

12. Bagosi, T., et al.: The *Ontop* framework for ontology based data access. In: Zhao, D., Du, J., Wang, H., Wang, P., Ji, D., Pan, J.Z. (eds.) CSWS 2014. CCIS, vol. 480, pp. 67–77. Springer, Heidelberg (2014). https://doi.org/10.1007/978-3-662-45495-4_6

13. Kharlamov, E., et al.: Ontology based access to exploration data at statoil. In: Arenas, M., et al. (eds.) ISWC 2015. LNCS, vol. 9367, pp. 93–112. Springer, Cham (2015). https://doi.org/10.1007/978-3-319-25010-6_6

14. Baader, F., Bienvenu, M., Lutz, C., Wolter, F.: Query and predicate emptiness in ontology-based data access. J. Artif. Intell. Res. **56**, 1–59 (2016)

15. Kogalovsky, M.R.: Ontology-based data access systems. Program. Comput. Softw. **38**(4), 167–182 (2012)

16. Calvanese D., De Giacomo G., Lembo D., Lenzerini M., Rosati R.: Ontology-based data access and integration. In: Liu, L., Özsu, M. (eds.) Encyclopedia of Database Systems. Springer, New York (2017). https://doi.org/10.1007/978-1-4899-7993-3_80667-1

17. De Giacomo, G., Lembo, D., Oriol, X., Savo, D.F., Teniente, E.: Practical update management in ontology-based data access. In: International Semantic Web Conference, pp. 225–242 (2017)

18. Rabhi, A., Fissoune, R.: WODII: a solution to process SPARQL queries over distributed data sources. Clust. Comput. **23**(3), 2315–2322 (2020)

19. Raimond, Y., Sutton, C., Sandler, M.B.: Automatic interlinking of music datasets on the semantic web. In: LDOW, vol. 369 (2008)

20. Ahlers, D.: Linkage quality analysis of GeoNames in the semantic web. In: Proceedings of the 11th Workshop on Geographic Information Retrieval, pp. 1–2. ACM, Heidelberg (2017)

Comprehensive Data Life Cycle Security in Cloud Computing: Current Mastery and Major Challenges

Kenza Chaoui[1]([✉]), Nadia Kabachi[2], Nouria Harbi[2], and Hassan Badir[1]

[1] IDS Team ENSAT, Abdelmalek Essaadi University Tangier, Tangier, Morocco
Kchaoui1994@gmail.com
[2] ERIC Laboratory, Lumière Lyon 1 University, Lyon, France

Abstract. One of the gravest concerns related to cloud computing pertains to data security. As businesses start on digital transformation, there is a clear requirement for privacy and data protection. Organizations today have more data, applications, and websites than they have ever had before. Data security has risen to the top of the priority list for cloud computing security. Although numerous solutions have been put forward, most of them exclusively target individual stages within the data life cycle, such as storage. This approach proves inadequate in effectively tackling the security challenges of cloud data, given that threats can arise at any phase of the data life cycle. Any security breach occurring during any stage of the data life cycle process has the potential to compromise overall data security. Hence, it becomes imperative to address data security across all phases of the data life cycle. This article's primary contribution lies in introducing a novel viewpoint concerning data security solutions aligned with the data life cycle. This perspective holds significant importance and can serve as a road map for crafting a comprehensive security strategy. The article conducts an exhaustive review of the complete data life cycle and identifies a research gap comprising unresolved challenges that could potentially serve as research inquiries for our forthcoming endeavors.

Keywords: Data life cycle · Data Security · Security issues · Cloud Computing

1 Introduction

Cloud computing is a virtualized system that allows users to access compute, storage, and software resources as well as servers from a single platform. Data management services are currently provided in the user's local environment, however, CSP Cloud Service Providers provide them remotely. Users may not know where, when, how, why, or by whom their data is seen or modified in a cloud environment because services are supplied in abstract form. Cloud computing, on the other hand, has several security risks. CSPs are also more vulnerable to

© The Author(s), under exclusive license to Springer Nature Switzerland AG 2024
M. Tabaa et al. (Eds.): INTIS 2022/2023, CCIS 1728, pp. 195–206, 2024.
https://doi.org/10.1007/978-3-031-47366-1_15

adversaries and hackers who can take advantage of these benefits. The cloud is vulnerable from a security and data privacy perspective, as sensitive user data is stored in a third-party CSP. [1] All these weaknesses and mistrust build a common element which is the issue of trust and safety between providers and consumers because Cloud Computing requires the trust of providers of cloud services. As a result, trust is one of the main factors for the adoption of this new paradigm. Conversely, there exists the possibility of data theft and malicious exploitation by the cloud provider itself. The paramount challenge in the realm of cloud services revolves around data security at its core, necessitating the safeguarding of sensitive information at the organizational level rather than relying solely on the cloud provider's security measures. The paradigm shift demands a focus on data-level security, empowering organizations to guarantee the protection of their data irrespective of its location. Consequently, it proves advantageous for each individual customer to proactively implement their own security protocols, independent of the offerings provided by service providers. When addressing data security, it becomes imperative to uphold the trio of confidentiality, integrity, and availability (CIA). Compromises in any of these aspects can significantly disrupt operations within cloud computing since data serves as the fundamental pillar of any business ecosystem. The prominence of one of these facets over the others is contingent upon the environment, application, context, or use case. Numerous solutions aimed at data security have been put forth; however, a majority of them fall short of encompassing all these security dimensions. Conversely, the challenge of data traceability arises, which involves tracking the data's state and movements. Without data traceability, ensuring the fulfillment of the remaining three criteria (CID) becomes uncertain. Our work will follow this structure: commencing with a comprehensive presentation of the current landscape of data protection and security methods within the data life cycle. Subsequently, we will delve into a detailed examination of the previous research, highlighting potential gaps. Finally, we will conclude by presenting our findings and outlining directions for future endeavors.

2   Data Life Cycle

Several distinct data life cycles have been proposed in the literature to aid businesses in selecting the most fitting and pertinent solutions for their specific contexts. Noteworthy among these are the CRUD life cycle [38], Life cycle for Big Data [39], IBM life cycle [29], DataOne life cycle [37], Information life cycle [30], CIGREF [31], DDI life cycle [32], USGS life cycle [29], PII life cycle [33], Enterprise data life cycle [34], and Hindawi life cycle [35]. All of these life cycles are comprehensively described and explored in [36]. Among these life cycles, certain pivotal stages consistently emerge, including creation, storage, utilization, sharing, archiving, and destruction [29]. Safeguarding data across all these life cycle phases is imperative, from its initial inception to eventual elimination. The stages of storing and archiving correspond to data-at-rest, utilization pertains to data-in-use, sharing aligns with data-in-transit, and the phase of destruction can be labeled as data-after-deletion.

These six stages are succinctly summarized in Fig. 1.

Fig. 1. A Data life cycle.

- **Creation** entails either the origination of a novel entity or the alteration of an existing digital data item. This phase can equivalently be referred to as the creation/update phase, encapsulating the modification aspect. The scope extends beyond documents or databases, encompassing a wide range of content, whether structured or unstructured. Within this phase, data is categorized and relevant permissions are established. It's noteworthy that data can be generated within the client or the cloud server environment.
- **Storage** involves the process of organizing digital data into a structured or unstructured storage repository, which can take the form of a database or a file. Typically, this occurs concurrently with the creation phase. Within this stage, it's crucial to align the classification of data and the configuration of security measures, encompassing access controls, encryption, and rights management.
- **Use** The data is accessed, manipulated, or utilized without making any modifications to the original dataset. These actions typically pertain to data retrieved and used by a user's computer or application. To ensure the integrity of such activities, various measures are in place, including detection controls like activity monitoring, preventive controls such as rights management, and logical controls that are commonly implemented within databases and applications.
- **Sharing** Data is shared with others, involving its exchange among users, clients, and collaborators. This stage incorporates a blend of detection and prevention mechanisms, encompassing encryption to ensure secure data transfer, logical controls, and application security measures.
- **Archiving** Data enters a dormant state, transitioning to long-term storage for archiving purposes. During this phase, a fusion of encryption management and profit management strategies is employed to guarantee data protection and availability.
- **Destruction**
  The information is permanently obliterated using either physical or logical techniques. To ensure a secure and comprehensive deletion process, tools are employed to identify and remove any lasting permanent copies.

3   Literature Review

The data must be secure throughout the life cycle of the data here are the existing works that are proposed in some phases of the data life cycle:

3.1   Secure Data Creation

In [18], The authors proposed a proxy re-encryption scheme with the support of a cloud, the authors proposed a protected cloud-assisted IoT data management system to preserve data confidentiality while collecting, storing, and accessing IoT data, taking into account the increase of users. Therefore, a secure IoT could handle most attacks from both IoT insiders and outsiders to break data confidentiality, in the meantime with communication's constant costs for IoT re-encryption anti-incremental scale.

In [19], a secure, adaptable, and effective system for storing and retrieving data is conceptualized, drawing on the synergies of fog computing and cloud computing methodologies. The paper outlines the key obstacles encompassing data refinement, data organization, searchable encryption, and dynamic data collection, and subsequently proposes fitting solutions to address these challenges. A tree of retrieval functions is designed to support effective and efficient privacy-preserving data search, precise data retrieval and an index encryption scheme based on the secure kNN algorithm are suggested. From a broader view, a flowchart including data mining and remote control is also presented.

In their work as described in [20], the authors introduced a blockchain framework within Mobile Ad hoc Networks (MANETs) to enhance the security of data collection processes. They propose a mechanism where the data collector can exercise control over payment by managing the extent of Route REQuest (RREQ) forwarding during route discovery. This approach ensures equitable distribution of rewards to all forwarders of control information (specifically RREQs and abbreviated Route REPlies, or RREPs). Simultaneously, the framework tackles collision threats through the implementation of secure digital signatures, cooperative receipt reporting, and defense mechanisms against spoofing attacks. The system goes beyond just offering incentives to participating nodes; it also thwarts potential forking and guarantees both efficiency and genuine decentralization. This achievement is realized by incorporating a groundbreaking Proof-of-Stake consensus mechanism that accumulates stakes through message forwarding.

A new data collection scheme called Secure Data was proposed in [21] to provide data protection and to protect the rights of the personal data of patients. The authors introduced the KATAN secret cipher algorithm as a measure to ensure communication security, which was further implemented on the FPGA hardware platform. The authors implemented secret cipher sharing and share repairing techniques to enhance the privacy of the KATAN cipher. Their evaluation demonstrates that the Secure Data scheme when subjected to attacks, exhibits effectiveness in terms of frequency, energy expenditure, and overall computational load. In [22], a secure data collection system known as SeDC was proposed. This system is built on compressive sensing principles and aims to enhance data privacy. It leverages an asymmetric semi-homomorphic encryption mechanism and reduces computational costs by utilizing a sparse compressive matrix. The asymmetric approach simplifies the distribution process and provides control over the secret key. The inclusion of homomorphic encryption enables cipher domain in-network aggregation, thereby enhancing security and achieving load balancing across the network. The sparse measuring matrix reduces both the computation cost and communication cost, which compensates for the increasing cost caused by homomorphic encryption.

3.2 Ensuring Secure Data Exchange

In [1], The authors proposed an advanced secure and privacy-preserving data-sharing system for smart cities based on blockchain. The proposed system ensures that personal user data is protected, safely stored, and accessible to stakeholders on the need to know the basis of smart contracts embedded in user-defined ACLlaws. Besides, they devised a solution named "PrivyCoin," manifested as a digital token, which empowers users to share their data with stakeholders and third parties. Additionally, they introduced "PrivySharing".

To meet specific criteria outlined in the EU GDPR. This encompasses aspects like data asset sharing, usability, and the capability to secure data owner consent purging. The empirical findings detailed in the article validate that a multi-Channel (multi-Ch) blockchain solution exhibits superior scalability compared to a single-Channel (single-Ch) blockchain system.

In a similar pursuit outlined in [3], an architecture for data usage auditing, based on blockchain, was introduced. This framework furnishes data controllers with indisputable proof of users' consent. The researchers assert the provision of user anonymity by permitting data owners (delegated to a Public Key Generator, PKG) to generate distinct public-private key pairs for each smart contract formed with a service provider or data processor, facilitating data sharing. Furthermore, they employed hierarchical ID-based encryption as a safeguard against unauthorized disclosure. While the data itself is stored off-blockchain, blockchain smart contracts are employed to store data hashes and data usage policies. Moreover, a specific smart contract is established between the data custodian and any other service provider or data processor. To enhance the security of data sharing within the cloud environment, the authors introduced a novel blockchain-powered attribute-based signcryption approach in their work [4]. This proposed scheme, known as BABSC, uniquely leverages blockchain technology and attribute-based signcryption to ensure both data confidentiality and its resistance to forgery. The evaluation segment of the study demonstrates that BABSC offers dual advantages: it reduces communication overhead and expedites decryption processes for end-users. BABSC additionally reinforces user access control, making it well-suited for cloud computing scenarios.

In [2], a blockchain-powered data-sharing platform named "SpeedyChain" was introduced, tailored for the context of a smart city ecosystem. The architecture of "SpeedyChain" places emphasis on expediting transaction settlement times, particularly beneficial for real-time applications such as smart vehicles. Additionally, the platform aims to ensure user privacy and provides safeguards against data tampering, guaranteeing data integrity and upholding non-repudiation principles.

In another context, detailed in [5], the authors proposed an encryption method termed "RS-IBE," which stands for revocable-capacity personality-based encryption. This approach facilitates identity revocation and cipher text updates concurrently, offering a pragmatic and consistent approach to establishing a cost-effective and reliable data-sharing system within cloud computing. This approach effectively blocks access to both previously and subsequently shared data by a revoked user.

In [6], the authors introduced a secure framework for sharing and distributing data within the public cloud. This approach relies on attribute-based and timed-release conditional identity-based broadcast, referred to as PRE. This innovative framework allows users to share data simultaneously with a designated group of recipients, utilizing identification markers such as email addresses and usernames. This approach offers both protection and convenience for data sharing within the public cloud environment. Employing fine-grained and timed-release CPRE, the framework empowers data owners to configure access policies for cipher text and time trapdoors. These configurations limit distribution conditions while allowing data outsourcing. The Cloud Service Provider (CSP) can successfully re-encrypt cipher text only if the data disseminator's attributes linked to the re-encryption key adhere to the access policy in the initial cipher text and are exposed to the time trapdoors within the initial cipher text. The outcomes of experimentation using a cryptography library with a focus on pairing have substantiated the system's efficacy and its capacity to provide robust protection.

In [9], the authors introduce a secure and efficient cloud data sharing scheme based on cipher text-policy attributes. This scheme facilitates the proxy's ability to transform a cipher text from one access policy, aligned with the requestor's attributes, to another cipher text governed by a new access policy. Yet, these systems do not account for scenarios where data access rights need to be granted to distinct user groups at different time intervals. Addressing this limitation, the authors of [10] propose a practical Trusted Time Agent-based approach to tackle this issue. This method employs a trusted time agent, rather than relying solely on the data owner, to uniformly grant access privileges at specific time points.

In [10], the authors put forth a secure scheme for data sharing and profile matching within mobile healthcare social networks (MHSN) operating in the realm of cloud computing. Within this framework, patients possess the capability to securely outsource their health records using identity-based broadcast encryption for cloud storage (IBBE). This enables them to effectively and securely share these records with a community of doctors. Additionally, the authors introduce a construction for conditional data re-encryption based on attributes. This construction empowers doctors who fulfill predefined criteria within the cipher text to grant authorization to the cloud platform. This authorization allows for the transformation of a cipher text into a new cipher text specifically tailored for specialists. Importantly, this process ensures that no sensitive information is exposed, maintaining the integrity of the identity-based encryption scheme. Furthermore, the paper presents a profile matching mechanism within the MHSN context, employing identity-based equality testing encryption. This mechanism permits patients to identify friends in a privacy-preserving manner, granting them flexible authorization to ward off guessing attacks on encrypted health records involving keywords.

Similarly, [10,11,17] have implemented IBBE to secure sharing confidential data with a community of users. The contrastive methods involve the sharing of cipher text with other users through the Proxy Re-Encryption (PRE) technique, where the ciphertext is re-encrypted. However, in [1,12,17], the doctor authorized by the patient is enabled to re-encrypt all the patient's health data. This differs from [11], where a similar approach is employed. [13] and [10] support re-encryption of conditional data. In particular, [13] and [10] follow the ABE approach that supports complex operations to describe the MHSN flexible condition. Further, [10,14–16] All help profile matching on cipher texts. Although [14] have obtained flexible authorization, two negotiated users generate the authorization token, which may not be valid in the MHSN. By identifying various trapdoors [10] and [15], the user may pick the data that will be matched according to their wishes.

3.3   Secure Data Deletion

In [28], the authors introduced an efficient attribute revocation scheme grounded in the Merkle Hash Tree structure, ensuring the verifiable deletion of data. When a user submits a deletion request to the cloud server, the linked files undergo re-encryption through the re-encryption key established by the trust authority. Concurrently, an updated root of the Merkle Hash Tree is communicated to the data owner as part of attribute revocation. This facilitates a means for the data owner to verify the successful deletion of the data. Furthermore, for Data Deletion Validation, the cloud data remains accessible to other users.

In [27] authors devised a finely-tuned data deletion system aimed at thwarting unauthorized data manipulation from cloud servers, safeguarding against hacking attempts, and ensuring comprehensive data erasure by cloud service providers. The system also incorporates a rank-based Merkle Hash Tree chain to verify the integrity and presence of data blocks on behalf of the user.

In [26], the authors introduced a data deletion framework tailored for cloud computing. This framework operates on a "trust-but-verify" basis, allowing users to validate the accuracy of encryption and deletion operations. Acknowledging the challenge in guaranteeing complete data deletion via software means, the authors propose a distinctive approach. They suggest the return of a digital signature, bound by a commitment to delete the corresponding secret key. This signature serves as evidence to hold the cloud service provider accountable if the deleted key resurfaces at a later stage.

In [25], the authors introduced a sophisticated scheme for outsourced data deletion, leveraging an invertible Bloom filter framework. This approach provides the capability for both public and private verification of storage and deletion outcomes. Notably, users can readily detect malicious actions undertaken by the cloud server with a high degree of certainty. Such detection becomes achievable when the cloud server fails to genuinely preserve or delete data and subsequently neglects to furnish corresponding evidence. Simultaneously, the proposed scheme maintains its computational complexity irrespective of the number of outsourced data blocks involved in data deletion and deletion outcome verification processes. This attribute renders the scheme exceptionally suited for scenarios requiring large-scale data deletion.

In [23], a novel framework for data deletion, based on blockchain technology, was introduced. This framework contributes to enhancing the transparency of the deletion process. Within this solution, regardless of the cloud server's intent, the data owner retains the ability to verify the outcome of deletion. Moreover, the proposed scheme ensures public verification through blockchain technology, all without the necessity of relying on a trusted third party.

In a separate study by the authors [24], a robust data deletion system was recommended. This system offers both verifiable data deletion and flexible control over access to sensitive information. The protocol ensures that during the deletion of cloud data and subsequent validation of its removal, only data owners and fog devices are engaged. This design choice imbues the protocol with practicality, taking advantage of low latency and real-time interaction capabilities with fog devices.

4   Research Gap in Data Life Cycle

When we talk about data security we must ensure the triplet of confidentiality, integrity and availability. Losses of confidentiality, integrity, and availability (CIA) can have a big impact on cloud computing operations because data is the backbone of any business. One of these aspects may prevail over the others depending on the environment, application, context or use case. Many data security solutions have been proposed, however, most of them do not cover all of these security aspects. On the other hand, there is the challenge of data traceability which is used to trace the state and movements of the data. Without it, there is no chance of being sure that the other three criteria (CID) are met. In addition, thanks to traceability, we can control and monitor what is happening and where the data is located, who has access to it, in what state it is, what process has it undergone, has it arrived? to destination?

The currently proposed data security solutions that aim to cover all three dimensions of security share a common characteristic: they tend to focus on individual stages within the data life cycle, which encompasses the entire process from data generation to its eventual destruction. Within this intricate process, a security vulnerability present at any stage could potentially compromise the overall state of data security. In the context of cloud computing, data is frequently in motion, transitioning between different locations. Alongside cloud storage, data is frequently transmitted to clients through networks that might lack adequate security measures. Regardless of where data resides, there is an inherent risk of encountering security challenges. Given these dynamics, it becomes imperative to incorporate data security considerations throughout all phases of the data life cycle. In our study, we contend that one of the paramount challenges within the data life cycle pertains to what is known as "data after-delete," more commonly referred to as data remanence. Following the deletion of storage media, there might persist certain physical attributes that enable the reconstruction of data. Establishing the data's pathway, commonly referred to as data lineage, holds significance for audit purposes within cloud computing. This is particularly pertinent in the context of public cloud environments, extending beyond the stages mentioned earlier. On the other hand. The currently proposed data security solutions that aim to cover all three dimensions of security share a common characteristic: they tend to focus on individual stages within the data life cycle, which encompasses the entire process from data generation to its eventual destruction. Within this intricate process, a security vulnerability present at any stage could potentially compromise the overall state of data security. In the context of cloud computing, data is frequently in motion, transitioning between different locations. Alongside cloud storage, data is frequently transmitted to clients through networks that might lack adequate security measures. Regardless of where data resides, there is an inherent risk of encountering security challenges. Given these dynamics, it becomes imperative to incorporate data security considerations throughout all phases of the data life cycle. In our study, we contend that one of the paramount challenges within the data life cycle pertains to what is known as "data after-delete," more commonly referred to as data remanence. Following the deletion of storage media, there might persist certain physical attributes that enable the reconstruction of data. Establishing the data's pathway, commonly referred to as data lineage, holds significance for audit purposes within cloud computing. This is particularly pertinent in the context of public cloud environments, extending beyond the stages mentioned earlier. There are challenges in that investigates securing data during the data restore operation and after restoring. Additionally, during investigating these challenges, confidentiality, integrity and availability (CIA) are considered, The challenges addressed can be summarized as follows: most of the existing SWs that are used to restore data deleted, retrieves a part of the deleted data and the cloud service consumer (CSC) can construct the reminder, and therefore all data are retrieved. Besides, the CSC can perform illegal operations (edit, delete) on the data retrieved which can lead to a crisis for other consumers, and these operations represent security breach issues. Furthermore, it's crucial to emphasize that there is currently no definitive method to guarantee the integrity of deleted data. The second challenge is preserving the privacy for the restored data, for example; when the data deleted, the access roles for authenticated users are also deleted, so when the data is restored, these roles must be maintained to maintain to uphold data privacy. Finally, within the dataset-in-use stage, there are unauthorized users who can guess the data creation standards and generate data that can be used in real operations.

5 Conclusion

Data security has become a paramount concern in the realm of cloud computing security. While numerous solutions have been put forward, a significant portion of these solutions focuses on addressing singular facets of security. In our proposition, we emphasize the imperative of encompassing data security considerations across the entirety of the data life cycle within the cloud environment. The primary contribution of this paper lies in its novel perspective on data security solutions, rooted in the framework of the data life cycle. This approach holds pivotal importance and can serve as a guiding framework for crafting comprehensive security solutions. Looking ahead, our future endeavors will involve a meticulous analysis of the research gaps evident within the data life cycle domain, as well as the implementation and realization of the proposed solutions.

References

1. Michelin, R.A., et al.: SpeedyChain: a framework for decoupling data from blockchain for smart cities. In: Proceedings of the 15th 750 EAI International Conference on Mobile and Ubiquitous Systems: Computing, Networking and Services, pp. 145–154. ACM (2018)
2. Wang, H., Song, Y.: Secure cloud-based EHR system using attribute-based 595 cryptosystem and blockchain. J. Med. Syst. **42**(8), 152 (2018)
3. Eltayieb, N., Elhabob, R., Hassan, A., Li, F.: A blockchain-based attribute-based signcryption scheme to secure data sharing in the cloud. J. Syst. Architect. **102**, 101653 (2020)
4. Gowri, M.K., Sowjanya, L., Durga, D.K.: Secure data sharing in cloud server using data revocation and identity based encryption. IEEE Trans. Cloud Comput. **6**(4), 1136–1148 (2018)
5. Zhou, Y., Deng, H., Wu, Q., Qin, B., Liu, J.: Identity-based Proxy ReEncryption Version 2: making mobile access easy in cloud. Future Gener. Comput. Syst. **62**, 128–139 (2016)
6. Shao, J., Wei, G., Ling, Y., Xie, M.: Identity-based conditional proxy reencryption. In: Proceedings of 2011 IEEE International Conference on Communications (ICC 2011), pp. 1–5 (2011)
7. Liang, K., Chu, C., Tan, X., Wong, D., Tang, C., Zhou, J.: Chosen-ciphertext secure multi-hop identity-based conditional proxy re-encryption with constant-size ciphertexts. Theoret. Comput. Sci. **539**, 87–105 (2014)
8. Liang, K., et al.: A secure and efficient ciphertext-policy attribute-based proxy re-encryption for cloud data sharing. Futur. Gener. Comput. Syst. **2015**(52), 95–108 (2015)
9. Rivest, R., Shamir, A., Wagner, D.: Time Lock Puzzles and Timed-release Crypto. Massachusetts Institute of Technology, MA, USA (1996)
10. Huang, Q., Yue, W., He, Y., Yang, Y.: Secure identity-based data sharing and profile matching for mobile healthcare social networks in cloud computing. IEEE Access **6**, 36584–36594 (2018)

11. Xu, P., Jiao, T., Wu, Q., Wang, W., Jin, H.: Conditional identity-based broadcast proxy re-encryption and its application to cloud email. IEEE Trans. Comput. **65**(1), 66–79 (2016)
12. Liang, K., et al.: A secure and efficient ciphertext-policy attribute-based proxy re-encryption for cloud data sharing. Future Generat. Comput. Syst. **52**, 95–108 (2015)
13. Yang, Y., Zhu, H., Lu, H., Weng, J., Zhang, Y., Choo, K.: Cloud based data sharing with fine-grained proxy re-encryption. Pervasive Mob. Comput. **28**, 122–134 (2016)
14. Qiu, S., Liu, J., Shi, Y., Li, M., Wang, W.: Identity-based private matching over outsourced encrypted datasets. IEEE Trans. Cloud Comput. **6**(3), 747–759 (2015). https://doi.org/10.1109/TCC.2015.2511723
15. Ma, S.: Identity-based encryption with outsourced equality test in cloud computing. Inf. Sci. **328**, 389–402 (2016)
16. Wu, L., Zhang, Y., Choo, K., He, D.: Efficient and secure identity-based encryption scheme with equality test in cloud computing. Future Generat. Comput. Syst. **73**, 22–31 (2017)
17. Zhou, Y., Deng, H., Wu, Q., Qin, B., Liu, J., Ding, Y.: Identity-based proxy re-encryption version 2: making mobile access easy in cloud. Future Generat. Comput. Syst. **62**, 128–139 (2016)
18. Wang, W., Xu, P., Yang, L.T.: Secure data collection, storage and access in cloud-assisted IoT. IEEE Cloud Comput. **5**(4), 77–88 (2018)
19. Fu, J.S., Liu, Y., Chao, H.C., Bhargava, B.K., Zhang, Z.J.: Secure data storage and searching for industrial IoT by integrating fog computing and cloud computing. IEEE Trans. Industr. Inf. **14**(10), 4519–4528 (2018)
20. Liu, G., Dong, H., Yan, Z., Zhou, X., Shimizu, S.: B4SDC: a blockchain system for security data collection in MANETs. IEEE Trans. Big Data **8**(3), 739–752 (2020)
21. Tao, H., Bhuiyan, M.Z.A., Abdalla, A.N., Hassan, M.M., Zain, J.M., Hayajneh, T.: Secured data collection with hardware-based ciphers for IoT-based healthcare. IEEE Internet Things J. **6**(1), 410–420 (2018)
22. Zhang, P., Wang, S., Guo, K., Wang, J.: A secure data collection scheme based on compressive sensing in wireless sensor networks. Ad Hoc Netw. **70**, 73–84 (2018)
23. Yang, C., Chen, X., Xiang, Y.: Blockchain-based publicly verifiable data deletion scheme for cloud storage. J. Netw. Comput. Appl. **103**, 185–193 (2018)
24. Yu, Y., Xue, L., Li, Y., Du, X., Guizani, M., Yang, B.: Assured data deletion with fine-grained access control for fog-based industrial applications. IEEE Trans. Industr. Inf. **14**(10), 4538–4547 (2018)
25. Yang, C., Liu, Y., Tao, X., Zhao, F.: Publicly verifiable and efficient fine-grained data deletion scheme in cloud computing. IEEE Access **8**, 99393–99403 (2020)
26. Hao, F., Clarke, D., Zorzo, A.F.: Deleting secret data with public verifiability. IEEE Trans. Dependable Secure Comput. **13**(6), 617–29 (2015)
27. Yang, C., Chen, Q., Liu, Y.: Fine-grained outsourced data deletion scheme in cloud computing. Int. J. Electron. Inf. Eng. **11**(2), 81–98 (2019)
28. Xue, L., Yu, Y., Li, Y.N., Au, M.H., Du, X.J., Yang, B.: Efficient attribute-based encryption with attribute revocation for assured data deletion. Inf. Sci. **479**, 640–650 (2019)
29. IBM, Wrangling big data: fundamentals of data lifecycle management (2013)
30. Lin, L., Liu, T., Hu, J., Zhang, J.: A privacy-aware cloud service selection method toward data life-cycle. In: 2014 20th IEEE International Conference on Parallel and Distributed Systems (ICPADS), pp. 752–759. IEEE (2014)
31. Bouteiller, S.: Business data challenges. How to manage company data to create value? CIGREF (2014)

32. Ma, X., Fox, P., Rozell, E., West, P., Zednik, S.: Ontology dynamics in a data lifecycle: challenges and recommendations from a geoscience perspective. J. Earth Sci. **25**(2), 407–412 (2014)

33. Michota, A., Katsikas, S.: Designing a seamless privacy policy for social networks. In: Proceedings of the 19th Panhellenic Conference on Informatics, pp. 139–143. ACM (2015)

34. Chaki, S.: The lifecycle of enterprise information management. In: Enterprise Information Management in Practice, pp. 7–14. Springer, Cham (2015). https://doi.org/ 10.1007/978-1-4842-1218-9_2

35. Khan, N., et al.: Big data: survey, technologies, opportunities, and challenges. Sci. World J. **2014**, 18 (2014)

36. El Arass, M., Tikito, I., Souissi, N.: Data lifecycles analysis: towards intelligent cycle. In: 2017 Intelligent Systems and Computer Vision (ISCV), pp. 1–8. IEEE, April 2017

37. Reed, A., Rezek, C., Simmonds, P.: Security Guidance for Critical Area of Focus in Cloud Computing V3.0, Cloud Security Alliance (CSA), pp. 1–177 (2011)

38. Yu, X., Wen, Q.: A view about cloud data security from data life cycle. In: International Conference on Computational Intelligence and Software Engineering (CiSE), pp. 1–4 (2010)

39. Demchenko, Y., De Laat, C., Membrey, P.: Defining architecture components of the Big Data Ecosystem. In: International Conference on Collaboration Technologies and Systems (CTS), pp. 104–112 (2014)

Author Index

Printed in the United States
by Baker & Taylor Publisher Services